Translating in the Local Community

This volume showcases different forms of natural and non-professional translation and interpreting at work at multilingual sites in a single city, shedding new light on our understanding of the intersection of city, migration and translation.

Flynn builds on work in translation studies, sociolinguistics, linguistic ethnography and anthropology to offer a translational perspective on scholarship on multilingualism and translation, focusing on examples from the superdiverse city of Ghent in Belgium. Each chapter comprises a different multilingual site, ranging from schools to eateries to public transport, and unpacks specific dimensions of translation practices within and against constantly shifting multilingual settings. The book also reflects on socio-political factors and methodological considerations of concern when undertaking such an approach. Taken together, the chapters seek to provide a composite picture of translation in a multilingual city, demonstrating how tracing physical, linguistic and social trajectories of movement in these contexts can deepen our understanding of the contemporary dynamics of multilingualism and natural translation and of translanguaging, more broadly.

This book will be of interest to students and scholars in translation and interpreting studies, sociolinguistics, multilingualism, linguistic anthropology and migration studies.

Peter Flynn (emeritus) lectured in Translation Studies and English at KU Leuven, Antwerp Campus, Belgium, from 2006 to 2020. He is a member of CETRA, and Research Fellow at UFS, Bloemfontein, South Africa.

Routledge Advances in Translation and Interpreting Studies

For more information about this series, please visit: www.routledge.
com/Routledge-Advances-in-Translation-and-Interpreting-Studies/
book-series/RTS

Translating in the Local Community

Peter Flynn

Routledge
Taylor & Francis Group

NEW YORK AND LONDON

First published 2023
by Routledge
605 Third Avenue, New York, NY 10158

and by Routledge
4 Park Square, Milton Park, Abingdon, Oxon, OX14 4RN

Routledge is an imprint of the Taylor & Francis Group, an informa business

© 2023 Peter Flynn

ISBN: 9781032426914 (hbk)
ISBN: 9781032426921 (pbk)
ISBN: 9781003363811 (ebk)

DOI: 10.4324/9781003363811

Typeset in Sabon
by codeMantra

Contents

Figures

Acknowledgements

I would first like to thank all those who were willing to cooperate in this project. They have given me hours and days of their valuable time and took pains to share their insights and have taught me things I could never have discovered on my own. Without them this book could never have been written. Though their names have been changed for reasons of anonymity, they will surely recognise their own voices or at least the sites their voices helped bring alive. I also like to thank my family for putting up with the usual persistent absent-mindedness I am afflicted with during such undertakings and Leander for valuable work on the referencing and bibliography. My sincere thanks as well go to all the colleagues and friends who have supported me over the years and encouraged me to finish this work. I will not mention you by name here for fear of forgetting any of you, but you know who I mean.

Part of the data used in Chapter 7 was analysed using a different method than in a previously published article (Flynn & van Doorslaer, 2015). I would like to thank the publishers for their kind permission to use the materials involved.

I would also like to thank the anonymous readers of the book proposal for their valuable feedback. Any flaws found in this endeavour are entirely my own.

Peter Flynn
Ghent, 1 October 2022

Introduction

This book, and the research it reports on, was directly inspired by the late Jan Blommaert's study of Berchem, the neighbourhood he lived in the city of Antwerp, Belgium (Blommaert, 2013). Though I had been toying with the idea for a while when reading the literature on linguistic landscapes, the project only took real form on reading Jan's book. There was a certain urgency to it that was first eclipsed by more pressing events in the day to day, only to be completely washed away seven years ago by what became known as the migrant crisis of 2015. The futility of pursuing the project and writing the book seemed more than obvious, its significance infinitesimal in comparison to the scale of the humanitarian disaster unfolding at the time. For sure, migration formed an integral part of the projected research but the urgency of the migration under scrutiny in this book simply paled in contrast to what was happening. In the meantime, the longstanding multilingual and multicultural interaction on public transport nonetheless continued to remind me of my original purpose, to which I now return.

Having come rather late in life to the world of academia and more particularly to the field of Translation Studies, I found myself faced at the start of this project with the prospect of five more years of active academic life before retirement. There was so much to explore and not enough time to do so. Having failed on a couple of occasions to be awarded research funding, and not wishing to face similar disappointment should I try again, I had decided to venture out on my own and conduct the research for this project where I could and whenever I could. So, I started by exploring my own neighbourhood in the city of Ghent (Belgium) and slowly began to visit other parts of the city in search of multilingual sites and people in the local community who would be willing to talk to me about their work or activities at such sites. This also involved collecting other forms of (translated) data, documentation and forms of institutional or "official" discourse on the sites being visited with a view to providing a composite picture of semiotic activity framing or related to translation.

Like all city dwellers no matter where we are in the world, we encounter multilingual communication on a daily basis in various media and forms. Once it comes to our attention, it is impossible to ignore and, like me, you will probably often find yourself eavesdropping on

DOI: 10.4324/9781003363811-1

conversations on the tram in cafés and public places trying to figure out which language is being spoken, often with a degree of approximation – Slavic, probably, but which language? Persian, it is that probing song-like intonation that catches the ear; an Indian language, yes because of that particular sibilant perhaps, but which? There are so many. You will also notice how children spice their home language with one of the languages of the country they are now growing up in. Like my former colleagues at Ghent University, you may find yourself trying to puzzle together the variety and prominence of languages in shop windows in certain neighbourhoods (Collins & Slembrouck, 2005) or in the small ads on the wall next to the counter. You will be puzzled by the multilingual information on flyers in chip shops, Chinese take-ways and cafés announcing the latest craze (De Vierman, 2019). By now, you will have probably noticed that sales are announced in block capitals in English as SALES and no longer in the local language. Why? It could be called an ongoing love affair with English in Flanders. You can hear it everywhere, especially on the radio, where prominent Flemish politicians, businesspeople and celebrities convince us of the urgency of their opinions and the course of action to take by spicing them with commonplace American expressions or lopsided English translations of commonplace Flemish expressions. Does this mean that the local population has suddenly converted to English? I doubt it. Does this mean you can go into any shop announcing SALES in the front window and demand to be served in English? I doubt it. Something else must be happening here and it has been happening against the backdrop of or in step with increased multilingualism. It could be argued that it both obscures and at the same time indexes the presence of increasing multilingualism. So using English in commerce is not simply an informative strategy to attract foreign customers through the lingua franca. Obviously, decisions were taken by the store owners in question, colour schemes and font sizes were decided upon, printers were contacted, etc. This was a conscious form of symbolic or more specifically iconic action that seemingly paid little heed to the language laws in place, something that would cause trouble in France where the Loi Toubon is designed to protect the French language in advertising and public media. This process of iconisation (Irvine & Gal, 2000), by which English no longer functions as its denotational self but as an element in selling particular lifestyles, by repackaging language ideological resonances of "English" as a whole.[1] But this highly visible item is just one element in a sea of perhaps less visible but certainly audible forms of multilingualism that we engage in, and which surround us on a daily basis. And translation, it is argued here, is an integral part of and at a given moment finds itself at a somewhat hidden centre of all this semiotic activity. Some might call translation a communicative hiccough, a glitch in a seemingly ubiquitous flow of communication that has somehow miraculously resolved language difference. SALES has now silently replaced solden/soldes without mention of translation. As mentioned above, other forms of semiosis and symbolic action, including iconisation, come into play here and will also be dealt with in the chapters that follow.

The purpose of this book is to add a humble corollary to the vast amount of work being done in contemporary sociolinguistics, multilingualism and translanguaging, linguistic ethnography and anthropology. The idea is to address a topic that is often sidestepped or for some reason left underexplored in such work, i.e. translation and its dynamics in multilingual contexts. This is not meant as criticism. On the contrary, the idea is to contribute to the debate and try to show how translation is practised against the backdrop of and through the continuously shifting multilingual sites that the above-mentioned scholars and many others explore with such energy and insight (viz. Pennycook & Otsuji, 2015). The very existence of translation as a practice presupposes multilingualism and translanguaging. It is argued here, however, that translanguaging, despite its importance both practically and theoretically, cannot resolve the problem of translation or fully explain its existence.[2] The term multilingualism is also problematic and has been challenged in the literature, especially with regard to heightened levels of mobility in present-day societies, which highlight real language practices and rightly call into the question fixed notions of languages and their supposed national borders:

> Recently, a number of terms have emerged, as scholars have sought to describe and analyse linguistic practices in which meaning is made using signs flexibly. These include, among others, flexible bilingualism (Creese and Blackledge, 2010); code-meshing (Canagarajah, 2011); polylingual languaging (Jørgensen, Karrebaek, Madsen, and Møller, 2011); contemporary urban vernaculars (Rampton, 2011); metrolingualism (Otsuji and Pennycook, 2011; translingual practice (Canagarajah, 2013; heteroglossia (Bailey 2012; Blackledge and Creese, 2014); and translanguaging (Garcia; Creese and Blackledge, 2011). The shared perspective represented in the use of these various terms considers that meaning-making is not confined to the use of "languages" as discrete enumerable, bounded sets of linguistic resources.
>
> (Blackledge & Creese, pp. 32–33 in Canagarajah, 2017)

The term multilingualism will be used throughout the book for reasons of simplicity and as a catch-all term for all of these practices. (Mundane) metrolingualism will be used, however, to encapsulate practices described in Chapter 5. It should be pointed out that despite these new insights and their related conceptualisations, the participants reported on in this book do use such descriptors as French, Dutch, Spanish and Lingala, which is also something that has to be taken into consideration (Silverstein, 1981, pp. 22–23).

The study is ethnographic[3] to the extent that it attempts to present translation as it is viewed and practised by those who were observed and spoken to and engaged with in the project, practically none of whom have had any formal training in translation. The study is also adjacent to or overlaps with a huge body of work on non-professional/natural translation and language brokering (Harris, 2013; Antonini et al., 2017). The focus here is slightly different, however, in that it attempts to build a composite, though by no means complete, picture of translation in multilingual settings in a single city, which, by the sheer diversity of its population (156 different nationalities[4]), is de-facto multilingual. In doing so, the study must engage with migration in some fashion and try to trace trajectories of movement, both physical and social, experienced by those reported on here. At the same time, it wishes to explore certain issues both methodological and others that have emerged from the research as it progressed or, at times and for long periods, when it failed to progress at all, and valuable data got irretrievably lost as a result of glitches with computers and flash drives.

What is presented in the chapters that follow is not a detailed blow-by-blow report of translation practices at all the sites visited. It comprises a selection of shorter pieces – seven in all – that highlight the shifting contexts and dynamics of a variety of translation practices, each with its own goals and purposes, based on the data gathered, observations made and conversations held in the city of Ghent over a period of seven years. The study is not exhaustive, nor does it claim or wish to be and hopefully it will encourage others to pick up where it left off, be it here in Ghent or other cities in Belgium or, who knows, in other cities around the world. In this regard, I would like to consider it as being fractal (Irvine & Gal, 2000) in the sense that the distinctions I manage to tease out in relation to translation across the various sites are reflected in and can be re-examined from other angles to provide a more complete picture, also given the knowledge that I have been attributed certain roles and have taken on various other roles depending on the encounter in each case.[5]

Again, this work is not only about translation, which is a very old chestnut, as translation is never only about itself. In fact, in one of the chapters (Chapter 3) translation is conspicuous by its very absence but it does, nonetheless, resound in the debate and the underlying reasoning and in so doing casts a shadow, if you will, or leaves a virtual imprint that belies its absence. In another chapter (Chapter 4), the evidence of translation is ephemeral and evaporates once the participants in an ad-hoc interpreting event go their separate ways, leaving behind then what I have termed a momentary chain lightning of indexicalities (Hanks, 1999; Silverstein, 2003). In others (Chapters 5 and 7), it extends into the multimodal and inter-semiotic in its attempts to transfer meaning. In Chapters 5, 8 and 9, it is a basic element in identity formation and in Chapter 8 it mainly serves not only as a mainstay of inclusion but also as a reminder of borders in public behaviour.

The title of each chapter gives an indication of the site under discussion. The subsections of each chapter address translation in relation to various genres and/or activity types including adjacent letters, games, menus, cookbooks, official documents, signage and beer mats. All of these items (and others besides) provide an anchor for a given generic activity or form each genre's entextualised/semioticised precipitate (Silverstein & Urban, 1996) and basis for translational and interpreting activity. The notion of precipitate is important in the whole work. As Silverstein and Urban note:

> To equate culture with its resultant texts is to miss the fact that texts (as we see them, the precipitates of continuous cultural processes) represent one, "thing-y" phase in a broader conceptualisation of cultural process.
>
> (Silverstein & Urban, 1996, p. 1)

Translation and interpreting are phases in this cultural process (Gal, 2015) and not merely the result of a narrow engagement with a previous text or thing-y phase. Further, a variety of concepts will be drawn on to analyse these translational phases and multilingual activity involved. Translation is understood here as an umbrella term that includes both interpreting and written translation. The study was written for both (PhD) students and TS scholars alike but also harbours the ambition of being accessible to a broader audience. As was mentioned above, the research reported on here was overshadowed by what has become known as the 2015 "immigrant crisis," a topic too vast to address here. However, the work could be understood as being grounded in forms of migration extant in the global north but then again not entirely so. What I wish to avoid are the implications of seeming superfluity that might be associated with the term global north. The pain, or indeed release, of migration is not specific to any geographical region. What the book does attempt to argue is that migration and subsequent translation are permanent states that need to be addressed as such instead of being understood as the result of temporary crises that will someday be miraculously solved by some political sleight of hand,[6] after which we will all return to our happy monolingual pre-Babylonian selves and homelands. The book was written by a migrant who settled in the city of Ghent and who is aware of the fact that the word migrant has a string of cognates and a variety of politically changed meanings that fluctuate, drift off into oblivion and resurface time and again. Much like the language of ethnic and national stereotypes (Leerssen in Beller & Leerssen, 2007, pp. 63–76), they are all interdiscursive constructs (Gal, 2015; see Chapter 3 and 5 for further illustration and debate) that become manifest in numerous ways, ranging from the slogans on banners at demonstrations for or against migrants to public policy on migration and its related language ideological underpinnings. But migration is as old as humanity. In the words of Seamus Heaney

> *Our pioneers keep striking*
> *Inwards and downwards*
> *Every layer they strip*
> *Seems camped on before*[7]

The sense of impermanence that stems from the words *camped on* and *before* demands our attention, not because the words point to a former impermanence that has since been resolved in the nation, but rather to an impermanence that is a constant, even at the heart of any nationalist or community project. This impermanence became real in the block of flats in Chapter 7, which has since been raised to the ground and its community dispersed, a policy not particular to the city of Ghent. It is also visible in shifts in and flows of (migrant) population in the city mentioned in Chapter 8.

The research reported on in this book was all conducted before the Coronavirus pandemic and also purposely ignores the internet and social media, even though they were ever-present, no matter where I turned during this study. Let us then consider this little book as trying to create a variegated picture of an already sedimented layer of social practices involving translation and interpreting that has long since been covered over by many further digitised layers of related semiotic activity. So the study is a translational archaeology of sorts. The layer reported on here also had its own global connections, as hopefully will become visible in the pages that follow.

Notes

1 Including the language of globalisation, business, trade and commerce, American popular culture.
2 For a discussion, see the Further Comments section in Chapter 5.
3 See Chapter 2 for a full discussion.
4 https://www.statistiekvlaanderen.be/sites/default/files/docs/LIIM-Gent. pdf – see page 6 of pdf for details (consulted 14/10/2021).
5 See also the section on Position in Chapter 2.
6 Britain's attempt to send migrants to Rwanda comes to mind.
7 From the poem 'Bogland' in Door Into the Dark, Seamus Heaney, 1969, Faber & Faber, London.

References

Blommaert, J. (2013). *Ethnography, Superdiversity and Linguistic Landscapes. Chronicles of Complexity* (Critical Language and Literacy Studies, [18]). Bristol/Buffalo, NY: Multilingual Matters.

Collins, J., & Slembrouck, S. (guest Eds.). (2005). Multilingualism and diasporic populations: Spatializing practices, institutional processes, and social hierarchies. *Special Issue of Language & Communication*, 25(3), 189–334.

De Vierman, A. (2019). *Non-professional Translation in the City of Antwerp.* Leuven: KU Leuven. Faculteit Letteren.

Gal, S. (2015). Politics of translation. *Annual Review of Anthropology,* 44 (1), 225–240. doi:10.1146/annurev-anthro-102214-013806

Hanks, W. (1999). Indexicality. *Journal of Linguistic Anthropology,* 9(1–2), 124–126.

Heaney, S. (1969). *Door into the Dark.* London: Faber & Faber.

Irvine, J. T., & Gal, S. (2000). Language ideology and linguistic differentiation. In P. V. Kroskrity (Ed.), *Regimes of Language: Ideologies, Polities and Identities* (pp. 35–83). Santa Fe, NM: School of American Research Press.

Leerssen, J. (2007). The poetics and anthropology of national character (1500–2000). In M. Beller & J. Leerssen (Eds.). *Imagology: The Cultural Construction and Literary Representation of National Characters. A Critical Survey* (p. 76). Amsterdam: BRILL.

Silverstein, M. (2003). Indexical order and the dialectics of sociolinguistic life. *Language & Communication,* 23, 193–229. doi:10.1016/S0271-5309(03)00013-2

Silverstein, M., & Urban, G. (1996). *Natural Histories of Discourse.* Chicago, IL: University of Chicago.

1   Basic Assumptions and Theoretical Underpinnings

The basic (theoretical) assumptions underpinning this study are both old and at the same time rather recent. They comprise approaches to and studies on genre as an activity type, cities and migration taken together,[1] globalisation and superdiversity and ethnography and, of course, non-professional[2] or rather natural translation. Each of these items will be set out in this and the following chapter and will also be drawn on in the various chapters of the book, where they will merge with or form the backdrop to more pertinent detailed analyses using conceptual tools that fit the specific type of translational action involved.

Genre as an Activity Type

Genre is understood as an activity or part of the activities framing it. Such a view is based on Vološinov (1973), Bakhtin (1986), Martin[3] (1984), Hanks (1987) and Wetherell et al. (2001), among others. This view takes us beyond classical definitions of literary genres to speech genres:

> Language is realized in the form of concrete utterances (oral or written) by the participants in the various areas of human activity. These utterances reflect the specific conditions and goals of each such area. ... Each sphere in which language is used develops its own relatively stable types of these utterances. These we may call genres.
>
> (Bakhtin, 1986, p. 60)

Wetherell, Taylor and Yates hold a similar view:

> Genres are diverse ways of acting, of producing social life, in the semiotic mode. Examples are: everyday conversation, meetings in various types of organizations, political and other forms of interview, and book reviews.
>
> (Wetherell et al., 2001, p. 235)

DOI: 10.4324/9781003363811-2

Vološinov ([1930] 1973) clearly recognised genre as an 'activity type' involving language use, as the following quote illustrates:

> Social psychology exists primarily in a wide variety of forms of the utterance of little *speech genres* of internal and external kinds – things left completely unstudied to the present. All these speech performances are, of course, joined with other types of semiotic manifestations and interchange – with miming, gesturing, acting out, and the like.
>
> (Vološinov, 1973, pp. 19–20)

Here already we can witness what is now known as the multimodal nature of human interaction, considered from the very outset to be interactional and mediated by social circumstance, in fact, as being embedded totally within the social and historical contexts in which they came about, a view which Vološinov shares with Bakhtin.

A similar view to Vološinov's is also commonly held in linguistic anthropology, as the following quote illustrates:

> Genres are not sets of discourse features,[4] but "orienting frameworks, interpretive procedures, and sets of expectations".
>
> (Hanks, 1987, p. 670)

The features of this tripartite definition are nascent in Vološinov's, for example. In the definition, the discourse features that were considered in the past as constituting genre are now subsumed under a broader definition of genre as activity, outside of which the discourse features identified or recognised as pertaining to a particular genre would make no sense. Elsewhere, Hanks also notes the following in relation to genre:

> Perhaps we should assume, in fact, that emergence is the basic mode of being of genres, and that category labels, like mnemonic devices, grow mainly out of retrospection. …, I will take genres to be defined by the interplay of formal linguistic features, native metalinguistic typifications and the actual practices in which the actors engage.
>
> (Hanks in Silverstein & Urban 1996, p. 161)

"Native metalinguistic typifications" and "actual practices" lead us directly to those involved in this book and to how they talk about what they are doing. The question then is where does any particular genre begin and, for the purposes of this work, how does genre relate to translation, for translation is a key element in all the instances of genre activities described in the seven cases examined in this book? Emergence is also key, as these events were not tightly scheduled, if at all. The main activity types and genres will become apparent in each case at each site reported on.

No matter how it is defined or conceptualised (see Blackledge & Creese in Canagarajah, 2017 for a list of conceptualisations), multilingualism is a feature of each of these sites, including translation, if and when it is needed to maintain communicative interaction during an activity (Flynn, 2014). The multilingual activities and related translation practices and products have been observed over a long period of time, which means that they have been subject to reflection. Such reflection has tamed the venture and limited the number of sites reported on, the justification for this being that other sites in the same city can be reported on with greater acumen by others who are more familiar with them over time than the present author.

From a theoretical perspective, Hanks's position on genre can be considered as belonging within a broader definition of practice (Bourdieu, 1984). In the TS literature, the link between translational norms (Toury, 1995) and Bourdieu's notion of habitus was posited by Simeoni. Daniel Simeoni has the following to say: "Indeed, norms without a habitus to instantiate them make no more sense than a habitus without norms" (Simeoni, 1998, p. 33). Hanks further ties the notion of habitus to genre:

> Genres then are key parts of habitus... Rather they embody just the kinds of schemes for practice that constitute the habitus. And like it they are unequally distributed among agents in any social world. For access to certain genres involves power and legitimacy and serves as a form of sociocultural capital.
>
> (1996, p. 246)

In relation to the habitus of the translator, one question we can ask regarding the translators and interpreters encountered during the course of this study is the following: when were they appointed that role, i.e. of (an ad-hoc) translator or interpreter and, consequently, at what moment did that realisation occur: why is it always me who gets asked to do this?

Cities, Migration and Natural Translation

A number of important works in Translation Studies address configurations of the nexus of city, migration and (natural) translation in some way or use the nexus as their point of departure. For example, Sherry Simon mainly approaches it from the angle of literary translation, which forms the modus operandi for her elucidating detailed studies of such cities as Montreal, Calcutta, Trieste, Barcelona and Czernowitz, among others (Simon, 2006, 2011). These studies bear witness to the central role of translation in cross-cultural production and the creation of new forms of expression and multicultural exchange. The cities she explores have/ had long since been hubs of encounter, despite the political upheavals they found themselves embroiled in, especially in pre-WWII central Europe.

Building on insights from both their work, Cronin and Simon's special issue (2014) introduces the idea of the translational city (see also Simon in Lee 2021) and collects studies on the city as a 'translation zone': "The term is used ...more specifically to refer to the cultural and geographical spaces that give rise to intense language traffic" (Cronin & Simon, 2014, p. 121).

Research that takes us beyond the confines of the city to document translation in its numerous forms can be found in the sweeping and intriguing historical study of the Habsburg monarchy by Michaela Wolf (2015). Wolf's meticulous work examines and describes the various configurations of translation at all levels of society in the former monarchy. In so doing she identifies what she calls 'habitualised' translation, i.e. translation as a matter of habit acquired by necessity by those in the lower orders of a highly stratified social hierarchy and

> part of the typical cultural configurations of multi-ethnic spaces. The perpetual recontextualizations brought about by these configurations and the diversity of their cultural imprints are vital factors in the characteristic concentration of cultural circulation in such spaces.
>
> (Wolf, 2015, p. 51)

Though hierarchies are less outspoken or visible and differently configured nowadays, the distinction Wolf makes between institutionalised and habitualised translation still holds today and informs the debate on "non-professional translation," albeit in other terms.

In her book on translation and migration, Moira Inghilleri (2017) explores the topic mainly in the context of the United States but also from a global and historical perspective. The work is philosophical in tone and draws on the apparatus of cultural studies to discuss the many links between translation and migration, which she examines through three lenses: (i) fluidity, hybridity, identity; (ii) reconfiguring 'us' and 'them' and (iii) translation and hospitality (Inghilleri 2017, pp. 18–31). In her closing discussion of "spaces of translational identity exploration," she returns Cronin's call for a "cosmopolitanism from below" (Cronin, 2006).

Lieven D'hulst and Kaisa Koskinen's edited volume (2020) is also historical in its approach to tracing translation policy "in the long 19th century." In their introduction, D'hulst & Koskinen stress the importance of translation as a "local practice" and purposely steer clear of a "national perspective[5]" with a view to continuing "this emerging spatially determined research tradition in Translation Studies, agreeing that one of the best possible loci to find evidence of such an interaction is the city" (D'hulst & Koskinen, 2020, p. 2). In the volume, the authors also provide their "answer to Michael Cronin's (2006, p. 14) call for micro-cosmopolitan thinking from below" (D'hulst & Koskinen, 2020, p. 1).

In the studies of non-professional translation collected in Antonini et al. (2017), migrant inmates comprise the focus of Rossato's chapter, for example, whereas Baraldi and Gavioli highlight "migrant-friendliness" among lay interpreters in medical consultations. The whole collection forms a state of the art on the topic of non-professional translation, while succeeding in bringing such types of translation and interpreting into the direct purview of TIS. Prior to this, Brian Harris's *Annotated Chronological Bibliography of Natural Translation Studies* (1913–2012) Harris bears witness to his long-standing dedication to the topic (Harris, 2013). The city also forms the backdrop to Judith Weisz Woodsworth's edited volume, *Translation and the Global City* (2021), which highlights the work of young scholars building on Simon's foundational research.

The wealth of material in *The Routledge Handbook of Translation and the City* (Tong King Lee, 2021) is too vast and detailed to discuss here, save to note that in relation to the nexus of city migration and translation it completes the picture set out by Suresh Canagarajah in *The Routledge Handbook of Migration and Language* (2017).

Given the scope and depth of these two handbooks, and other research besides, translation and the 2016 "migration crisis" will not be dealt with here. The literature on the nexus of city, migration and translation discussed above forms the foundation for the studies in this book. Such notions as 'translation zone,' and 'habitualised' and 'local' translation and the view of building a cosmopolitanism from below, though perhaps not explicitly mentioned, have all helped frame the studies in some way. It is hoped that, as this work unfolds, certain patterns or at least observations emerging from this small-scale urban inquiry will be of use in understanding a couple of elements of the nexus of city migration and translation. Understanding the migration "crisis" will require much more research and reflection, especially regarding the multiple ramifications of the use of the word "crisis" in the first place.

Non-professional translation, language brokering, natural translation, native translation and 'habitualised' and 'local' translation: all of these are similar concepts and indicate that there is a considerable amount of 'non-professional' present in our societies, especially in contexts where city and migration come together. The fact that such similar concepts exist means that they stress different aspects of the phenomenon: the specific characteristic of brokerage, the 'naturalness' of translating or the fact that it has been internalised as a habit. Despite Toury's critical remark that he is "far from convinced that there is a need for this added compartmentalization in our field" (Toury, 2012, p. 277, footnote 1, referring to Brian Harris's blog on all these topics), we believe that this terminological diversity enriches the analysis potential of the discipline when dealing with this type of non-professional translation and interpreting. In a similar vein to translanguaging (space) and translation (space), this terminological diversity reflects the interest shown by scholars from a number of different but adjacent disciplines in the phenomenon of multilingualism in cities and the translation practices that "naturally" belong to it. The questions and outcomes discussed above are also very much in line with work conducted by many other scholars within non-professional translation such as Faulstich Orellana (2009). In the meantime, as discussed above, non-professional translation and interpreting has become the object of research within mainstream TS, as is witnessed by volume (Antonini et al., 2017) along with recent conferences[6] on the topic outside of NPIT.

In outlining its various forms, Harris has the following to say:

> Nevertheless, the selection of the major ones given above[7] should be enough to show incontrovertibly that non-professional translation is very widespread, probably more so than the professional kind, and exists in fields that are just as varied. Furthermore, it is not limited by age, education, culture or historical period, and does not require prior training in translating. Readers are asked to bear in mind that the blog is descriptive and not prescriptive: it aims to paint broadly the translation scene as it is and not as it ought to be.
>
> (Harris in Antonini et al., 2017, p. 42)

The term non-professional translation still remains problematic because the activity it encompasses is defined negatively in relation to its opposite number, professional translation. But the term professional translation itself is of fairly recent coinage and brings with it a whole set of assumptions, a pertinent one being that professional translators have to have training in Translation Studies. This was seldom the case for the vast majority of "professional" translators up until recently. In contrast, much like cooking, "non-professional" translation is a regular, if not daily practice for many people. The focus here, however, is on how such translation is illustrative of social practices of various types and the omnipresence of multilingualism in cities. One final assumption that needs to be mentioned here is that the analyses will also draw on basic concepts from Translation Studies. These concepts will be dealt with as they arise and brought into play with others as the analysis requires, as will become clear in the chapters that follow.

Globalisation and Superdiversity

Increasing levels of globalisation and resulting levels of complexity in encounter have led to what Vertovec (2006) calls "superdiversity." A lot has been written on the topic since but globalisation and superdiversity are approached here mainly through the lens of language use and translation. Though it is obvious to assume that globalisation and superdiversity are related, we can hardly argue that they are recent or unprecedented or that globalisation and superdiversity coincide completely and were indeed instantaneous (Mufwene,[8] 2004). The impact of globalisation[9] and subsequent superdiversity (Blommaert, 2013, inter alia) on multilingualism in our cities is slowly being mapped out mainly within what could broadly be termed contemporary sociolinguistics, though this is certainly not the only area of study involved.

How to frame the phenomenon of multilingualism and translation in a globalised superdiverse city, and again what to call it, is a topic of hot debate (Pennycook & Otsuji, 2015; Canagarajah 2017; Lee, 2021). How to factor translation into the whole debate is even more problematic as the literature on language use and superdiversity in the city often sidesteps the issue or fails to take it on board, despite the omnipresence of translation in everyday life. This has been largely compensated for by Lee's handbook, however. It is, nonetheless, important to consider translation against the backdrop of increased multilingualism and try to frame it as such. As was mentioned in the introduction, those studying multilingualism have mainly resorted to the concept of translanguaging: "Translanguaging is the act performed by bilinguals of accessing different features of various modes of what are described as autonomous languages … Therefore, translanguaging goes beyond what has been termed codeswitching, although it includes it" (Garcia, 2009, p. 140).

Not unlike Gumperz's concept of repertoire (Gumperz, 1964), particularly in the way it was understood by Hymes in his seminal article (Hymes, 1972), translanguaging is a particularly useful notion as it enables us to encapsulate everyday multilingual practices without having to describe such practices in terms of separate, often unrelated languages. An equally interesting and related concept is that of translanguaging space[10] (Li Wei, 2011, p. 1223), which he describes as "a space for the act of translanguaging as well as a space created through translanguaging." Following Li Wei's reasoning, not only does the space[11] exist, but it is also created, negotiated and maintained by the activity of translanguaging. Hence, it follows that these spaces propagate themselves, as it were, and behave in certain ways all of which Pennycook and Otsuji and their fellow researchers have been trying to bring into focus in their studies of Sydney and Tokyo, among other places (Pennycook & Otsuji, 2015). These notions offer us ways into the maze of everyday multilingualism and also tie in with concepts coined within TS like translation zone and translation spaces that were discussed in the previous subsection that go beyond the rigid boundaries of discrete languages and predicated on population differences.

Though they do not theorise translation in the way it is theorised in TS, it seems obvious to assume that translational activities occur in such settings. Though Pennycook and Otsuji place a very clear emphasis on the flux and ever-changing nature of multilingualism in cities, it is important to point out that translation, whether it is ad hoc or not, predicates certain roles in communicative interaction and longer spans of time during which these roles can develop and take shape (Stovel et al., 2011). Though translanguaging does not theorise translation per se, it neither includes nor excludes it. In fact, Wei's understanding of translanguaging space bears strong resemblance to a concept coined at an earlier date by Michael Cronin called 'translation space':

> [e]verything, from small local theatres presenting translations of plays from different migrant languages to new voice recognition and speech synthesis technology producing discreet translations in wireless environments to systematic client education for community interpreting to translation workshops as part of diversity management courses in the workplace.
>
> (Cronin, 2006, p. 68)

In relation to time span, Cronin argues elsewhere (Cronin, 2008) that, wherever translation is needed, it slows down time and belies the instantaneous flux of globalised communication highlighted and analysed in Pennycook et al. (2015) or in Blommaert (2013). So it could be argued that translation spaces are further manifestations of translanguaging spaces that have incorporated various degrees of language brokering, ad-hoc interpreting or translation or even more permanent varieties of the same that have become part of the local economy in all its various aspects (see the discussion in Chapters 3 and 4).

So following Mufwene (2004), it seems important to point to existing networks of exchanges and sociocultural and commercial activities that facilitated recent forms of globalisation and related superdiversity. The networks explored in the chapters are much less visible than those of multinationals and multimedia conglomerates, but they do exist and become visible in the exchanges discussed below. That they involve translation implies that there is a time differential in relation to layers of migration. Being able to translate which is not quite the same thing as being bi- or multilingual first involves acculturation in such settings and practices and this takes time as well. It also involves the allocation and distribution of translational and language roles and competences in social interactions (Gumperz, 1964; Hymes, 1972; Toury, 1995; Blommaert, 2001; Harris, 2013). Indeed, this does not sit well with the notion of instant communication implicit either in globalisation or in superdiversity.

To conceptualise the individuals in such translanguaging or translation spaces, Michael Cronin draws on notions such as "denizen" and "common ground" as useful ways of understanding migration and migrant communities in urban neighbourhoods:

> In opposition to the figure of the citizen we find the notion of the "denizen," ... where a denizen is a person who dwells in a particular place and who can move through and knowingly inhabit that place (our emphasis). Therefore, Common Ground dedicates itself to

encouraging the proliferation of vernacular, ideographic, and connotative descriptions of local places that can take the form of place myths, stories, personal associations, and celebrations of various kinds, (www.commonground.org.uk).

(Cronin, 2008, p. 267)

These two concepts create room for multinational and multi-ethnic experiences of the same cities and their various neighbourhoods. This of course begs the question: why the opposition between citizens and denizens? It seems plausible that one could be both at the same time (see discussion of Chapters 3 and 8 inter alia). It is also the case that often less visible dynamic interactions between the two occur in those areas of cities not immediately associated with the 'translation zone.' Cronin is quick, therefore, to point to an all too hasty adherence to the rhetoric of globalisation:

> The inability to translate thus foregrounds a cultural blindness on the part of the traveller who finds he is not so much an empowered citizen of the world as the unwilling denizen of a place. In this sense, the failure to translate reinstates the importance of a particular kind of time in overly spatialized and visualized models of the global.
>
> (Cronin, 2008, p. 269)

Cronin's concerns are echoed indirectly in an early ethnographic study of globalisation. In relation to globalisation, drawing on numerous studies of sites with global connections, Burawoy et al. (2000) make a tripartite distinction between imaginations, forces and connections in tracing various types of interconnected global practices, which in turn dismisses any claim to easy linearity or immediate global access in global processes. They stress the importance of each of these factors as the following quote illustrates:

> Just as global connections are transnational, global imaginations are post-national in that they react against the nation, reinvigorate the local, demand regional autonomy, or clamour for universal identities... Even if it is true, pace Appadurai, that global imaginations have emancipated themselves from the nation state and that the cultural is rapidly disconnecting from the nation state, which should not blind us to the latter's continuing influence in the realm of forces and connections.
>
> (Burawoy et al., 2000, pp. 34–35)

When migrants move to a city they often come into contact with local housing authorities and may be lucky to find accommodation in municipal housing complexes (see Chapters 6 and 8 for a more complete discussion). They also often have connections in the neighbourhoods they move to, as will be illustrated in Chapter 4. It is in such places that citizens encounter denizens and, after a certain period of time, where denizens may become citizens of the host country. These places and other public facilities like local clinics and hospitals are and continue to be sites of multilingual encounter and hence translation. This has been reported on in the literature (viz. Angelelli, 2010, or Cox & Lázaro Gutiérrez, 2016, inter alia) and continues to be a focus of study in superdiverse cities.

The interaction of these two forces – new and more complex forms of migration, and new and more complex forms of communication and knowledge circulation – has generated a situation in which two questions have become extremely hard to answer: who is the Other? And who are We? The Other is now a category in constant flux, a moving target about whom very little can be presupposed; and as for the We, ourselves, our own lives have become vastly more complex and are now very differently organised, distributed over online as well as offline sites and involving worlds of knowledge, information and communication that were simply unthinkable two decades ago. According to Blommaert, superdiversity is driven by three keywords: mobility, complexity and unpredictability (Blommaert, 2013, pp. 5–6).

Though Blommaert (2013) researched "linguistic landscapes" in the Berchem area of Antwerp, Belgium, in more recent works he pointed to how these landscapes have global reach and are connected by invisible lines to various places throughout the globe (Blommaert, 2018). His comments on migrant and local populations and the multilingual interactions involved are therefore highly relevant for this study. In this respect, it must be noted that mobility is both spatial and social and that migration and settlement must also be viewed from a longitudinal and temporal perspective, and this includes how local population flows are enmeshed with migration flows. Though Blommaert does not theorise translation in his study of Berchem, Koskinen has already explored the link between such linguistic landscapes and translational spaces in her study of the suburb of Hervanta in Tampere, Finland (Koskinen, 2012).

So, next to the other perspectives explored above in framing the debate on the topic of this book, globalisation and superdiversity and their resultant translation spaces can be regarded as forming a backdrop for the case studies discussed below, each of which give a more situated view of a given site and the discursive and translational spaces they create. It should be noted however that the two terms will not be taken for granted or used as blanket terms. It would seem advisable in the studies that follow to see how to use the two terms with caution and not simply rely on their explanatory power but rather see what forms they take on in the sites under scrutiny.

Notes

1 This does not mean that migrants move exclusively to cities. For a study of migrants in the Italian countryside see Translating the Village by Andrea Ciribuco (2020).

2 An unhappy term.

3 Martin's work belongs in the framework of (Hallidayan) Systemic Functional Linguistics which can be traced back further to Firth (and Malinowski) who lay at the origin of an '"enduring and distinctive vision of language study" in twentieth-century Britain' (Stubbs, 1996, p. 22 quoted in Kenny, 2001 – Firthian Linguistics) – a tradition that has always taken the social dimensions of language use into account. In a similar vein, Wetherell et al.'s work belongs within discourse analysis, "a hybrid field of inquiry" (Slembrouck, 1998–2004), which studies language in use/language in social situations and stems from a number of disciplines within the social sciences. More specifically, Wetherell's work belongs within Discursive Psychology and draws on the work of Sacks and Goffman. Hanks's work belongs squarely within linguistic anthropology which according to Duranti (2008, p. 5) "…is the understanding of the crucial role played by language (and other semiotic resources) in the constitution of society and its cultural representations."

4 This approach to genre is epitomised in Crystal & Davy (first published in 1969), some of the chapters of which are entitled, The Language of Conversation, The Language of Religion etc. The authors remarked back in 1969 that:" we must remember here that the term 'genre' has never been given a precise, generally agreed definition, and is regularly used to refer simultaneously to varieties operating at different degrees of theoretical abstraction – for example, 'poetry' v 'prose' as well as 'essay' v 'short story', which are subcategories of prose" (p. 75). Despite the refinement of analysis in the book, genre can be equated more or less with varieties of 'text' (spoken or written). For a more general discussion of text and text-types see also Dressler (1978).

5 The default unit of measure underlying most forms of cross-comparison in any comparative approach to linguistics and literary studies and the mainstay of translation studies, informing such concepts as norms and systems, source and target, etc.

6 See Translating the Neighbourhood, an online conference organised by Andrea Ciribuco and Anne O'Connor (NUI Galway) and Non-professional interpreting and translation: advancement and subversion, a panel at the upcoming quite Congress in Oslo in 2022.

7 For a detailed overview of the literature on non-professional translation and interpreting, see Harris (2013).

8 For a fascinating lecture see https://www.youtube.com/watch?v=Ger PWSqSCww.

9 On the need for translation studies and other disciplines in studying the sociolinguistics of globalisation and migration, see Slembrouck (2011).

10 For a detailed discussion of the term in relation to language and migration, see Christina Higgins (2017) on Space, Place and Language, in Chapter 5 Part 1 of the Routledge Handbook of Migration and Language.

11 See the section on Zones Places and Spaces in Some Tentative Conclusions for a discussion.

References

Angelelli, C. V. (2010). A professional ideology in the making: Bilingual youngsters interpreting for their communities and the notion of (no) choice. *Translation and Interpreting Studies*, 5(1), 94–108.

Antonini, J. R., Cirillo, L., & Rossato, L. (2017). *Non-professional Interpreting and Translation: State of the Art and Future of an Emerging Field of Research* (Benjamins translation library 129). Amsterdam: John Benjamins.

Bakhtin, M. M. (1986). *Speech Genres and Other Late Essays*. (C. Emerson & M. Holquist, Eds. and V. W. McGee, Trans.). Austin: University of Texas Press.

Baraldi, C., & Gavioli, L. (2017). Intercultural mediation and "(non)professional" interpreting in Italian healthcare institutions. In R. Antonini et al. (Eds.) *Non-professional Interpreting and Translation* (pp. 83–106). Amsterdam/Philadelphia, PA: John Benjamins Publishing Company.

Bauman, R. (2002). The ethnography of genre in a Mexican market: Form, function, variation. In P. Eckert & J. Rickford (Eds.), *Style and Sociolinguistic Variation* (pp. 57–77). Cambridge: Cambridge University Press. doi:10.1017/CBO9780511613258.004

Blackledge, A., & Creese, A. (2017). Translanguaging in mobility. In S. Canagarajah (Ed.), *The Routledge Handbook of Migration and Language* (pp. 31–46). London/New York: Routledge.

Blommaert, J. (2013). *Ethnography, Superdiversity and Linguistic Landscapes. Chronicles of Complexity* (Critical Language and Literacy Studies, [18]). Bristol/Buffalo, NY: Multilingual Matters.

Blommaert, J. (2018). *Durkheim and the Internet*. London: Bloomsbury Publishing Plc.

Bourdieu, P. (1984). *Le sens pratique*. Paris: Editions de Minuit.

Burawoy, M., Blum, J. A., George, S., Gille, Z., Gowan, T., Haney, L., Klawiter, M., Lopez, S. H., O' Riain, S., & Thayer, M. (2000). *Global Ethnography. Forces, Connections, and Imaginations in a Postmodern World*. Berkeley: University of California Press.

Canagarajah, S. (Ed.). (2017). *The Routledge Handbook of Migration and Language* (1st ed., Routledge Handbooks in Applied Linguistics). London: Routledge.

Ciribuco, A. (2020). Translating the village: Translation as part of the everyday lives of asylum seekers in Italy. *Translation Spaces*, 9(2), 179–201. doi:10.1075/ts.20002.cir

Cox, A., & Lázaro Gutiérrez, R. (2016). Interpreting in the emergency department: How context matters for practice. In F. Federici (Ed.), *Mediating Emergencies and Conflicts* (Palgrave Studies in Translating and Interpreting, pp. 33–58). London: Palgrave Macmillan UK.

Cronin, M. (2006). *Translation and Identity*. London/New York: Routledge.

Cronin, M. (2008). Downsizing the world: Translation and the politics of proximity. In A. Pym M. Shlesinger, & D. Simeoni (Eds.), *Beyond Descriptive Translation Studies: Investigations in Homage to Gideon Toury* (pp. 265–276). Amsterdam/Philadelphia, PA: John Benjamins Publishing.

Cronin, M., & Simon S. (2014). *Introduction: The City as Translation Zone*. New York: Blackwell/Wiley.

Crystal, D., & Davy, D. (1997). *Investigating English Style*. London: Routledge.

D'hulst, L., & Koskinen, K. (2020). *Translating in Town: Local Translation Policies During the European 19th Century* (L. D'hulst & K. Koskinen, Eds.). New York: Bloomsbury Academic.

Dressler, W. U. (Ed.). (1976). *Current Trends in Text Linguistics*. Berlin/New York: Walter De Gruyter.

Duranti, A. (2008). *Linguistic Anthropology* (Cambridge Textbooks in Linguistics). Cambridge: Cambridge University Press.

Faulstich Orellana, M. (2009). *Translating Childhoods. Immigrant Youth, Language, and Culture* (The Rutgers Series in Childhood Studies). New Brunswick, NJ: Rutgers University Press.

Flynn, P. (2014). Using the concept of genre to frame translational practices. Innovative info-technologies for science. *Business and Education*, 1(16), 26–30.

Garcia, O. (2009). Bilingual education in the 21st century: A global perspective. *Translation Studies*, 7(2), 119–132.

Gumperz, J. J. (1964). Linguistic and social interaction in two communities. *American Anthropologist*, 66(6), 137–153. http://www.jstor.org/stable/668168

Hanks, W. F. (1987). Discourse genres in a theory of practice. *American Ethnologist*, 14(4), 668–692. http://www.jstor.org/stable/645320

Hanks, W. F. (1996). *Language and Communicative Practices*. Boulder, CO: Westview Press.

Harris, B. (2013). An Annotated Chronological Bibliography of Natural Translation Studies with Native Translation and Language Brokering 1913–2012. https://www.academia.edu/ 5855596/Bibliography_of_natural_translation (last accessed 25/10/2020).

Higgins, C. (2017). Space, place and language. In S. Canagarajah (Ed.), *The Routledge Handbook of Migration and Language* (pp. 102–116). London/New York: Routledge.

Hymes, D. H. (1972). On communicative competence. In J. B. Pride and J. Holmes (Eds.), *Sociolinguistics. Selected Readings* (pp. 269–293). Harmondsworth: Penguin.

Inghilleri, M. (2017). *Translation and Migration* (New Perspectives in Translation and Interpreting Studies). London: Routledge.

Kenny, D. (2001). *Lexis and Creativity in Translation. A Corpus-based Study*. Manchester: St. Jerome.

Koskinen, K. (2012). Linguistic landscape as a translational space: The case of Hervanta, Tampere. In J. Vuolteenaho, L. Ameel, A. Newby, & M. Scott (Eds.), *Language, Space and Power: Urban Entanglements Studies across Disciplines in the Humanities and Social Sciences 13* (pp. 73–92). Helsinki: Helsinki Collegium for Advanced Studies.

Lee, T. K. (2021). *The Routledge Handbook of Translation and the City* (Routledge Handbooks in Translation and Interpreting Studies). London/New York: Routledge.

Martin, J. R. (1984). Language, register and genre. In C. F. Geelong (Ed.), *Children Writing: Reader* (ECT Language Studies: Children Writing) (pp. 21–30). Vic: Deakin University Press.

Mufwene, S. S. (2004). Colonization, globalization, and the future of languages. In J. Bindé (Ed.), *The Future of Values. 21st-Century Talks* (pp. 161–165). Paris/ New York: UNESCO Publishing/Berghahn Books.

Pennycook, A. & Otsuji, E. (2015). *Metrolingualism: Language in the City*. London/New York: Routledge (Taylor and Francis).

Rossato, L. (2017). From confinement to community service: Migrant inmates mediating between languages and cultures. In R. Antonini et al. (Eds.), *Non-professional Interpreting and Translation* (pp. 157–176). Amsterdam/ Philadelphia, PA: John Benjamins Publishing Company.

Silverstein, M., & Urban, G. (1996). *Natural Histories of Discourse*. Chicago, IL: University of Chicago Press. http://www.academia.edu/5855596/Bibliography_of_natural_translation (last accessed 16/05/2018).

Simeoni, D. (1998). The pivotal status of the translator's habitus. *Target*, 10(1), 1–39.

Simon, S. (2006). *Translating Montreal: Episodes in the Life of a Divided City*. Montreal: McGill-Queen's University Press.

Simon, S. (2011). *Cities in Translation: Intersections of Language and Memory*. London/New York: Routledge.

Slembrouck, S. (2011). Globalization theory and migration. In R. Wodak, B. Johnstone, & P. Kerswill (Eds.), *The SAGE Handbook of Sociolinguistics* (pp. 153–164). London: Sage.

Slembrouck, S. (2022). What Is Meant by Discourse Analysis. https://www.english.ugent.be/da (consulted 25/09/2022).

Stovel, K., Golub, B., & Milgrom, E. M. M. (2011). Stabilizing brokerage. In Proceedings of the National Academy of Sciences of the United States of America. http://www.pnas.org/content/early/2011/12/13/1100920108.full.pdf (last accessed 27.12.2011).

Toury, G. (1995). *Descriptive Translation Studies- and Beyond*. Amsterdam/Philadelphia, PA: Benjamins.

Vertovec, S. (2006). The emergence of super-diversity in Britain (Working Paper No. 25). Centre on Migration, Policy and Society. Oxford: University of Oxford.

Vološinov, V. N. (1973). *Marxism and the Philosophy of Language* (Studies in Language) (L. Matejka and I. R. Titunik (Trans.) and M. Silverstein (Ed.). New York/London: Seminar Press.

Wei, L. (2011). Moment Analysis and translanguaging space: Discursive construction of identities by multilingual Chinese youth in Britain. *Journal of Pragmatics*, 43(5), 1222–1235. doi:10.1016/j.pragma.2010.07.035

Weisz Woodsworth, J. W. (Ed.). (2021). *Translation and the Global City: Bridges and Gateways* (1st ed.). Routledge. https://doi-org.kuleuven.e-bronnen.be/10.4324/9781003094074

Wetherell, M.; Taylor, S., & Yates, S. J. (2001). *Discourse as Data a Guide for Analysis*. Milton Keynes: The Open University.

Wolf, M. (2015). *The Habsburg Monarchy's Many-Languaged Soul: Translating and Interpreting, 1848–1918* (Benjamins Translation Library, Volume 116). Amsterdam/Philadelphia, PA: John Benjamins Publishing Company.

2 Approach and Positioning

Having presented an overview of basic assumptions and theoretical underpinnings in the previous chapter, it is now time to turn to the overall approach used in this study, and the position, both personal and professional, adopted in conducting it.

Approach

Any study of natural translation and interpreting, wherever such natural translation and interpreting might occur, can of late be considered as falling within the remit of Translation Studies. The task might seem easy enough: find some natural translation and interpreting data, frame the data theoretically and subject them to scrutiny using existing TS methods of analysis and see what the results are. Surely there are enough methods and models? Why venture into other areas of study, like sociolinguistics, for example, and then why ethnography? The answer lies first in the matter of finding data. How do you find it? Running experiments, no matter how ecologically sound the circumstances, would put an awful lot of strain on naturalness. Then there's the problematic notion of data and what it consists of as such. Next comes the matter of framing that data theoretically. The previous chapter already provides a set of theoretical underpinnings, and we haven't even got started yet. Translation theory will certainly be of use as will TS methods of analysis but will only go part of the way in trying to understand the "natural" in natural translation and interpreting and how it is articulated at the various sites under study. Concepts from sociolinguistics and elsewhere will help broaden the canvas. But to get a fuller picture with a higher resolution, ethnography is needed, both as a point of departure and as a guiding light with a view to providing a final result.

But this gives rise to another, perhaps more pertinent question. If the focus is on natural translation and translation and interpreting practices why not opt for linguistic ethnography or its American equivalent linguistic anthropology as a general approach, as they are clearly closer in terms of area of study and method? Though my doctoral research fell squarely within the domain of linguistic ethnography, its main focus was on literary translators and their translation practices. For the last

DOI: 10.4324/9781003363811-3

16 years since then, I've been involved in Translation Studies but always had a clear and continuing interest in ethnography, particularly in relation to translation practices. Regarding linguistic ethnography, a basic tenet of this study adheres to is

> that the contexts for communication should be investigated rather than assumed. Meaning takes shape within specific social relations, interactional histories and institutional regimes, produced and construed by agents with expectations and repertoires that have to be grasped ethnographically.
>
> (Rampton, 2007, p. 585)

Another point it shares with linguistic ethnography is the following: it is

> an interpretive approach which studies the local and immediate actions of actors from their point of view and considers how these interactions are embedded in wider social contexts and structures. According to Erickson (1990, p. 92), interpretive approaches are necessary because of the 'invisibility of everyday life' which when held at arm's-length can empirically serve 'to make the familiar strange'.
>
> (Copland & Creese, 2015, p. 12)

While acknowledging linguistic ethnography "as a site of encounter" (Rampton, 2007, p. 585) in which this study might find a place, it would be dishonest, however, given my own academic trajectory and long-term involvement in TS, to claim that it is a linguistic ethnography. It would be equally dishonest to call it an ethnography in linguistic anthropological terms, even though it shares their basic points of departure and epistemology, which are discussed in detail in the following section of this chapter.

In terms of overlap with linguistic ethnography and anthropology, this study uses ethnography to discover and contextualise translation and interpreting practices at a number of sites in a city. It then turns to models and concepts developed within Translation Studies to make "translational sense" of these practices. The next step is to further explicate these practices by drawing on a set of concepts taken from an extensive toolkit used by linguistic ethnographers and sociolinguists. Hopefully, this will help fill a gap and constitute a reconnect or redress an imbalance of sorts. It is argued here that filling the gap requires considering theoretical developments in Translation Studies over the past 30 years. In developing its critical apparatus, Linguistic Ethnography has tended to focus on translanguaging rather than on translation and interpreting,[1] which is no criticism as studies of translanguaging are highly insightful for TS scholars (Beres, 2015). Though attention is paid to translation in Linguistic Anthropology, it also tends to focus on problems and theoretical considerations arising from fieldwork (viz. Duranti, 2008, p. 154), which in themselves are important, as the following quote illustrates:

If we conceive of translation as the mere exercise of matching words or phrases in one language with those of another, we are likely to miss one of the main contributions of the anthropological study of language, namely, the idea that for anthropologists the activity of translating is intimately related to ethnography, to the contextualization of words within the activity and the larger socio-political and cultural systems in which their speakers participate.

(Duranti, 2008, p. 154)

Here, Duranti highlights the intimate relationship between translation and ethnography – and also between the anthropologist as translator and as ethnographer. But is the "contextualisation of words within the activity and the larger socio-political and cultural systems in which their speakers participate" not one of the daily tasks of translators and interpreters[2]? Also of considerable importance are contributions, from a semiotic perspective, to thinking on translation by Silverstein (Silverstein in Rubel & Rosman, 2003) and Gal (2015), especially in relation to indexicality. These contributions echo and run parallel to studies of transfer in TS (see the section on Transfer and Transduction in Chapter 3 for more details). However, these writings do not approach translation and interpreting as everyday social practices in themselves or as elements or focal points of possible ethnographies "of communication" (Hymes, 1977). Hanks does recognise this as such, however (Hanks, 2014), as does Gal (2015). It still could be argued that translation and interpreting practices fall under the remit of 'linguistics' in linguistic anthropology or linguistic ethnography. This is probably true, but the task of rhyming TS and these areas of study is too vast an exercise to undertake here and not the purpose of this book. In contrast, ethnographies of translation or interpreting remain feasible ventures both practically and theoretically and they might spark incremental debates in the "site of encounter" (Rampton, 2007, p. 585) and elsewhere in time to come.

Before discussing ethnography in more detail it is important to note the book's connection with (indebtedness to) sociolinguistics and its links to ethnography as conceptualised in work by John Gumperz and Dell Hymes (viz. Gumperz & Hymes, 1972; Hymes, 1977, inter alia). The approach to sociolinguistics espoused here follows the line set out and developed in their work and that of others too numerous to mention here. Underlining the importance of and tracing developments in this work would take up too much space. What is required to coalesce with the study of natural translation and interpreting is a sociolinguistic view that takes migration, globalisation and superdiversity into account. This is the view taken by Jan Blommaert in building on Hymes's work:

The sociolinguistic approach, Hymes continues, involves a shift 'from focus on 'structure to focus on function – from focus on linguistic form in isolation to linguistic form in human context' (Hymes, 1974, p. 77). And it is this sociolinguistic approach ... one that considers language as organized not just in a linguistic system but in a sociolinguistic system, the rules and dynamics of which cannot be automatically derived from considering their linguistic features; and one that so examines language in an attempt to understand society. (See Hanks, 1996; Agha, 2007; Blommaert, 2005 for elaborate discussions.) An ethnographically formulated sociolinguistics, seen from that angle, is a critical social science of language.

(Blommaert, 2010, p. 3)

Further in proposing *a* sociolinguistics of globalisation, he speaks literally of building "on the shoulders of others," and goes on to "categorically opt for a sociolinguistics of resources, not of languages," and notes that "mobility is a central theoretical concern in this sociolinguistics of resources" (Blommaert, 2010, pp. 21–22). The focus on resources will fit opportunely into the discussion of the practices described in different cases, especially in Chapters 4 and 7, and is an emergent category alongside mobility in all the cases in the book.

Ethnography, Theorising and Emergence

Ethnography first needs to be defined, which is a thorny task in itself. According to the website of the American Anthropological Association, "Ethnography[3] involves the researcher's study of human behaviour in the natural settings in which people live." This covers just about anything in human affairs, but in our case, it involves studying people's translation and interpreting practices in situ. Such studies have mainly been conducted by scholars outside the domain of anthropology proper (Flynn, 2005; Koskinen, 2008; Duflou, 2016; Tesseur, 2017; Van Rooyen, 2018; Brewis, 2019). Writing in the late 1990s, Agar notes the following by way of tentative explanation for the growing interest in ethnography outside of anthropology:

Ethnography, the former province of anthropologists and sociologists, is now entering the mainstream of United States social research. The reasons for the shift are numerous, but many of them boil down to a simple pair of questions- "Who are these people" and "What are they doing?" My guess is that in a time of dramatic and continual change, a time when organizations and institutions have become unsure of the nature of the world and their role in it, ethnography looks like a useful way to find some answers, because it features discovery and learning of other human perspectives and ways of living, rather than the controlled testing of previously derived hypotheses.

(Agar, 1997, p. 1155)

Translation scholars have been part of that "mainstream" for some time already, in the same way they have absorbed theories and models from other areas of study in the humanities and elsewhere. Regarding the questions of "who these people" are and "what they are doing," ethnographies of translation and interpreting have so far included studies of literary translators in the Netherlands and Flanders (Flynn, 2005), conference interpreters and translators working for the European institutions (Koskinen, 2008; Duflou, 2016), translators working for international NGOs (Tesseur, 2017), people working at community radio stations in South Africa (Van Rooyen, 2018) and university students and lecturers at a South African university (Brewis, 2019).

To gain insight into how to go about asking these two basic questions in ethnographic terms, we turn to Clifford Geertz's classical explanation:

> And it is understanding what ethnography is or more exactly what *doing ethnography is,* that a start can be made towards grasping what anthropological analysis amounts to as a form of knowledge. This, it must immediately be said, is not a matter of method. From one point of view, that of the textbook, doing ethnography is establishing rapport, selecting informants, transcribing texts, taking genealogies, mapping fields, keeping a diary, and so on. But it is not these things, techniques and received procedures that define the enterprise. What defines it is the kind of intellectual effort it is: an elaborate venture in, to borrow a notion from Gilbert Ryle, 'thick description'".
>
> (Geertz, 1973, pp. 5–6)

The items listed in the textbook view of doing ethnography can be re-imagined and also quite easily transposed into useful aspects of method (Flynn, 2010, pp. 116–119) in an ethnography of translation and interpreting practices. Completing the list of activities involves doing field-work and participant observation, which are further discussed below. Attention however has to be paid to Geertz's warning in the quote about ethnography not being "a matter of method." There is more to undertaking 'an elaborate venture in … "thick description"' than completing the tasks on the list. Thick description is a matter of uncovering what Geertz called "a stratified hierarchy of meaningful structures" (Geertz, 1973, p. 7) emerging from a study. This has to do with the "form of knowledge" anthropology seeks to generate, which is empirical (Marcus, 1998, p. 18) or as Eriksen reminds us in commenting on early social scientists inspired by Hume's philosophy "who would rather travel into the social world itself in order to obtain first-hand experience through the senses (empirical means, literally, 'based on experience')" (Eriksen, 2001, p. 10). Regarding the generalisable knowledge generated by an ethnography, Geertz remarks: "what generality it contrives to achieve grows out of the delicacy of its distinctions rather than the sweep of its abstractions" (Geertz, 1973, p. 25).

It also has to do with ethnography's relation to theory or rather to theorising. There are two important points to take into account in this respect. First there is a certain research logic upon which ethnography is based, according to Agar:

> Ethnography is "abductive," a term invented by Charles Peirce (Hookway, 1992), one of the founders of American pragmatism. Abduction is about the imaginative construction of a "p" that implies an observed "q," or, to put it in our terms, about the modification or development of a frame that explains a rich point. Abduction is a research logic that features the development of new theoretical propositions to account for material that the old propositions didn't map onto. Ethnography is theory generating...
>
> (Agar, 1997, p. 1162)

A "rich point" is something that happens during fieldwork that an ethnographer doesn't understand, something that requires further inquiry. How can this be explained? What is the p underlying the q, as it were? Second, as also Agar points out:

> "theory" in the received view refers to a coherent literature about some domain of human life, a literature that consists of concepts and the propositions that link them. Theory, in fact, is the source of the hypotheses that the received view sets out to test. Ethnography is often associated with "description" rather than "theory," but that is an error. Theory in ethnography grows out of the data in an emergent way, since it organizes the concepts and relationships uncovered during ethnographic research.
>
> (Agar, 1997, p. 1164).

Agar's remarks on theory apply to how the theoretical framework of this work was put together in general and also to the sets of analytical concepts brought into play in the various chapters, thereby foregrounding the methodological importance of description and emergence. They also fit in with what was unknown and discovered during fieldwork. There was always an element of surprise both during fieldwork and afterwards when poring over notes and remarks or transcribing and analysing the materials: "participant observation makes it possible for surprises to happen, for the unexpected to occur" (Agar, 1997, p. 1157). Agar summarises the whole process in very concise terms:

> any trajectory in the ethnographic space will run on the fuel of abduction. You'll read or see how surprises came up, how they were taken seriously, and how they were explained using concepts not anticipated when the story started.
>
> (Agar, 2006, paragraph 66)

How the cases are presented, and the rationale of their presentation grew as the study progressed. And were not decided on beforehand or in keeping with strict chronology of when the fieldwork was carried out. There are seven cases in the book. Each case deals with (different) instances of natural translation/interpreting in a given situation or at a given site. So the site, the people and their translational activities are always the point of departure in each case. A site or situation first has to be described, – yes, I'm an old-fashioned Touryan descriptivist but also follow Marcus's point on description being basic to ethnography that "describe, interpret, and discover new relationships and processes embedded in the world" (Marcus, 1998, p. 18). Only after or during description does a model of analysis suggest itself, something that fits the translational situation involved along with its sociocultural/sociolinguistic contours. As the events described are "embedded in the world" they first have to be identified as such. As Goodwin notes,

> an event being seen, a relevant object of knowledge, emerges through the interplay between a domain of scrutiny and a set of discursive practices being deployed in a specific activity … It is not possible to work in some abstract world where the constitution of knowledge through a politics of representation has been magically overcome.
>
> (Goodwin, 1994, pp. 606–607)

This is a deliberate methodological stance that also tries to take into account the emergent nature of social interaction and resulting translation. Susan Gal even argues the following in her own work and also in relation to translation itself:

> The term [translation], I suggest, points usefully to a whole family of semiotic processes. They purport to change the form, the social place, or the meaning of a text, object, person, or practice while simultaneously seeming to keep something about it the same. These writings share the key insight that different social worlds—including those of scholars—emerge through forms of communication that presume and often mark practices, objects, genres, and texts as recontextualizable, thereby mediating among the domains of knowledge/action that the communications themselves play a role in enacting and separating.
>
> (Gal, 2015, p. 226)

It is only during or after description that concepts from TS, sociolinguistics and elsewhere come together in the course of analysis. It is a process of discovery whereby the immediacy of translational interaction suggests ways of being transformed into an academic account. This process of discovery, and of connecting the materials of the study to sources in the literature, runs through to the very end in the conclusions. As Geertz notes:

> The ethnographer "inscribes" social discourse; he writes it down. In doing so, he turns it from a passing event, which exists only in its own moment of occurrence, into an account, which exists in its inscriptions and can be reconsulted.
>
> (Geertz, 1973, p. 19)

Even in the case of the school to which a questionnaire was sent beforehand (Chapter 8), the process of discovery remains vital. Though we are convinced that we know what we are asking, this never means that we ourselves grasp the full set of implications of our own questions, let alone how they will be understood by others. Respondents will forever draw our attention to something new or to other ways of understanding what we ask (Briggs, 1986). Analysis may have a cumulative effect as the separate analyses of the various cases evolve. Patterns of multilingual/translational behaviour may emerge across the various sites, along with ways of describing them, or they may not, which is also worth noting.

Next to the above and once again following Geertz, any ethnographic account "must be cast in terms of the constructions we imagine [they] place upon what they live through and the formulae[4] they use to define what happens to them" (Geertz, 1973, p. 15). Similarly, Silverstein argues for an understanding of "the properties of ideologies and ethno-theories, which seem to guide participants in social systems, as part and parcel of those social systems, which must be understood as meaningful" (Silverstein, 1981, pp. 22–23). This further opens the door to a discussion of local and learned forms of knowledge or what Kenneth Pike termed *emic* and *etic* views of the world (Pike, 1966). This distinction plays out in chapters of the book in terms of how participants talk about their activities (their own meta-commentaries) in conjunction with how they are described in scholarly terms in the analysis. This distinction is still tricky as it may create the illusion that people's meta-commentaries are not learned, which is not the case. They are just different and hence may escape the attention of a researcher who is too busy taking care of business and talking shop, i.e. not paying attention, as Hymes notes.

Ultimately, the term ethnography is used to describe how this study came about, how it took shape, and what it ended up being, but the term is used with a degree of caution and trepidation even and always will, particularly when used by someone from outside of anthropology proper. The approach used is ethnographic in that it attempts to give an account of translation as it is understood and practised by the people involved in the study, hence to the extent that it comprises studies *with* and not just *of* the participants in the project (Ingold, 2018, pp. 13–14).

Ethnography: Contestations and Complications

Despite the clarity of Geertz's outline ethnography as thick description, what doing ethnography entails has been contested and has become further complicated over time. These contestations can be understood typically in terms of conceptual engagement with and problematisation of models and theory, on the one hand, and engagement with the practicalities of fieldwork and how these experiences, interactions and observations map back onto ongoing theoretical discussions, on the other hand. As scholars from the 'mainstream' it is important for us to keep these things in mind when it comes to doing ethnography.

Fieldwork and Ethnography

Doing ethnography means *being there* after all, even though 'there' is a shaky notion at best, as will be discussed in the section on multi-sited ethnography below. In outlining the key characteristics of the way ethnography works, Agar notes,

> First, *I was there*. When an ethnographer takes an interest in some comer of the world, he or she goes out and encounters it first hand. In the jargon this is called participant observation, an awkward term that simply codes the assumption that the raw material of ethnographic research lies out there in the daily activities of the people you are interested in, and the only way to access those activities is to establish relationships with people, participate with them in what they do, and observe what is going on.
>
> (Agar, 1997, p. 1157)

Being a participant and an observer didn't always coincide in my case. Establishing rapport was not initially for the purposes of study, either. In most of the situations, participation came long before conscious observation, which involved my switching from being an insider to being an outsider of sorts, after which participation and observation became self-conscious and even awkwardly academic (see the section Position below). I was there and being there was vital to the ethnographic exercise, but what this means or how one is there is by no means straightforward. We turn to Dell Hymes to illustrate the point. Hymes's ethnographic work is of particular interest as he used ethnography to study language practices directly. He makes a distinction between doing fieldwork and doing ethnography, even though fieldwork is basic to be what an ethnographer does.

> It is important to distinguish between "ethnography" and "fieldwork." There are two related reasons for this. First, "field work"

is a suitable general term for any contact with people as sources of information; second, and most important, not all "field work" in this sense is ethnography" in the sense I intend. There are again two reasons.

First, contact, having been there, is not enough...If the anthropological methodology in field work is effective, it is based on more than being there, however romantic some of us may make the field work experience sound...This brings us to the second way in which I should like to restrict the term -"ethnography." I should like to give "ethnography" the connotation of inquiry that is open to questions and answers not foreseen, for which possible observations need not be pre-coded, and for which the test of validity need not fit within a pre-structured model.

(Hymes, 1980, pp. 73–74)

The distinction Hymes makes could probably be explained in terms of the difference between a more straightforward qualitative study (gathering data in the field and analysing it according to a pre-structured and predetermined model) and an ethnography in which the researcher is particularly attentive to emergent factors in the interactions she is witnessing and participating in.

Participant Observation and Ethnography

The distinction Ingold makes is not between fieldwork and ethnography but between ethnography and participant observation and related understandings of data (Ingold, 2018, pp. 11–14). This seems strange as, ordinarily speaking, no ethnography is possible without participant observation. The distinction seems to stem from understandings of what ethnography has come to mean in sociology, i.e. a means of data collection, which Ingold rejects, so much so that he ends up seriously distancing himself from ethnography in that form (see Ingold, 2017, pp. 21–26; 2018, pp. 120–121). Ingold raises the problem of data and the term's association with quantitative methods of analysis and further explains his understanding of the nature and purpose of participant observation:

Though literally a datum is a thing given (from the Latin *dare*, 'to give'), in the vocabulary of science it has come to mean that which is there for the taking – a 'fact' that has already precipitated[5] out from the ebb and flow of life in which it once was formed...

Should we regard participant observation ... as a method for collecting data that are not quantitative but qualitative, cannot be tabulated in numbers, expressed in measurements or compiled in statistics? ... Yet something makes me uneasy about the idea of 'qualitative data.' For the quality of a phenomenon can only lie in its presence – in the way it opens up to its surroundings, including we who perceive it. The moment we turn the quality into a datum, however, the phenomenon is closed off, severed from the matrix of its formation.

(Ingold, 2018, pp. 12–13)

In stressing the importance of involvement in the field, much in the same way Hymes does, he drives his point home:

To repeat, participant observation is a way of studying *with* people. It is not about writing other lives, but joining with them in the common task of finding a way to live. Herein I contend lies the difference between ethnography and anthropology. Thus for the anthropologist, participant observation is absolutely *not* a method of data collection. It is rather a commitment to learning by doing, comparable to that of an apprentice or student.

(Ingold, 2018, p. 14)

This reasoning chimes with Agar's who notes: "participant observation makes it possible for surprises to happen, for the unexpected to occur" (Agar, 1997, p. 1157) and further that

Any trajectory in the ethnographic space will run on the fuel of abduction. You'll read or see how surprises came up, how they were taken seriously, and how they were explained using concepts not anticipated when the story started.

At this juncture, it is worth going all the way back to Geertz's remark all those years ago about ethnography not being a matter of method but an exercise in "thick description" (Geertz, 1973, pp. 3–30).

Surely this echoes what Ingold is insisting on and points again to the importance of a consistent engagement with the field?

In a similar vein in relation to scholars from the "mainstream," Marcus also expressed concern about the relative "thinness" of certain ethnographies conducted within cultural studies in which

The space of potential discovery and increased understanding of processes and relationships in the world (which require a bedrock of very thick description indeed) is taken over by a discourse of purpose and commitment within a certain moral economy. While the latter is essential to any contemporary critical ethnography it cannot be developed at the expense of contributions to ethnographic knowledge that describe, interpret, and discover new relationships and processes embedded in the world.

(Marcus, 1998, p. 18)

Marcus also returns to Geertz in casting ethnography in terms of the "bedrock" of thick description, once again echoing the sense of commitment and attentiveness visible in the quotes discussed so far.

Rapport and Complicity

Another area of contestation and complication is that of "establishing rapport" and what it entails, as it has generated a considerable body of comment in anthropology over the years.[6] Establishing rapport is fraught with difficulty and is not to be taken for granted. As Ingold remarks: "anthropologists often stress the importance, in fieldwork, of establishing rapport. But rapport can mean both friendship and report. Is it right to befriend people to write them up?" (Ingold, 2021, p. 13). Ingold's play on words stems from the distinction between ethnography as research process during which participants are befriended and ethnography as a written product during which these friendships may be forgotten. Friendship, however, is not the only form of rapport possible. Its later neglect or betrayal in written ethnography is not the only or most obvious outcome either. This is certainly not the case with regard to many of the participants in this book. Again, Ingold is using this play on words to draw our attention to something he considers vital to participant observation:

> *Taking others seriously* is the first rule of anthropology. This doesn't just mean attending to their deeds and words. More than that, we have to face up to the challenges they present to our assumptions about the way things are, the kind of world we inhabit and how we relate to it.
>
> (Ingold, 2021, pp. 14–15)

Ingold's point is also an ethical one, which is visible in his rejection of the idea of treating people as mere sources of possible data. Rapport and remaining sensitive to those we are interacting with also reminds us that we are also involved in more ways than one, as Tusting and Maybin point out:

> the researcher as participant observer is part of what is going on [...] and part of the nexus that makes action possible (Scollon & Scollon, 2007). Sensitivity to the implications of this is at the heart of the ethnographic endeavour. The involvement of the ethnographer in social action, coupled with the impossibility of divorcing the self from the process of interpretive praxis, mean that the researcher is inevitably part of, and shapes, the research that is being produced. This reflexivity is an issue in all social scientific research, but one which is not necessarily thematised in other areas in the way that ethnography problematises it.
>
> (Tusting & Maybin, 2007, p. 578)

The views expressed by Tusting and Maybin are part of a long ongoing debate on rapport. Marcus (1998, pp. 105–131) reflects at length on the nature of rapport and its troubled history, and on how it can be cast more pragmatically in terms of collaboration between researcher and participant. But he also shows how it always had that shadow side of complicity from the outset in moving from the "outside" to the "inside" in research. In tracing the history of the use of the term "rapport" in anthropology, Marcus notes the following in relation to complicity:

> Likewise, as the figure frequently evoked in past critiques of field-work to probe the ethical problems of a too-innocent figure of rap-port, complicity specifically plays to and constructs a different and more complex sense of the substance of the ethnographer-subject relationship.
>
> (Marcus, 1998, p. 121)

He explores complicity not only in the (negative) sense of being an accomplice but also and more pertinently in terms of how it articulates a growing awareness of the increased complexity of rapport,[7] especially in contemporary research into increasingly complex globalised local relations:

> In contrast, while it begins from the same inside-outside boundary positioning [as rapport], investment in the figure of complicity does not posit the same faith in being able to probe the "inside" of a culture (nor does it presuppose that the subject herself is even on the "inside" of a culture, given that contemporary local knowledge is never only about being local).
>
> (Marcus, 1998, p. 118)

He does not propose that rapport be replaced by complicity:

> The figure of rapport has always been acknowledged as being too simplistic to stand for the actual complexities of fieldwork, but it has had—and continues to have—great influence as a regulative ideal in professional culture.
>
> (Marcus, 1998, pp. 126–127)

The "great influence [of rapport] as a regulative professional ideal" is also the reason for its continuous critique and such critique stems more from the actual practicalities and complications of establishing rap-port and their consequences (as a standard of professional practice) than its contemplation and problematisation as a theoretical concept as such. This critique seems to run parallel with far-reaching reflections on the subject[8] conducting and engaged in fieldwork (Bourdieu, 2001, pp. 173–184) and equally on what is understood in fieldwork as context as partly given and partly co-constructed – see for example the discussion of scale in Chapter 5. Complicity hence serves as a corrective in that it is a constant reminder of the complexity underlying any form of rapport.

Contestations and complications are common in any field of study.[9] The ones outlined in this section probably sound familiar to most scholars in some form or another as they basically reflect a honing of the tools of both theory and practice over time. There is a tendency to forget this when we borrow concepts from other disciplines.

Ethnography and Time

Many years of interaction and observation has gone into this little work. Time and its vagaries has played an important role in the study – something which contemporary academics have very little of in their daily tasks of writing up projects and reports and applications for funding, outside of all their other tasks and duties. The project reported on here was done outside of those many tasks and without university or government funding, which certainly delayed its completion. Young researchers be advised: the time needed to do this type of research is at odds with expectations regarding publication turnaround and career planning. Time is of the essence in ethnography because you need plenty of it, even to waste.

For example, time spent is presented as part of Blommaert's credentials in his ethnography of superdiversity and linguistic landscapes in Berchem. After mentioning his and his family's long-term commitment to his neighbourhood and to grass-roots movements within it, he notes the following:

> My ethnographic engagement with this neighbourhood, therefore, is in is most literal sense longitudinal and participant observation; it is, in fact 'ethnographic monitoring' in the most immediate sense of the term (Hymes, 1980; Van der Aa, 2012; Van der Aa & Blommaert, 2011). It has enabled me to witness and capture both the objective and subjective features of the area, to participate in processes of change and transformation – and experience such processes, and to maintain an extensive network of contacts and resource people in the neighbourhood. The neighbourhood has been my learning environment for about two decades now.
>
> (Blommaert, 2013, p. 21)

Very few scholars can present such credentials, certainly not academics starting off their career. The time scale involved allowed him to witness and reflect on growing superdiversity and multilingualism close at hand in his own neighbourhood. But you still need the professional distance and acumen to spot and analyse such emerging practices. It would be disingenuous, however, to set this as a standard and expect it from others, but it does stress the importance in ethnography of time spent, both inside and outside the halls of academe.

To make this a little less daunting, we can make a loose distinction between the time of lived experience in a neighbourhood and the time spent actually conducting the study (including the activities on Geertz's list above). But an awful lot of time can go into what is classically known as establishing and maintaining rapport, with little or no "data" to show. Is this time wasted?

Partly because of the very shortage of time in academic circles, and perhaps as a result of fashion and a penchant for catch-all buzz words, the term 'ethnography' or 'ethnographic research,' has become shorthand in Translation Studies for time spent interviewing participants, after which all engagement with ethnography's "developed form of empiricism" is neatly sidestepped or simply ignored. As Translation Studies is continuously looking beyond its own confines in search of useful concepts in priming its multidisciplinary ethos, translation scholars are expected to keep abreast of debates in other areas of study. So, time spent also means staying abreast of these debates. My trepidation and caution in calling this study ethnographic also stems from this, as is probably more than obvious by now.

Next to the above there is the real time of translation and interpreting practices and the various interactions they emerged from and the seeming abolition of time in their description and analysis. This is what Eriksen (2001, pp. 32–33) calls the "ethnographic present" most ethnographies are written up in – as if the events described and analysed have become frozen in time in some eternal present that somehow give them the aura of immovable fact in contrast to the historical sociocultural flux from which they emerged. Bourdieu warns us of the dangers of moving from the real time of practice to its conspicuous absence in science:

> Passer du schème pratique au schéma théorique, construit après la bataille, du sens pratique au modèle théorique, qui peut être lu soit comme un projet, un plan ou une méthode, soit comme un programme mécanique, ordonnance mystérieuse mystérieusement reconstruite par le savant, c'est laisser échapper tout ce qui fait la réalité temporelle de la pratique en train de se faire. La pratique se déroule dans le temps et elle a toutes les caractéristiques corrélatives, comme l'irréversibilité que détruit la synchronisation ... Il y a un temps de la science qui n'est pas celui de la pratique. Pour l'analyste, le temps s'abolit ...
>
> (Bourdieu, 1980, pp. 136–137)

Passing from a schema of practice to that of theory, constructed after the battle, from a sense of practice to a theoretical model which can be read either as a project, a plan or a method, or as a mechanical programme, a mysterious prescription mysteriously reconstructed by the scientist, is allowing to escape all that makes up the temporal reality of practice in its process of being made. Practice takes place in time and has all its correlative characteristics, such as the irreversibility that synchronisation destroys… There is a time of science which is not that of practice. For the analyst, time abolishes itself …

(my translation)

Factoring time into our theoretical models has caused us to contest the very notion of synchrony, especially that of any language system (see Blommaert, 2010, pp. 4–6 for example). The debate on synchrony and diachrony is almost as old as Saussure's distinction itself (see Matejka in Vološinov, 1973, pp. 165–167), which shows that once formulated concepts have a habit of sticking around. This should not prevent us from taking Bourdieu's advice and heighten our awareness of and attention to the contingencies of the day to day and to the flux of time and emergence in context.

Multi-sited Ethnography

The study as a whole can be called multi-sited, first for the following practical reason: it includes a social housing scheme, an inner-city primary school, street corner social work, public transport, an Italian restaurant, an Irish pub, the city registration office, in the same city, it must be noted. From a theoretical perspective, it fits and resonates with many of the observations made by Marcus on the multi-sitedness and the social complexities the term encapsulates (Marcus, 1998, pp. 79–104). In quoting Marcus (1995, 2011) in his opening remarks on multi-sited ethnography (MSE), Paolo Boccagni notes three basic understandings of the term:

> Firstly as "a shorthand for all ways of doing ethnographic fieldwork in more than one site;"
> Secondly, as "a focus on the processual connections between sites," and
> Thirdly, as "an attempt to reconstruct the system of relations and trans-local interdependencies that coproduce any particular social setting or phenomenon
>
> (Boccagni, 2019, p. 2)

In relation to this study, the ambitions expressed in the second and third understanding can only be attempted in part and the possible outcomes remain unknown at this juncture outside of commonalities of approach and method used across the seven cases. Though the "particular social phenomenon" under scrutiny is natural translation and interpreting, it still remains to be seen whether "processual connections between sites" or a "system of relations and trans-local interdependencies" can be laid bare that "co-produce" natural translation and interpreting. This is perhaps too ambitious a goal to attempt but hopefully some traces of connections or relations and interdependencies may emerge towards the end of the study.

In the meantime, Marcus's thoughts were kept in mind as the study evolved across its various sites. As Marcus notes:

> Multi-sited research is designed around chains, paths, threads, conjunctions, or juxtapositions of locations in which the ethnographer establishes some form of literal, physical presence, with an explicit, posited logic of association or connection among sites that in fact defines the argument of the ethnography.
>
> (Marcus, 1998, p. 90)

The "logic of association or connection" defining the argument of the ethnography was particularly that of translation witnessed and participated in by a co-migrant at the various sites under study.

For Marcus, doing multi-sited ethnography involves "following" any number of phenomena (people; the thing; the metaphor; the plot story or allegory; the life or biography; or the conflict) across various sites (Marcus, 1998, pp. 90–95). What I was following was particular forms of language practice among people in multilingual settings. This meant going from one place to another in search of these practices, which multi-sited ethnography provides for. As Boccagni remarks,

> Whenever social and cultural phenomena are not reducible to one-site observation, due to their emergence in multiple locations or to their inherent mobility, MSE has come to the fore as an almost self-evident option.
>
> (Boccagni, 2019, p. 4)

Translation and interpreting practices are not restricted to a single site and are shaped by the particular contexts of the sites in question, along with the constellations of multilingualism they go along with and from which they emerge. These are all things that cannot be assumed as given beforehand – like assuming that only English is spoken in an Irish pub – and have to be found out in each particular case. To substantiate the claim to multisitedness beyond the actual number of sites, whether these practices are inter-connected, what Boccagni calls "a matter of in-betweenness, rather than only of multisitedness" (Boccagni, 2019, p. 5) also remains to be seen.

Positioning – Personal and Professional

This section addresses my position both personal and professional regarding the sites presented in the chapters that follow and how the research was conducted. The sites I studied in detail were chosen for their links with my being a migrant and with the (migrant) circles I move in. This only became really clear when working my way through all the materials I had collected during the research and then further upon reflection, mainly in retrospect, as this migrant position remained obscured by my professional academic interest in the project.

As a migrant, I am more like a long-term denizen (Cronin, 2008) than a native inhabitant of a multilingual neighbourhood (Blommaert, 2013), but we can rightly ask whether this makes any real difference when it comes to analysis. Nonetheless, the fact that I am not a native of the city or country was well known to most concerned in this study and was also something I shared with many of them. Except for one case (Chapter 4), all of the participants I addressed and informed prior to commencing the project agreed to participate and allowed me to interview them and be an observer at the site in question. All their names were anonymised in the interests of privacy.

Specifically in relation to this study as such, I'd been around long enough to generate the trust needed to present myself to those concerned in a new guise, i.e. that of a researcher looking into instances of translation in everyday life, an innocent albeit curious exercise, on the face of it. This involved leaving behind roles the participants were familiar with and allowing them to see my academic side, of switching from insider to outsider, as it were, which is particularly so in Chapters 3, 5, 6 and 7, as I already knew most of the participants socially and professionally. In contrast, the encounter in Chapter 4 was spontaneous and completely unpredictable. The participants involved remain unknown to each other, except for the two teenage friends. Ostensibly we were all passengers on a tram, heading our various ways, each with their own purpose. In Chapter 8, in explaining the purpose of my visits to the school, I presented myself beforehand squarely as an academic interested in translation and conducted myself as such during the encounters. This nonetheless involved drawing on and referring to our shared experiences as teachers (of migrant origin) working with migrants or students of migrant origin.

In Chapter 9, I became the subject of my own inquiry, while also observing and participating in translational and interpreting practices as they unfolded during several visits to the city office. My role in the chapter was that of someone seeking to rectify or have confirmed their status as a resident of the country, something which most of those around me were also seeking to do at the time. As in Chapter 4, none of those present were aware of my "ulterior motives" as an academic, but these motives were not "ulterior" or hidden from the outset. Sometimes opportunities present themselves and you have to get into character as quickly as possible, i.e. by keeping channels of observation open alongside those of participation. For example, the interaction on the tram seemed too important in its typical "everydayness" to pass over, which meant my memorising and noting the details as soon as I got home. This can be attributed to a form of *déformation professionelle,* but also to training and experience, which is explored in the first section of Chapter 4. The interactions in Chapter 9 took place intermittently over a period of several months, yet the decision to report on them stems from the same initial reflex. It was also a matter of making the best of a bad job after having let my residence permit unknowingly run out – a clear reminder that I am still a migrant. There was also a need to understand the "bureaucratic" side of identity construction and maintenance I had unwittingly been drawn into and had to deal with. The people working there are involved with the practicalities of identity on a daily basis; as such they are involved in the business of making who you think you are correspond with who you are officially. I was like anyone else going there trying to sort out their papers, so rather than bemoaning my lot, I took the opportunity to try and make sense of it all, but again mainly from a translational perspective.

With regard to conducting such research with any degree of success, I'd also been around long enough to understand which choices might be viable and prove fruitful. Again in retrospect, my main justification for choosing these particular sites is that I "discovered" them academically in surprising new ways, despite knowing (about) them already in various other ways. This happened because I was able to take a certain distance from them and view them professionally as an outsider. As Marcus remarks: "the anthropologist really has to find something out she doesn't really know, and she has to do it in terms ethnography permits in its own developed form of empiricism" (Marcus, 1998, p. 18). This "developed form of empiricism" along with the "rapport" (Geertz, 1973, p. 6) or indeed "complicity" (Marcus, 1998, pp. 105–131) that terms like "insider" and "outsider" are predicated upon, have already been tackled in the previous sections of this chapter. However, I wish to state here in advance that I believe in each case that I came across things involving natural translation and interpreting as a social practice I didn't know, which taking an outsider position allowed me to discover. This does not mean that they are new, as such practices have been reported on elsewhere (Harris, 2013) but perhaps not in the same configurations or tied together in the same way or viewed against the sociolinguistic backdrop or woven into the sociocultural fabric in which they occurred. It is for the reader to judge if this is actually the case.

Positioning permeates the whole approach discussed in the various sections of this chapter so far, the way the project was carried out, including interaction with the participants and how the materials I managed to gather thanks to them were dealt with and written into this book. It is the task of the researcher, much like that of a translator, to provide a careful adequate account of the activities observed, while at the same time carrying over the nuances found in the distinctions the participants made in relation to their own language and translational practices.

So, ultimately, the reason for using ethnography as an overall approach is epistemological in the sense of its particular way of knowing, so cogently formulated by Geertz, Marcus and others and discussed above. It is also practical in terms of the basic set of steps ethnography offers in conducting research. It is also ethnographic in the way it takes surprises and people seriously and attempts to represent the natural translation and interpreting practices observed and experienced at the various sites.

The way into the nexus of city, translation and migration in this study has been through (Geertz, 1973, p. 15) and with (Ingold, 2021, pp. 13–14) the people involved, including myself. Its point of departure is the local community and the people living there and moves from there outwards to other parts of the city in tracing instances of natural translation and interpreting that belong to networks of response that in turn are framed by trajectories of practice that are both local and global at the same time. In this respect, it is not the purpose to provide a unified view of the macro-social order in and through the dynamics of micro-social translational interactions but rather to uncover a modicum of order across the various sites at the heart of which lies translation, in what, on the face of it, seems rather random chaotic city life.

Notes

1   For example, though translation is mentioned in the index under translanguaging and discussed by way of extensive example in the entry on Heteroglossia, it is not theorised to any serious extent; neither is interpreting.
2   A similar point is also made in Gal (see Gal, 2015, p. 226).
3   https://www.americananthro.org/ParticipateAndAdvocate/Content. aspx?ItemNumber=1652 (09/08/2022).
4   See especially Chapter 3, but also Chapters 5, 6 and 8.
5   For text as precipitate or sedimentation see Silverstein and Urban (1996, p. 5).
6   Viz. Marcus (1998) on rapport and complicity, p. 105–131 and the series of articles in Qualitative Inquiry, Volume 7 Number 4, 2001, including Marcus (2001, pp. 519–528).
7   See Marcus on affinity (1998, pp. 97–98, 118–119, 122–123) and activism (1998, pp. 243–244) for example.
8   For a detailed discussion of various understandings of reflexivity, including Bourdieu's, see Marcus (1998, pp. 181–202).
9   For a detail discussion of what "real" ethnography might be, see Agar (2006).

References

Agar, M. (1997). Ethnography: An overview. *Substance Use & Misuse*, 32(9), 1155–1173.

Agar, M. (2006). An ethnography by any other name… [149 paragraphs]. Forum qualitative sozialforschung / forum: *Qualitative Social Research*, 7(4), Art. 36. http://nbn-resolving.de/urn:nbn:de:0114-fqs0604367

Beres, A. M. (2015). An overview of translanguaging. 20 years of 'giving voice to those who do not speak'. *Translation and Translanguaging in Multilingual Contexts* 1(1), 103–118. https://doi-org.kuleuven.e-bronnen.be/10.1075/ttmc.1.1.05ber

Blommaert, J. (2010). *The Sociolinguistics of Globalization* (Cambridge Approaches to Language Contact). Cambridge: Cambridge University Press.

Blommaert, J. (2013): *Ethnography, Superdiversity and Linguistic Landscapes. Chronicles of Complexity* (Critical Language and Literacy Studies, [18]). Bristol/Buffalo, NY: Multilingual Matters.

Boccagni, P. (2019). *Multi-Sited Ethnography.* SAGE Research Method Foundations. doi:10.4135/9781526421036842870

Bourdieu, P. (1980). *Le sens pratique.* Paris : Les éditions de minuit.

Bourdieu, P. (2001). *Science de la science et réflexivité.* Paris: Raisons d'Agir.

Brewis, C. (2019). Die produksienetwerk van 'n getolkte lesing binne die universiteitskonteks: 'n etnografiese ondersoek (Doctoral Dissertation KU Leuven & University of Stellenbosch).

Briggs, C. (1986). *Learning How to Ask: A Sociolinguistic Appraisal of the Role of the Interview in Social Science Research* (Studies in the Social and Cultural Foundations of Language). Cambridge: Cambridge University Press. doi:10.1017/CBO9781139165990

Ciribuco, A. (2020). Translating the village: Translation as part of the everyday lives of asylum seekers in Italy. *Translation Spaces,* 9(2), 179–201.

Copland, F., & Creese, A. (2015). *Linguistic Ethnography.* SAGE Publications Ltd. doi:10.4135/9781473910607

Cronin, M. (2008). Downsizing the world: Translation and the politics of proximity. In A. Pym, M. Shlesinger, & D. Simeoni (Eds.), *Beyond Descriptive Translation Studies. Investigations in Homage to Gideon Toury* (pp. 265–276). Amsterdam/Philadelphia, PA: Benjamins.

Duflou, V. (2016). *Be(com)ing a Conference Interpreter: An Ethnography of EU Interpreters as a Professional Community* (Benjamins Translation Library 124). Amsterdam: John Benjamins Publishing Company.

Duranti, A. (2008). *Linguistic Anthropology* (Cambridge Textbooks in Linguistics). Cambridge: Cambridge University Press.

Erickson, F. (1990). Qualitative Methods. In R. L. Linn & F. Erickson (Eds.), *Research in Teaching and Learning: Volume Two* (pp. 77–194). New York: Macmillan.

Eriksen, T. (2001). *Small Places, Large Issues: An Introduction to Social and Cultural Anthropology* (Third ed., Anthropology, Culture and Society). London: Pluto Press.

Flynn, P. (2005). *A Linguistic Ethnography of Literary Translation: Irish Poems and Dutch-Speaking Translators.* Gent: Universiteit Gent. Faculteit letteren en wijsbegeerte.

Flynn, P. (2010). Ethnographic approaches. In Y. Gambier & L. van Doorslaer (Eds.), *Handbook of Translation Studies* (Vol. 1, pp. 116–119). Amsterdam/Philadelphia, PA: John Benjamins.

Gal, S. (2015). Politics of translation. *Annual Review of Anthropology,* 44 (1), 225–240. doi:10.1146/annurev-anthro-102214-013806

Geertz, C. (1973). *The Interpretation of Cultures. Selected Essays.* New York: Basic Books.

Goodwin. C. (1994). Professional vision. *American Anthropologist*, 96(3), 606–633. doi:10.1525/aa.1994.96.3.02a00100

Gumperz, J., & Hymes, D. H. (1972). *Directions in Sociolinguistics: The Ethnography of Communication* (J. J. Gumperz & D. H. Hymes, Eds.). New York: Holt, Rinehart and Winston.

Hanks, W. (2014). The space of translation. *HAU Journal of Ethnographic Theory*, 4(2), 17–39. doi:10.14318/hau4.2.002

Harris, B. (2013). An Annotated Chronological Bibliography of Natural Translation Studies with Native Translation and Language Brokering 1913–2012. https://www.academia.edu/ 5855596/Bibliography_of_natural_translation (last accessed 25/10/2020).

Hymes, D. (1977). Foundations in sociolinguistics: An ethnographic approach. *Tavistock*.

Hymes, D. (1980). *Language in Education: Ethnolinguistic Essays*. Washington, DC: Center for Applied Linguistics.

Ingold, T. (2017). Anthropology contra ethnography. *HAU Journal of Ethnographic Theory*, 7(1), 21–26. doi:10.14318/hau7.1.005

Ingold, T. (2018). *Anthropology: Why It Matters*. Cambridge: Polity.

Koskinen, K. (2008). *Translating Institutions: An Ethnographic Study of EU Translation*. Manchester: St. Jerome.

Marcus, G. (1995). Ethnography in/of the world system. *Annual Review of Anthropology*, 24, 95–117. doi:10.1146/annurev.an.24.100195.000523

Marcus, G. (2011). Multi-sited Ethnography: Five or Six Things I Know About It Now. In S. Coleman & P. Hellerman (Eds.), *Multi-sited Ethnography: Problems and Possibilities in the Translocation of Research Methods* (pp. 16–33). London: Routledge.

Marcus, G. E. (1998). *Ethnography Through Thick and Thin*. Princeton, NJ: Princeton University Press.

Marcus, G. E. (2021). *Ethnography Through Thick and Thin*. Princeton, NJ: Princeton University Press. https://doi-org.kuleuven.e-bronnen.be/10.1515/9781400851805

Matejka, L. (1973). On the first Russian prolegomena to semiotics. In V. N. Vološinov (Ed.), *Marxism and the Philosophy of Language* (pp. 161–174). Cambridge/London: Harvard University Press.

Pike, K. L. (1966). Etic and emic standpoints for the description of behavior. In A. G. Smith (Ed.), *Communication and Culture: Readings in the Codes of Human Interaction* (pp. 152–163). New York: Holt, Rinehart, & Winston.

Rampton, B. (2007). Neo-Hymesian linguistic ethnography in the United Kingdom. *Journal of Sociolinguistics*, 11(5), 584–607.

Scollon, R., & Scollon, S. W. (2007). Nexus analysis: Refocusing ethnography on action. *Journal of Sociolinguistics*, 11(5), 608–625. doi:10.1111/j.1467-9841.2007.00342.x

Silverstein, M. (1981). The limits of awareness. Working Papers in Sociolinguistics 84, June 1981.

Silverstein, M. (2003). Translation, transduction, transformation: Skating "glossando" on thin semiotic ice. In P. G. Rubel & A. Rosman (Eds.), *Translating Cultures: Perspectives on Translation and Anthropology* (pp. 75–105). Oxford: Berg.

Tesseur, W. (2017). Incorporating translation into sociolinguistic research: Translation policy in an international nongovernmental organisation. *Journal of Sociolinguistics*, 21, 629–649.

Tusting, K., & Maybin, J. (2007). Linguistic ethnography and interdisciplinarity: Opening the discussion. *Journal of Sociolinguistics*, 11(5), 575–583.

Van der Aa, J. (2012). Ethnographic monitoring: Language narrative and voice in a Caribbean classroom. PhD dissertation. Tilburg University.

Van de Aa, J., & Blommaert, J. (2011). Ethnographic monitoring: Hymes's unfinished business in education. *Anthropology & Education Quarterly*, 42(4), 319–334.

Van Rooyen, M. (2018). Investigating translation flows: Community radio news in South Africa. *Across Languages and Cultures*, 19(2), 259–278.

Vološinov, V. N. (1973). *Marxism and the Philosophy of Language* (L. Matejka & I. R. Titunik, Trans.). Cambridge/London: Harvard University Press.

3   A Street Corner

The brevity of this chapter is simple to explain but this does not detract from its importance in the overall scheme of the book. The materials collected for this part of the study were irretrievably lost following a computer crash. When I went in search of the backup, I discovered that the audio files had become corrupted as well and could not be accessed. This double blow was very disappointing for a number of reasons. First, the data comprised several conversations, including a long in-depth interview with, and further observations made by Brian,[1] a social worker[2] all recorded during several encounters over a short period of time. I have known Brian for many years and was aware of his work helping the homeless and migrants living in difficult circumstances in "less well known" parts of the city. The data contained many insightful remarks on language use and translation and bore evidence of his unique stance on the role of language in the difficult situations in which he works among the homeless. Some time had passed since our conversations and the research project had come to a standstill as a result of other urgent business at the job and setbacks we all share. I felt ashamed of my negligence and postponed telling him about the loss of all the wonderful material he had shared with me. I knew we could never replicate our conversations, but I did pluck up the courage to go and talk to him about the glitches. He just laughed when I told him. I apologised and explained how his data formed a key position in the whole project. It was a sort of alpha point from which the whole construction unfolded and somehow returned. This was not because he was the first person I had spoken to. In fact, he was only the eighth,[3] and hence the last, but his observations reconfigured the composite picture of multilingualism and natural translation that was slowly emerging from my research. He was surprised that I could remember so much of what he had told me, so I decided to try and reconstruct some of his main arguments from memory. This was a sad lesson in the misguided trust I put in modern electronics and a reminder that notepads, pens and markers will continue to be indispensable in this line of work.

So, I have nothing to show in the form of interview transcripts, or other remarks and observations recorded on my smartphone to back up what will be described and discussed in the following pages. All that can be presented here is a report on the main points that emerged from the

DOI: 10.4324/9781003363811-4

encounters and a sketchy reconstruction of a narrative on the importance of three basic activities that formed the centrepiece of his whole reasoning on language and its place in the difficult work he does among the homeless. These three basic activities are cooking, sports and music.

Le degré zéro de la traduction

In "Le degré zéro de l'écriture" (Barthes, 1972), Roland Barthes posited a form of literary writing that *"ne trouvait plus de pureté que dans l'absence de tout signe proposant enfin l'accomplissement de ce rêve orphéen : un écrivain sans littérature"* (Barthes, 1972, p. 9) *[could only find purity in the absence of all sign, proposing at last the accomplishment of that Orphean dream: a writer without literature – my translation].* This form of writing emerged gradually following a cycle of progressive literary solidification resulting in absence (Barthes, 1972, p. 9). Barthes work, ostensibly an examination of the troubled relationship between writing (and writers) and society, or more particularly between writing as a set of historically recognisable literary signs (Barthes, 1972, pp. 25–40) and speech and its unpredictable variety (Barthes, 1972, pp. 58–61), sounded a chord in the course of my conversations with Brian. In analogy to Barthes's "degré zero," I consider the stance that emerged from Brian's views as a recognition of a sort of "degré zero" or absence, not in literary writing but in language use and translation in particular, but viewed from a very different angle. The absence referred to in Barthes work is the result of literature becoming detached from its writers. In Brian's case, in contrast, the absence was in the language encountered by those he works with, which was inherently destructive from the outset, especially those destructive forms of language use and everyday symbolic violence (Thapar-Björkert et al., 2016) found in troubled homes, at the various stages of (forced) migration and even in such official forms ostensibly designed to alleviate distress (Maryns, 2006).

This results in a basic distrust of and cautious approach to language use among the people Brian tries to help. It puts into question the need for (a specific) language as a basic form of communication, not to mention the desire for or presence of translation. In his view, translation in any shape or form is not immediately essential to (intercultural) communication and understanding among people, even when they do not speak the same language or share a common language. It might only come into the picture at a later stage in the development of communication among those who have come to know each other and who are involved to some degree in shared activities or work. This is a departure from standard views in the literature on the role of translation in intercultural communication, but it is highly understandable in the particular context discussed here. Some who have only just arrived in the country are struggling with the new language and the levels of proficiency they are expected to reach in such a short period of time[4] (Khan & McNamara in Canagarajah, 2017, pp. 451–467). Many of the people he works with and helps, both newly arrived and local, have literacy issues or have been disadvantaged or hurt by language in some way or other when growing up. The reasons for this are various and have been well documented in the literature (Collins & Blot, 2009), so it is not the purpose here to discuss them in any detail. Suffice it to say that the homeless people Brian tries to help stem from various sections of society that reflect the multilingual and multicultural make-up of the city.

In his efforts to help them, he often finds himself at odds and at loggerheads with official bodies in the city. This tension is often played out in terms of language and shows up the gap between official discourse and ways of speaking about the homeless and the socially challenged and what Brian sees as the pressing urgency of immediate action without too much discursive or administrative convolution. My asking (rather academic) questions like "we know that our cities and neighbourhoods are increasingly multilingual and multicultural: what is your experience?" Or "how does translation fit into all of this?" to someone in such a situation seems vain and supercilious at best. Given the urgency and the immediate needs of the people in such precarious situations, these questions seem simply beside the point. Or perhaps not. Inquiring into and reflecting on the basic preconditions for asking such questions and not asking them lightly is something worth doing, as this might lay bare a whole range of unchallenged assumptions upon which theoretical debates on the (power) roles of translators and interpreters are based. The need for translation and interpreting in precarious situations is beyond doubt and has been demonstrated and argued for extensively in the literature.[5] However, assuming that translation and interpreting are needed from the outset and insisting that these services be provided might prevent translation scholars from seeing the needs in a given situation and then understanding what might best fit. This is another reason why ethnographies of translation and interpreting are important (viz. Brewis, 2022, Tesseur, 2022, Van Rooyen, 2022). There is a sense of embarrassment that comes from asking seemingly silly questions, and a stab of conscience from being out of step with the needs of the homeless and with the realities they face, i.e. Brian's primary concern. In this humiliating and humbling moment you are cast back and painfully reminded of that basic question: what does this mean to them, if anything at all? In our particular case, translation: a very sobering thought for a translation scholar. It is a small price to pay on the way towards obtaining a small degree of understanding. Hopefully, this account will do justice to Brian's point of view.

Forms of Life – Music, Cooking and Sports

In terms of language use and translation, the situation Brian finds himself in is perhaps less visible in the literature. This does not make them any less relevant. As mentioned already, encountering Brian's "degré zero" stance regarding language use and subsequent translation was a very sobering experience. One of the directions it points in is the availability of resources. As Blommaert points out, resources are a much-neglected aspect of context:

> Resources and the way in which they feature as elements of social structure are often 'invisible' contexts in discourse analysis. Illiterates will not show up in analyses of written discourse; their perceptions of 'news' and 'politics' do not feature in analyses of newspaper reporting. Such analyses are not about, nor for them. [...] However, the importance of resources lies in the deep relation between language and a general economy of symbols and status in societies. One does not just 'have' or 'know' a language; there is a complex and highly sensitive political-economic dynamics of acquisition and differential distribution behind such seemingly innocuous phrases.
>
> (Blommaert, 2001, p. 23)

According to Brian, there are resources other than language that precede and lower the thresholds or negotiate the obstacles of language use and even translation, namely a set of activities that promote a sense of (as yet to be articulated) community. The activities Brian engages in with the people he helps are cooking, music and sports (not necessarily football). He considers them basic to existence and prerequisites for any form of social cohesion and understanding, no matter where you come from. Each constitutes a point of encounter both material and symbolic/semiotic, a form of practice that can be engaged in openly and to which each individual can make their own contribution.

Cooking, music and sports, both as activities and as forms of expression, can lay claim to a certain degree of semiotic 'universality' (moves on a pitch, ways of cooking, chord shapes, drum patterns) that goes beyond the confines of any given historical language or sign system and also beyond the immediate need for translation; at least, according to Brian, this is the way they are perceived and hence rendered valid communally by those involved.

These activities have sets of rules that were not necessarily mediated through the new language encountered by the immigrant or subjected to the regulations of the standard form of any language expected from locals and immigrants alike (in this case Dutch). This does not mean they are unmediated, however. Taken individually, each of these activities can also be viewed from a highly professional angle and considered in terms of its own sophisticated (national) history, "grammar[6]" and set of practices,[7] hence in a way that would perhaps bar participation from the outset to the people Brian works with.

At another basic human level, i.e. that of sustenance, art and play viewed as coterminous aspects of life, they can form a yet-to-be-negotiated yet advantageous open space (de Certeau, 1984, pp. 117–118). So Brian's retreat from discrete languages towards activity as a basis for understanding is similar to Wittgenstein's:

> *19 "It is easy to imagine a language consisting only of orders and reports in battle ... – And to imagine a language is to imagine a form of life."
>
> (2009, p. 11ᵉ)

Wittgenstein goes on to equate language games to forms of life:

> 23. ...There are *countless* kinds; countless different kinds of use of all the things we call "signs", "words", "sentences". And this diversity is not something fixed, given once for all; but new types of language, new language games, as we may say, come into existence, others become obsolete and get forgotten... The word *"language-game"* is used here to emphasize the fact that the *speaking* of language is part of an activity, or of a form of life.
>
> (Wittgenstein, 2009, pp. 14ᵉ–15ᵉ)

As activities, cooking, sports and music can be considered forms of life with their own language games ranging from the most basic to the highly complex. But these games and related forms of life are not predicated on a single historical (national standard) language and grammar but involve more complex situated forms of semiotic interaction linked to an activity, i.e. no single language holds the linguistic prerogative over an activity like cooking, sport or music, etc. These activities also bring with them genre perceptions and sets of discourses that shift across languages and cultures, but the activities they are part of remain more or less accessible to all participants, each with their own point of entry and each with their own understanding of how best to play a game (sport), musical instrument or cook a dish and how to describe the state of play in any of the three and why. In Brian's context, the three activities can be considered as "forms of life" involving "language games" which find their expression interactionally and interculturally, but not in any specific language. The multilingual activities that emerge from these shared activities over time would be best encompassed by Gumperz's notion of repertoire and the related notion of (multilingual) speech community (Hymes, 1972), no matter how precarious. But we are not there yet.

Let us first return to Brian's insistence on shared activity as the foundation of communication and understanding and then bring in Wittgenstein again: "205 ... Shared human behaviour is the system of reference by means of which we interpret an unknown language" (Wittgenstein, 2009, p. 88ᵉ). Moving quite in the opposite direction by way of possible analysis, this also brings us to Quine's famous piece on meaning and translation and the following quote:

> It would be trivial to say that we cannot know the meaning of a foreign sentence except as we are prepared to offer a translation in our own language. I am saying more: that it is only relative to an in large part arbitrary manual of translation that most foreign sentences may be said to share the meaning of English sentences, and then only in a very parochial sense of meaning, viz. use-in-English. Stimulus meanings of observation sentences aside, most talk of meaning requires a tacit reference to a home language in much the way that talk of truth involves tacit reference to one's own system of the world, the best that one can muster at the time.
>
> (Quine in Venuti, 2000 p. 111)

The situation the linguist finds himself in Quine's speculative piece, i.e. of being involved in 'radical translation,' is not unlike that of the migrant and others involved in the activities Brian organises. No one would question the reflex in such encounters of attempting to translate "the foreign sentence" into one's own language. But, even if we consider the sentence as a unit of meaning, it can be asked whether it is a useful point of departure in "foreign" exchanges or any exchanges for that matter. Why raise this issue if this has long been shown not to be the case in various forms of discourse analysis and interactional sociolinguistics? Mainly because the sentence[8] is still the basic unit of analysis and practice in translation training. The sentence, however, excludes all the other forms of semiosis that are brought into play in such exchanges, and equally in Brian's activities, the resources Blommaert was speaking of above and elsewhere (Blommaert, 2001, p. 102).

There is another fundamental difference between Wittgenstein's and Quine's position. Though both could be typified as thought experiments,[9] the former posits "shared human behaviour as the system of reference by means of which we interpret an unknown language" whereas the latter takes the sentence as the measure of comprehension. Brian's activities can easily be encompassed by Wittgenstein's formulation but are rendered almost impossible by Quine's. The sentence is Quine's point of departure and the major architectural element in the piece as a whole, which perhaps stems from his interest in formal logic to the exclusion of various forms of gesture and multimodal meaning-making that are evident in his essay.

Quine's speculation on meaning and its translation in decontextualised sentences pushes such meaning even further away from the related possible worlds they might belong to. As Hanks & Severi (2014, p. 5) points out, "Quine posits a monolingual native speaker who is evidently incapable of formulating meaning statements in his own language."

Though Quine's experiment can be considered typical in some respects as it involves the ethnographic practice of glossing words and stringing them together into a sentence, it seems to shove aside actual anthropological (translational) practices, which are often collaborative. In the context of Brian's activities it would seem to preclude or render highly difficult the capacity of language users of finding similarity (through translation) based on how they relate to the same activity and context, no matter how different the languages present are from each other. This is in fact the migrant's plight, and at the same time perhaps a gift. It is also the plight and possible gift of the non-migrant homeless person. There is no such thing as a complete cultural or, more specifically, linguistic tabula rasa, as Quine seems to suggest in his exercise. Each person brings her own understandings to the activity or as Hanks would put it, their own "orienting frameworks, interpretive procedures, and sets of expectations that are not part of discourse structure, but of the ways actors relate to and use language," and other semiotic means in the activities concerned (Hanks, 1987, p. 670). It must also be remembered that these frameworks, procedures and expectations are culture specific, which will result in variation and potential friction in terms of the outcomes of Brian's activities. Next to this, it is not, to borrow a phrase from Auden,[10] a matter of "being hurt into" language – in our case into (the new) language – but rather a matter of easing the hurt caused by language by viewing it, as Wittgenstein did, as an element of activity and not as something that precedes and defines it. I believe this to be Brian's goal, which is why the notion of "le degré zero" of translation was proposed in the first place. Translation in such circumstances will have to be engaged with from another perhaps less obvious angle, i.e. in terms of transfer (D'hulst, 2012) or transduction (Silverstein, 2003; Gal, 2015). Before doing so, we must first return to Gumperz and to repertoire and speech community.

Repertoires on the Move

In an article on Gumperz's discourse strategies, Susan Gal (2013) points to how, since their conceptualisation, both repertoire and speech community and other terms proposed by Gumperz have undergone various stages of redefinition to fit and match shifting sociolinguistic configurations brought on by various forms of social change including globalisation. In this respect, speech community is understood in more flexible terms as encompassing what are now known as communities of practice (originally Lave & Wenger, 1991). Repertoire has since been aligned theoretically with register and the related terms of "enregisterment" or "the social processes that create registers" (Gal, 2013, pp. 120–121). Blommaert and Backus (2013) have since examined repertoire from the perspective of superdiversity and also in relation to "learning" languages, all of which proves useful for our understanding of Brian's activities. Blommaert and Backus (2013, p. 15) define repertoires as "individual, biographically organized complexes of resources, and they follow the rhythms of actual human lives."

They point to how language learning is a never-ending process during which we learn to *speak as* the person we are constantly becoming, socially speaking (Blommaert & Backus, 2013, p. 15).

Expressed in terms of acquiring resources and of "learning" and inclusion, the participants in Brian's activities can be considered as having followed staggered socialisation processes across various cultural sites over which they may have had little control. This is in stark contrast to underlying assumptions and exigencies of integration[11] or more commonly held views on language learning. Moreover, much like language acquisition, (language) socialisation is often framed in monocultural terms, which obscures various types of socialisation extant in and across cultures (Ochs in Duranti, 2001, p. 228). Ochs also points to how socialisation is not always a conscious concerted effort and "may be fleeting – as when one interlocutor momentarily asks another for directions or points out some hitherto unnoticed phenomenon" (Ochs in Duranti, 2001, p. 227). The understanding is that, though the term is mainly used to address young people in any given society, socialisation, like language learning never actually ends and at times can prove challenging.[12] As mentioned above, Brian's take on sport, cooking and music is that these activities provide a "space" (de Certeau, 1988, pp. 117–118) and related opportunities for people to "learn" by doing through working and interacting with others and not by being immediately told what to do.

Space is understood here in de Certeau's terms. As he remarks

> Space is composed of intersections of mobile elements. It is a sense actuated by the ensemble of movements deployed within it. Space occurs as the effect produced by the operations that orient it, situate it, temporalize it, and make it function in a polyvalent unity of conflictual programmes or contractual proximities. On this view, in relation to place, space is like the word when it is spoken...
>
> (de Certeau, 1988, p. 117)

The space sketched by de Certeau is full of meaning-making within which socialisation occurs at each participant's pace, as do changes, shifts and extensions to each one's repertoire. Again it must be stressed here that repertoire is not a monolingual concept, i.e. only consisting of resources in one language. Neither are those participating in Brian's activities expected to "become integrated" in Flemish society by demonstrating competence in Dutch. The sense of belonging Brian wishes to create through the activities is not of that order. But does not mean however that this might not be one of the possible outcomes. Without describing the complexity they use to illustrate their point, we concur with Blommaert and Backus (2013, p. 28) when they argue that:

> [r]epertoires are thus indexical biographies, and analyzing repertoires amounts to analyzing the social and cultural itineraries followed by people, how they manoeuvred and navigated them, and how they placed themselves into the various social arenas they inhabited or visited in their lives.

The space Brian helps create is both a haven and a potential storehouse of resources for its participants. Though Brian tries to pre-empt possible language violence in his activities, it cannot be denied that various forms of language and cultural expression are present among the participants from the outset. This coming together of various types of (staggered) socialisation and (hurt or partially silenced) repertoires in the interactions is offset by a toning down of language in favour of activity. But for the activities to work, some (other) form of semiotic exchange has to take place, as de Certeau's notion of space suggests. The complexity outlined thus far, along with the potential it generates, has to be engaged with, no matter how implicitly. Given the variety of repertoires and indexical biographies, some form of translation can be considered a basic element of this process, but how are we to approach it in these circumstances? Translation can be understood as an acquired resource that accrues to a participant's repertoire (see the discussion in Chapter 5 Further Comments) – another possible outcome of Brian's activities. It can also be considered a general practice that is engaged in to varying degrees by participants in the activities. How can we deal with this? Two conceptualisations were proposed above: (assumed) transfer and transduction. Each grounds translation in its context, the former by freeing translation from its centuries-old binary strictures, something which even the notion of cultural translation fails to do. The latter does so by bringing in iconic and indexical aspects of meaning-making, without which any form of exchange or transfer would be impossible, especially in Brian's activities.

Transfer and Transduction

We will address transfer first. D'hulst offers four arguments in favour of transfer, three of which apply directly to the situation being discussed here. First, according to D'hulst

> since transfer is a process that may combine several types of relations, one cannot assume a one-to-one relationship between a source and a target, nor take for granted that such a relationship is spontaneously recognized by contemporary agents as a token of a

given type of transfer, let alone that it is considered a "necessary" or "sufficient" feature of transfer by those agents.

(D'hulst, 2012, p. 142)

Though clearly couched in the discourse of translation studies, the argument problematises basic assumptions about translation and at the same time offers us a nascent methodology to investigate it, a methodology, it must be added, that leans very strongly in the direction of ethnography and working with the agents involved in an attempt to understand processes and practices related to translation as a form of transfer. Given the complexity of the interactions and potential uptakes among the participants in Brian's activities, transfer seems an opportune means of encapsulating it.

Second, D'hulst notes the following:

the transfer concept suggests a one-way process, whereas sociologists and cultural ethnographers (e.g. Fitzgerald, 2006) have convincingly shown that interacting cultures are interdependent, so that bi- or even multi-directionality may become a determining factor in the relative importance, the forms, and the content of transfer flows.

(D'hulst, 2012, p. 142)

The interdependence and multi-directionality pointed to here fit the picture as far as Brian's activities are concerned.

D'hulst's fourth and final point is that

since transfer is an opaque process – partly invisible, partly mental, and therefore only partly observable – some of its features may, at least using the techniques of investigation currently available, escape the scholar's (and practitioner's) grasp.

(D'hulst, 2012, p. 142)

By drawing our attention to the opaque nature of transfer as a process, D'hulst causes us to pause and reflect on the dangers of assuming we know what translation constitutes simply because we have so many models of analysis to rely on. Models, much like the translations they purport to analyse are always partial or blind in some respect. My conversations with Brian led me beyond the opaque into the complex processes discussed above. Without his help they would have remained just that, opaque, if not to say invisible, which is exactly the point D'hulst is making, as I understand it of course. Transfer can remain purposely opaque in Brian's activities: the opaquer and the less obtrusive the better. This opaque unobtrusive transfer Brian is aiming for has to rely on other forms of semiotic exchange. This brings us to the second concept that proves useful in exploring the semiotic complexity of Brian's activities: transduction, as understood by Silverstein (Silverstein in Rubel

& Rosman, 2003; Gal, 2015). Silverstein posits a narrower view of the term as applying to iconic and indexical aspects of the translation of ethnographic texts whereas Gal takes a broader perspective and considers it also as applying to the translation of practices as a whole. Both the narrower and broader views are of interest to us here.

According to Silverstein, in transduction, "one form of organised energy is asymmetrically converted into another kind of energy" (Silverstein in Rubel & Rosman, 2003, p. 83). This energy is housed in iconic and indexical aspects of language and other forms of semiotic use, some of which is lost during the conversion process as a result of 'friction,' etc. This takes the focus away from perhaps more straightforward matter-of-fact "denotational" meaning found in explanation or giving instructions for example. It hence leaves room for less obvious though immediately tangible aspects of meaning-making like expressions of surprise or appreciation following a good move on a pitch, or at the appearance or taste of dish or the switch to a beat or rhythm that may trigger a chain of associations among the players and listeners. Such forms of meaning-making (and their possible translation among the participants) are clearly what Brian is after in his activities. As Silverstein himself puts it:

> These indexical and iconic values of words and expressions in co(n)textualized texts constitute a distinct area of problems we must consider for the would-be translator, because they rely on a different approach to "translation" than the clear-cut areas of Saussurean and deictic denotation, one that takes account of rather distinct semiotic properties.
>
> (Silverstein in Rubel & Rosman, 2003, p. 83)

Though Silverstein is clearly addressing anthropologists as translators, we can also ask who the translator(s) are in Brian's activities. There is perhaps a more well-defined division of labour among anthropologists and those they engage with in relation to fieldwork and cultural translation.[13] This is far from clear and certainly less unidirectional in the case of Brian's activities. Factoring in the iconic and indexical does make it much easier to understand Brian's motivations for focusing on action.

Here is Gal's take on the term: "Transduction, recognized as an analogical process, opens ways of understanding the productivity that characterizes many phenomena grouped under the rubric of "translation" (Gal, 2015, p. 233). Interestingly, D'hulst also draws our attention to the notion of analogy in relation to transfer when quoting Even-Zohar:

> Our accumulated knowledge about translation indicates more and more that translational procedures between two systems (languages/literatures) are in principle analogous, even homologous, with transfers within the borders of the system. The hypothesis of analogy/

homology has been formulated before, notably by Jakobson (1959),
but no consequences have ever been drawn for translation theory.
(Even-Zohar, 1990, p. 3 in D'hulst, 2012, p. 140)

Gal takes analogy beyond the language and literary systems Zohar[14]
focused on back in the 1990s: "By extending the analytical reach of
transduction from linguistic expression to other social practices, we see
the role of cultural models in generating value" (Gal, 2015). Her notion
of cultural models is in line with Zohar's discussion later on in the late
1990's (Even-Zohar, 1997) however, and a cultural or national border
is present in the discussion in each author's case. This is not the case
in Brian's activities. In the age of superdiverse cities, such borders have
been transported to and tacitly reconstructed in and between neighbourhoods, but this might be forcing the issue somewhat, as national and
cultural borders have always been porous and shifting from the outset.
If we consider transduction as applying to social practices (Gal, 2015)
within the space of Brian's activities, then transfer is indeed multidi-
rectional. The transduction involved in such transfer backgrounds the
denotational in favour of the iconic and indexical, as Silverstein might
have put it.

The notions of cultural models and practices also remain useful touch-
stones in tracing and understanding strands of exchange between participants during sports, cooking and music making. As noted previously
these cultural models and practices are being exchanged not only across
national and cultural borders but also across and within superdiverse
communities and neighbourhoods. The people Brian works are members
of these superdiverse communities, no matter how challenged their sense
of language and belonging might be.

The above discussion is based on recollections of my conversations
with Brian.

Further Comments

Even though the materials were lost, Brian's generosity has allowed me
to explore the complexity involved in his views on committed social action and his focus on music, cooking and sports as the way to go about
doing his social work. I have tried to remain loyal to his stance and goals
and have let them guide my reasoning throughout the analysis presented
above. Hopefully in doing so, I have managed to offer some reflections
on and ways into understanding the initial resistance I experienced when
approaching Brian on the role of translation in his work. His resistance
is not based on a rejection of knowing and knowhow however, far from
it. Despite my good intentions, I was on the obtuse side of the equation,
working for a knowledge machine that was mainly interested in feeding
itself. Nevertheless, Wittgenstein's forms of life offered a way into his
activities and transfer and transduction a path beyond the denotational

towards iconic and indexical forms of exchange and meaning-making that belong there. Forms of life and related language games offer us a sensitive way of framing and understanding the possibilities of Brian's work. In his discussion of Wittgenstein's notions of forms of life and language game, Duranti points out that 'the notion of "language game" is thus a *working* notion' (Duranti, 2008, p. 239). This sits well with Brian's stance in that his is both a way of working, literally speaking and also a rejection of any form of further theorising beyond its usefulness for the work at hand. Duranti further remarks that

Through the concept of language game, he [Wittgenstein] invites us to look at the context of what speakers do with words and for this reason constitutes an insight into what linguistic anthropologists are interested in.

(Duranti, 2008, p. 239)

Duranti suggests that language game might be considered a unit of analysis, which seems useful as it draws our attention to words used in a particular context and resultant meaning-making. This is obviously important when it comes to translation and interpreting and hence hardly worth mentioning. However, as Wittgenstein sees language games as part of forms of life, it would seem appropriate to start from forms of life as the encompassing unit in the same manner as we would when working (translating/interpreting) within a given genre[15] and considering the language expectations it brings with it. The 'degré zéro de la traduction' proposed at the beginning of this chapter is perhaps a forced analogy but it has served a somewhat intuitive category by which to approach translation in this case. It was meant to index not just the absence of translation as such but the absence of immediately recognisable or rather acceptable signs to translate in or out of, beyond those of (verbal) hurt and violence.

Notes

1 Purposely rendered anonymous for reasons of privacy.
2 Straathoekwerker: literally, a street corner worker in Dutch.
3 Not all the data found its way into this work: only seven cases were used.
4 Here is a link to the city website for "naturalisation" https://in-gent.be/voor-jou/inburgeren.
5 Viz. the Co-Minor IN/QUEST project https://www.arts.kuleuven.be/english/rg_interpreting_studies/research-projects/co_minor_in_quest or Translators Without Borders https://translatorswithoutborders.org/.
6 The idea of regarding the items of a recipe as elements of syntax being articulated into a culinary sentence.
7 Viz. the plethora of cookbooks built on the culinary reputations of chefs but also on cultural and national stereotypes visible in such terms as *French cuisine*.
8 As Vološinov remarked all those years ago:

"language as a ready-made product (ergon), as a stable system (lexicon, grammar, phonetics) is, so to speak, the inert crust, the hardened lava of language creativity, of which linguistics makes an abstract construct in the interests of the practical teaching of language as a ready-made instrument.

(Vološinov, 1973, p. 48)

9   For a critique of Quine's piece see Hanks and Severi (2014).
10 "Mad Ireland hurt you into poetry." From W.H. Auden's In Memory of W. B. Yeats (From Another Time by W. H. Auden, published by Random House. Copyright © 1940 W. H. Auden).
11 A buzzword in Flemish language and cultural policy
12 The vociferous public debate on 'wokeness' is a case in point.
13 Put in extremely simplistic terms, engaging with members of a social group, reporting on fieldwork, and adding to the body of anthropological knowledge.
14 It must be noted that Even-Zohar has long since broadened the scope of research and thinking on transfer. For a discussion of transfer, see Even-Zohar (1997) an article in which he connects transfer with what he calls "cultural repertoire" (no reference to Gumperz) by drawing on work in semiotics by Lotman and others. The forms of transfer he mentions are not far removed from Gal's in her discussion of the transduction of practices. For a comprehensive discussion of transfer, see Shaul Levin's chapter, Heeding the Call for Transfer Theory in van Doorslaer and Naaijkens (2021).
15 See the discussion in the section on forms of life and genres in Some Tentative Conclusions below.

References

Barthes, R. (1972). *Le Degré zéro de l'écriture*. Paris : Ed. Du Seuil.
Blommaert, J. (2001). Context is/as Critique. *Critique of Anthropology*, 21(1), 13–32.
Blommaert, J., & Backus, A. (2013). Superdiverse repertoires and the individual. In I. de Saint-Georges & J. J. Weber (Eds.), *Multilingualism and Multimodality: Current Challenges for Educational Studies* (pp. 11–32). Rotterdam: Sense.
Brewis, C. (2022). Some material aspects of an interpreted university lecture. Translation and Interpreting Studies, Translation and Interpreting Studies, 2022.
Collins, J., & Blot, R. (2009). *Literacy and Literacies: Texts, Power, and Identity* (3rd print). Cambridge: Cambridge University Press.
de Certeau, M. (1988). *The Practice of Everyday Life*. Berkeley/London: University of California Press.
D'hulst, L. (2012). (Re)locating translation history: From assumed translation to assumed transfer. *Translation Studies*, 5(2), 139–155.
Duranti, A. (2008). *Linguistic Anthropology* (Cambridge Textbooks in Linguistics). Cambridge: Cambridge University Press.
Even-Zohar, I. (1990). Translation and transfer. *Poetics Today*, 11(1), 73–78.
Even-Zohar, I. (1997). The making of culture repertoire and the role of transfer. *Target*, 9(2), 355–363.
Gal, S. (2013). John J. Gumperz's discourse strategies. *Journal of Linguistic Anthropology*, 23(3), 115–126.
Gal, S. (2015). Politics of translation. *Annual Review of Anthropology*, 44 (1), 225–240. doi:10.1146/annurev-anthro-102214-013806

Hanks, W. F. (1987). Discourse genres in a theory of practice. *American Ethnologist*, 14(4), 668–692. http://www.jstor.org/stable/645320

Hanks, F., & Severi, C. (2014). Translating worlds: The epistemological space of translation. *HAU Journal of Ethnographic Theory*, 4(2), 1–16. doi:10.14318/hau4.2.001

Hymes, D. H. (1972). Models of interaction and social life. In J. J. Gumperz & D. H. Hymes (Eds.), *Directions in Sociolinguistics: The Ethnography of Communication* (pp. 35–71). New York: Holt, Rinehart & Winston.

Jakobson, R. (2000 [1959]). On linguistics aspects of translation. In L. Venuti (Ed.), *The Translation Studies Reader* (pp. 113–118). London/New York: Routledge.

Khan, K., & McNamara, T. (2017). Citizenship, immigration laws and language. In S. Canagarajah (Ed.), *The Routledge Handbook of Migration and Language* (pp. 451–467). London/New York: Routledge.

Lave, J., & Wenger, E. (1991). *Situated Learning: Legitimate Peripheral Participation*. Cambridge: Cambridge University Press.

Levin, S. (2021). Heeding the call for transfer theory. In T. Naaijkens & L. van Doorslaer (Eds.) *The Situatedness of Translation Studies*. Leiden: Brill. doi:10.1163/9789004437807_006

Maryns, K. (2006). *The Asylum Speaker. Language in the Belgian Asylum Procedure* (Encounters v. 7). Manchester: St. Jerome Publishing.

Ochs, E. (2001). Socialization. In A. Duranti (Ed.), *Key Terms in Language and Culture* (pp. 227–230). Oxford: Blackwell.

Quine, W. V.O. (2000 [1957]). Meaning and translation. In L. Venuti (Ed.), *The Translation Studies Reader* (pp. 94–112). London/New York: Routledge.

Silverstein, M. (2003). Translation, Transduction, Transformation: Skating "Glossando" on Thin Semiotic Ice. In P. G. Rubel & A. Rosman (Eds.), *Translating Cultures: Perspectives on Translation and Anthropology* (pp. 75–105). Oxford: Berg.

Tesseur, W. (2022). *Translation as Social Justice: Translation Policies and Practices in Non-governmental Organisations* (New Perspectives in Translation and Interpreting Studies). New York: Routledge.

Thapar-Björkert, S., Samelius, L., & Sanghera, G. S. (2016). Exploring symbolic violence in the everyday: Misrecognition, condescension, consent and complicity. *Feminist Review*, 112, 144–162. http://www.jstor.org/stable/44987257

Van Rooyen, M. (2022) Alternative journalism and translation. In E. Esperança Bielsa (Ed.), *The Routledge Handbook of Translation and Media* (pp. 446–458). London/New York: Routledge.

Wittgenstein, L. (2009). Philosophical Investigations (Revised 4th ed., G. Anscombe, Trans.). Chichester: Wiley-Blackwell.

4   A Tram

Apart from a few rudimentary notes, the translational picture discussed in this chapter was painted from memory, not because the data were lost or corrupted and hence rendered useless but because the data were ephemeral[1] and came and went in the matter of a number of tram stops, along with the people I encountered. In her study of tram 12 in the city of Antwerp, Ruth Soenen (2006) examines relations on the tram from the dual perspective of diversity and the ephemeral. In outlining the various types of fleeting relations (positive and negative) encountered on the tram, she also points to how private and public realms and what she calls "the parochial realm" are co-present and shift into each other through various interactions, also those involving mobile phones (Soenen, 2006, pp. 4–5). She notes that

> Ephemeral relationships have an ambiguous character and bypass the dichotomies of strong and weak ties, of being and becoming. Instead, they have at their disposal a potentially unlimited number of ways of relational forms.
>
> (Soenen, 2006, p. 6)

Ephemeral relations seem to belong to another category than strong and weak ties but may result in either, though not necessarily. As I understand it, configurations of ties and relations on the tram are connected to the realms that come into play in what she calls "a city on wheels" (Soenen, 2006, p. 11). When it comes to diversity or superdiversity, one might wonder what the relevance of the "parochial realm" might be. In a Flemish context, belonging to the same parish evokes a whole set of indexical presuppositions and entailments (Silverstein, 2003) outside of nominally frequenting the same church. As is discussed further below, the parish/neighbourhood is often the first point of encounter between "locals" and "migrants." But as Blommaert (2013) points out, these encounters have been going on for generations. So the indexical presuppositions evoked by parish (e.g. growing up and playing on the same street, going to the same school, playing for the same team, working in the same factory[2] and so on) are not necessarily church centred or merely "local." In the meantime, local centres of worship have also diversified and globalised. Next to this, new centres of worship have sprung up in the wake of various diasporas moving into

DOI: 10.4324/9781003363811-5

neighbourhoods, all of which have a global reach. These centres of worship (still) function as important social actors in the local community and rearticulate the notion of the parochial in present-day terms (Blommaert, 2013, pp. 90–107). In this respect, enactments of the parochial realm on the tram are potentially as superdiverse as those that fall squarely within the public realm where mainly (diverse) strangers meet. I am convinced that the invocation of some type of "parochial realm" or notion of common neighbourhood played a crucial role in the case discussed in this chapter.

Regarding trams, my point of ingress is slightly different but of course interwoven with the above. As was mentioned in the introduction, I spend a lot of time on public transport and am always drawn to the various "accents" and "languages" heard on buses, trams and trains on a daily basis. The instance of translation discussed below was not the result of my eavesdropping, however. It involved the author directly, along with three other participants in the translational exchange. To paraphrase Ingold, this little piece of data was given and not taken (Ingold, 2018, p. 12). Following Ingold, I remain cognisant and appreciative of the gift and wish to do it justice as I have attempted to do in the previous chapter. Before discussing the case in detail, I would like to make a short digression and draw an analogy between translators and ethnographers and then provide the framing narrative for the translational event being discussed. In drawing the analogy, I will at the same time hopefully demonstrate the sociolinguistic complexity underlying the translational exchange. In terms of understanding the event, there is also a groundedness and resourcefulness among the participants I wish to talk about, which once explained, is actually rather easy to understand.

Of Translators and Ethnographers

As I understand it, ethnographers and translators[3] in the broad sense of the term share a sort of persistent and structured curiosity that coincides with and may even precede any form of official training. Without this curiosity the world would be a dull place and speech and other forms of communication an impenetrable surface rather than a constant source of fascination.

Imagine an ethnographer and an interpreter on an early morning bus or tram full of school children and people on their way to work. They too are on their way to work but, in the meantime, both would probably be involved in the ancient art of eavesdropping, for professional purposes, of course. They would be trying to identify "languages" and manners of speaking, noticing accents, intonations and particular gestures or how people, both young and old, pepper their speech with words and phrases from the official local language. The tram unloads its groups of pupils at the various schools along the way; some people get off at the train station to go to work in other cities, while the women stay on till they reach the last stop in the leafy neighbourhoods where they work. The ethnographer might be musing on how social stratification is enacted spatially in terms of the different types of school and workplaces the tram stops outside and will try to establish connections between social and intra- and inter-city mobility. The interpreter might be wondering about what languages are spoken in the playgrounds of the various schools and how they manage without interpreting or how the women on their way to the leafy neighbourhoods are getting along with courses in Standard Dutch they have to follow. Both the ethnographer and the translator assume these women are migrants, and this is where the job starts. Both are ostensibly watching the same set of interactions however but reading them in different ways.

The idea then is to merge the two characters and bring translation and interpreting into the mix, not as an aspect of ethnographic writing (Silverstein in Rubel & Rosman, 2003) or interpreter training (Pöchhacker, 2021) and related language acquisition (Tian & Link, 2019), but as emerging nodes of sociocultural ramification that can teach us something about our city or neighbourhood and what goes on there.

A Visit to a Kurdish Bakery

What follows now is the framing narrative that situates the translational encounter, an encounter I would argue that is more than commonplace:

We were having visitors over for lunch and were thinking of something interesting to serve our guests. Following a process of elimination – not that, not that, we did that the last time, no not that either – we decided to get some gözleme and other treats from the Kurdish bakery on the corner of Sint-Salvatorstraat in our old neighbourhood. I volunteered to go and headed up the street to catch tram 4 to what is now known as the Turkish part of town, one of several. It was Saturday morning, and the town was abustle with shoppers. Passing our old street along the way, I got off at the bottom of Sleepstraat and walked across to the bakery. There I was greeted by the usual smiling faces and placed my order for lunch. As usual, I came out with more than I planned to buy, also because the baker always adds a few items for free, including *simit* and *pide*. We have fond memories of the area and the generosity of our Turkish neighbours at Eid and other important moments in the year. Loaded with bags, I crossed to the other side of the street and waited for the tram to take me home.

A Letter #1 – By Happenstance

When the tram arrived, I got on and found an empty seat near the front. At the next stop, a lady got on and asked (in English), 'do you mind if I sit next to you.' What a pleasant day this is turning out to be, I thought to myself and quickly said 'yes of course, please do.' The woman sat down and immediately produced a letter which she unfolded and flattened. She then turned to the two girls sitting behind us and addressed them in Turkish. The woman was clearly in a hurry and needed some information quickly. She pointed at a paragraph in the letter, which set off an impromptu translation session on the tram. This involved the two girls reading the paragraph out loud in Dutch and discussing translation possibilities in Turkish. In the time it took the tram to pass the next stop, they had pieced together a fair translation of the paragraph. This also involved scanning other parts of the letter to gain more co-text and context. For this they used the same approach. But then came the urgent task of telling the lady what she needed and where she had to get off – something they only discovered by scanning and translating the letter. This was in fact the next (third) stop. I was able to help at this stage of the exchange and pointed the lady in the right direction.

The woman thanked the girls profusely, and also thanked me for the directions but mainly for letting her sit near the girls. She then inserted the "source text" into her handbag, made it off the tram in time and headed off in the direction of a nearby hospital. When the doors closed, one of the girls said to the other (in Dutch) "zij is een Bulgaarse, zeker weten."[4]

The girls got off the tram in the centre of town and I continued on to the stop at the top of my street. Much like many such interpreted events, all traces of 'translation' had evaporated into thin air or into a handbag in this instance. What did linger a little longer in the tram, however, was the aroma of savoury Kurdish pastries. I never saw these people again, but I continue to witness translation on public transport and also take part in it myself.

An Interpreting Event and Its Chain Lightning of Indexicalities

Taken together and separately, (1) the woman first addressing me in English, and (2) the girl's remark, set off a momentary chain lightning[5] of indexicalities, but before we go into that, we first have to have a closer look at the translational exchange on the tram. At the heart of the impromptu translational exchange or interpreting event is what we might call "sight translation." According to Čeňková (2010), sight translation or prima vista is "one of the basic modes of interpreting [...]" and is used "in a wide range of work situations." It comprises a "dichotomous process of language transfer from the source language (SL) into the target language (TL) as well as from a written into an oral form." This fits the picture so far. Sight translation can be used for a variety of purposes. Čeňková (2010) provides an outline of events at which it might be used, all of which are professional, as is to be expected. These bring with them a set of professional norms (Chesterman, 1993) and expectations including natural speed of delivery and clarity, non-interference from the SL, etc. In professional situations, preparation time and the prior availability of documents would also be essential factors, if expectations are to be met correctly. Given the urgency however, professional norms were not an immediate issue on the tram. The documents were not delivered beforehand but presented on the spot to the surprise of the two newly designated ad-hoc interpreters.

We can speculate about the randomness of this designation. We can also speculate about why she addressed me, quite elegantly I might add, in English. The woman clearly had a purpose in sitting down beside me and had already spotted the two girls when she got onto the tram. How did the woman know these girls spoke Turkish? She obviously did and also assumed that they spoke Dutch as well. But how did she know I spoke English, for that matter? Judging from my account of the translation event, all of the above proved to be the case.

This has something to do with the groundedness and resourcefulness I mentioned above. Such basic assumptions regarding potentialities of communication are usually considered as being typical of what you might call local interactions with people with whom we have grown up in our own neighbourhoods. People might then comment on ease of understanding and of someone's typical way of speaking etc., but typical ways of speaking aren't necessarily monolingual, if at all. This little interpreting event on a tram passing through a Turkish neighbourhood in Ghent bears witness to these basic assumptions being multilingual, and to how people read and engage with a potentially multilingual situation.

Conceptually speaking, it shows us once again how important repertoire is, also in helping us put aside monolingual takes on everyday speech. Translation is also one of the discursive features that emerges from this interaction. I was not given or arranged beforehand, as in professional sight translation situations.

As far as helping the woman was concerned, accuracy, an important aspect of professional sight translation, was also an important factor in the interaction. This does not mean that there was no slippage and renegotiation of translational meaning in the exchange, something that would be probably frowned upon or considered as time consuming in professional situations. The source text was a letter addressed to the woman, but this piece of evidence disappeared into the lady's handbag and cannot be relied on here to prove a point. Moreover, only a part of the "source text" was relevant in the interpreting event, even though the girls did scan other parts of the letter for further clarification. So could we call it a partial sight translation of a partial source text, perhaps?

Though they were used more often than not to explore and conceptualise translation (practices) in contrast to interpreting,[6] the various factors[7] of Hans Vermeer's Skopos theory (Nord, 1997)[8] come in quite handy in encapsulating the event described above. First, in outlining the factors of the theory, Vermeer replaced the common term source text by a rather vague one, *offer of information*. The term is not at all vague, however, when viewed in this context, as the letter was presented, albeit briefly, to the interpreters along with a request for translation/clarification and then very soon after that stored away in the woman's handbag. As a term, *offer of information* seems perhaps better suited to anticipate possible translational outcomes and cover such ephemeral exchanges. Even though they involve well-known genres like letters, when seen as offers of information, what happens with them in terms of translation is quite different from textbook translational expectations and professional procedures. This is mainly due to the leeway and leverage the term provides in encompassing less obvious forms of interpreting like these. In this way and despite much criticism, Vermeer helped translation dislodge itself from its text-centred conceptualisations and related procedures, even in literary translation. Moreover, professional translators, be they familiar with Vermeer's theory or not, also know that there is more to professional expectations than meet the eye and that these expectations often remain unarticulated, as is often the case with the *translation brief* or set of instructions issued by the principal in a translation event. The *skopos* or purpose of the exchange was to translate/ explain part of a letter but the *translatum*, as Vermeer calls it, was not a target text at all. It was an interpretation of part of the letter together with a set of instructions relating to that part of the letter, along with directions on how to get to the hospital, the need for which only became apparent from scanning the rest of the letter and only translating part of it.

I am not arguing that this does not happen in professional situations; I merely want to point out that the term and the others proposed in Skopos theory are quite flexible in encompassing the interpreting event discussed here, including its result. More importantly, the way the terms are conceived leaves the door open for other elements that heave into view. It could be argued that Vermeer and Reiss were trying to anticipate or make room for other aspects of translation by positing a set of somehow vague or abstract concepts. Their vagueness or level of abstraction, rather than being indicative of objectivity and so-called scientific practice and language use, can also be understood as potentially allowing us to factor in other less visible elements of the process.[9] In this respect, the assumptions the woman made when she got onto the tram, though unarticulated, somehow seem as obvious as asking a professional translator to do a job for you. This brings me to the chain lightning indexicalities I mentioned at the beginning, as they help shed light on these assumptions.

In his ground-breaking article, Silverstein proposes the notion of indexical order and its centrality "to analysing how semiotic agents access macro-sociological plane categories and concepts as values in the indexable realm of the micro-contextual. Through such access their relational identities are presupposed and creatively (trans)formed in interaction (Silverstein, 2003, p. 193). In making that remark, 'Zij is een Bulgaarse, zeker weten,' (She's a Bulgarian, for sure) she drew on the macro-sociological designation Bulgarian, to explain something she had detected in how the woman spoke Turkish in this micro-context. This also places the woman in the Turkish-speaking Bulgarian community in the city, a conclusion she indeed drew from her manner of speaking, which begs the question: how did she know that and say so with such assuredness?

To explain what her assuredness might be based on, we first have to turn briefly to studies of migration flows from Eastern and Central Europe over the past ten to fifteen years (Touquet & Wets, 2013), which clearly document the influx of migrants into Belgium and offer us a basic rationale for where they have settled. In their 2013 study on migration from

Eastern Europe, Touquet and Wets mention that 30% of all migrants to Belgium of Bulgarian origin live in Ghent – the highest concentration in the country (Touquet & Wets, 2013, p. 32). Among these are Bulgarian Roma, Turkish-speaking Muslims from the northeast of Bulgaria (Touquet & Wets, 2013, p. 70). Those who now live in and helped create Turkish neighbourhoods in Ghent either descend from Turkish migrants or arrived as Turkish "guest workers[10]" in the 1960s (De Bock, 2015).

The neighbourhood that forms the context for this chapter is in and around the Sleepstraat, a former working-class area of Ghent. Generally speaking, working-class areas are the first areas of encounter between migrants and locals, something that is easy to illustrate by picking any city at random: viz. Moore St and the North inner city of Dublin (Ireland) and the presence there of the African diaspora is a relatively recent example once spurred on by the now defunct Celtic tiger. There are plenty of other examples, but the point is that this is a pattern[11] in many a city that needs further examination by people outside of populist politics as these politicians have preyed on the frictions generated by these encounters and have failed to notice the positive forms of cultural expression that emerge from them. It is no coincidence either, given their long-standing cultural links, that the Bulgarians sought contact, work and accommodation in the Turkish neighbourhoods of Ghent. The irony is that these Bulgarians did not arrive as "guest workers" "invited" by the Belgian state but as members of the European Union exercising their right under the freedom of movement of people within the Union to go in search of employment.

Now, to return to the two girls on the tram, the likelihood is strong that they had previously interacted with Turkish-speaking Bulgarians and had picked up on their patterns of speech.[12]

Even though we cannot prove this in any real sense, the girl's remark, by itself, has enough indexical clout to suffice. To repeat Silverstein's point, the macro-social category '(she is a) Bulgarian' emerged as a value from and was indexed by the micro-contextual interpreting exchange on the tram. Let us follow Silverstein's complex and intricate logic here to further back up the point:

> Micro-sociological contexts are in a sense composed of a dynamic structure-in play of these categorical distinctions (see Silverstein, 1992; 1993; 1998). And indeed, interactional happenings are social-actional "events" of (to a degree determinately) interpretable cultural meanings only to the degree they "instantiate"—indexically invoke—such macro-sociological partitions of social space, in terms of which cultural values can thus be said to be indexically "articulated."
>
> (Silverstein, 2003, p. 202)

'Bulgarian' sets up a 'macro-sociological partition,' as Silverstein argues, but at the same time it sets up a form of distinction in inclusion set off by the indexical information in the woman's voice, something I as an interlocutor could not pick up on as it was not part of my repertoire. All I knew was that it was Turkish from hearing the language in my neighbourhood over the years.

In contrast, because of the way the woman addressed me in English, my indexical invocation of her was of a quite different order. To me she was "a well-spoken Brit," perhaps with a migrant background, which again was impossible to prove. Again as Silverstein puts it, both the girl and I "socio-culturally identified (from the presuppositional point of view) or placed, as it were (as an indexical entailment of language use)" the woman as belonging to or coming from at least two different places at the same time (Silverstein, 2003, p. 202).

This added an extra layer to her 'indexical biography,' (Blommaert and Backus, 2013, p. 28) not simply by placing her outside the neighbourhood but by further muddying the waters in relation to possible origins in this indexical biography. In contrast to being identified by the girl as "a Bulgarian," what caused me to identify her as a "well-spoken Brit" was a particular register I picked up on when she asked me if she could sit down next to me on the tram. The process of acquiring such a register or enregisterment, as it is known (Agha, 2007), ties in nicely with Silverstein's notion of indexical order. In discussing register and its formation, Agha (2007, p. 147) notes that

> A register formation is a reflexive model of behavior that evaluates a semiotic repertoire (or set of repertoires) as appropriate to specific types of conduct (such as the conduct of a given social practice), to classifications of persons whose conduct it is, and, hence, to performable roles (personae, identities) and relationships among them.

In a similar vein, what the girl and I were doing was drawing on some notion of voice quality and ways of speaking as indexing a certain social status or origin or, as Agha would put it, we were appealing to "metapragmatic stereotypes[13] of speech, i.e., culture-internal models of utterance indexicality associated with speech variants" (Agha, 2007, p. 148). This resonates with Silverstein's attention to a "tropic" reading of speech and how it "is characteristic of a folk- or ethno-metapragmatic view of the indexical facts" (Silverstein, 2003, p. 203). I assume that this also applies to our readings of the woman's speech.

There is nothing unusual about this indexical or register[14] work; in fact, we all do it all the time – indexing people by the way they speak and placing them somewhere both socially and "geographically" as a result. What emerges is a momentary view from the varying perspectives of the two girls and I on what in this case is the woman's "indexical biography," or a glimpse of "the social and cultural itineraries" she has followed (Blommaert and Backus, 2013, p. 28). This chain lightning of indexicalities and related registers also lights up the sociolinguistic backdrop against which this itinerary is taking place. Depending on the interlocutor, this was either clearly anchored in a Turkish neighbourhood in Ghent and the semiotic relations obtaining there. Or it had an even broader canvas of encounter that also involved England in some way. In the context of the interaction on the tram, those involving English perhaps belong in the "public realm" (Soenen, 2006). The semiotic relations obtaining in the Turkish neighbourhood of Ghent, or as was suggested at the beginning of this chapter, those involving an invocation of the "parochial realm" (Soenen, 2006) were probably instrumental in making the interpreting event possible. When getting on to the tram, the woman also made use of these semiotic relations in identifying the two girls as possible ad-hoc interpreters, which is central to the discussion here.

So, I think it is safe to argue from the above case, particularly in relation to the resourcefulness and groundedness mentioned earlier, that in various forms of natural translation and interpreting, similar semiotic (iconic and indexical) work will probably help set up and maintain possible natural translation or interpreting encounters. There is much more to it than a simple initial denotational request for translational help with some language issue – in this case a paragraph in a letter. The chain lightning of indexicality described above is probably typical of most encounters but in this case it moved out from a chance encounter on a tram that was sparked by a need for translation. We were able to trace the filigree of its implications as they disappeared in perhaps more real terms into the Turkish neighbourhood and at the same time into imaginations about England.

Further Comments

You might wonder, in terms of reliability of data, why I didn't choose to discuss one of my own translations on public transport. Reliability doesn't sit well with the ephemeral and the momentary, however, and the case discussed above does highlight these two factors in translational exchanges on public transport. I also chose the above interpreting exchange because I believed at the time that it said something specific about the no 4 tram route in terms of translation activity. I've long since changed my mind on the matter, as no specific route can lay claim to being the route where the most translation takes place. My reasoning for focusing on tram no 4 was that, while criss-crossing the city centre, the route passed through neighbourhoods with high concentrations of migrants. The same could be argued for the no 3 bus route, but all of this only tells part of the story. As I pointed out in the analogy at the beginning of this chapter, journeys to and from work and school, etc. create daily networks of scaled language activities including translation and interpreting. I am convinced, however, given the possibility of chance encounters and the ephemeral nature of the exchanges that it is more common a feature of public rather than private transport. As a colleague of mine pointed out however, no public transport route or mode of public transport can be excluded from this, which means we have to factor in people travelling to and from the villages in the greater Ghent conurbation, who also include migrants who work in and around the "big houses" in these villages. In the meantime, I believe it is safe to add interpreting and translation practices, at least in some small measure in this study, to the long list of components comprising repertoire and hence a person's indexical biography (Blommaert & Backus, 2013).

Notes

1 Soenen also uses the term fleeting (Soenen, 2006). For a typology of passengers on public transport in the cities of Split and Zagreb, see Tomić, Relja & Popović: Ethnography of urban public transport: A tale of two cities in Croatia. *Anthropological Notebooks* 21(1), 37–59 (2015).
2 All of these activities also have to be further articulated in terms of gender, age, etc.
3 Not all trained translators go on to translate and there are many professional translators who have no formal training in translation. See Flynn (2005) on the idea of an epiphany of translation.
4 "She's a Bulgarian, for sure."
5 In the sense that it comprises and lights up various momentary connections and branches.
6 See Pöchhacker (2017) for a study of simultaneous interpreting from a Skopos theory perspective.
7 Vermeer proposed five main factors that obtain in any translation situation: 1. Skopos; 2. Offer of information; 3. Translatum; 4. Commission; 5 Translation brief. The theory was further explored and worked out by Reiss.
8 For an examination of the relevance of Skopos theory for translation practices through an ethnography of literary translation, see Flynn (2004, 2005).
9 In similar way Bourdieu refused to surrender to demands to further specify terms like field, habitus etc., arguing that their supposed vagueness would be resolved empirically in each case.
10 For an interesting discussion on the notion of "guest worker" and its specific vagueness and on how superdiversity can be used as a means for examining past migration, see De Bock (2015).
11 See also De Bock on migration channels and immigration statuses in relation to Ghent (De Bock 2015, pp. 587–592).
12 In this respect, crossing is also prevalent among teenagers in Ghent schools (Rampton, 2005).
13 See the discussion of "accent" identification and stereotypes in the next chapter.
14 It is interesting to note that in explaining processes of enregisterment, Agha uses a typical set of functional wh-questions, something that is basic to functional approaches to translation, Skopos theory being a functionalist theory of translation. See Agha here: https://www.youtube.com/watch?v=XEr Ustf0wUg&t=5351s (29/11/2021).

References

Agha. (2007). *Language and Social Relations* (Studies in the Social and Cultural Foundations of Language; 24). Cambridge: Cambridge University Press.
Blommaert, J. (2013). *Ethnography, Superdiversity and Linguistic Landscapes. Chronicles of Complexity* (Critical language and literacy studies, [18]). Bristol/Buffalo, NY: Multilingual Matters.

Blommaert, J., & Backus, A. (2013). Superdiverse repertoires and the individual. In I. de Saint-Georges & J. J. Weber (Eds.), *Multilingualism and Multimodality: Current Challenges for Educational Studies* (pp. 11–32). Rotterdam: Sense.

Čeňková, I. (2010). Sight Translation Prima vista. *Handbook of Translation Studies*, 1, 320–323. Current revision: 2016.

Chesterman, A. (1993). "From 'is' to 'ought': Laws, norms and strategies in translation. *Target*, 5(1), 1–20.

De Bock, J. (2015) Not all the same after all? Superdiversity as a lens for the study of past migrations. *Ethnic and Racial Studies*, 38(4), 583–595. doi:10.1080/01419870.2015.980290

Flynn, P. (2004). Skopos theory: An ethnographic enquiry. *Perspectives*, 12(4), 270–285.

Flynn, P. (2005). *A Linguistic Ethnography of Literary Translation: Irish Poems and Dutch-Speaking Translators*. Gent: Universiteit Gent. Faculteit letteren en wijsbegeerte.

Ingold, T. (2018). *Anthropology: Why It Matters*. Cambridge/Medford, MA: Polity Press.

Nord, C. (1997). *Translation as a Purposeful Activity: Functionalist Approaches Explained* (Translation Theories Explained, 1). Manchester: St Jerome Press.

Pöchhacker, F. (2017). Simultaneous interpreting: A functionalist perspective. *HERMES - Journal of Language and Communication in Business*, 8(14), 31–53.

Pöchhacker, F. (2021). Pathways in interpreter training: An Austrian perspective. In P. Šveda (Ed.), *Changing Paradigms and Approaches in Interpreter Training: perspectives from Central Europe* (Routledge Advances in Translation and Interpreting Studies, pp. 43–64). London: Routledge.

Rampton, B. (2005). *Crossing: Language & ethnicity among adolescents* (2nd ed., Encounters). Manchester: St. Jerome.

Silverstein M. (2003). Indexical order and the dialectics of sociolinguistic life. *Language & Communication*, 23, 193–229. doi:10.1016/S0271–5309(03)00013-2

Silverstein, M. (2003). Translation, transduction, transformation: Skating "glossando" on thin semiotic ice. In P. G. Rubel & A. Rosman (Eds.), *Translating Cultures: Perspectives on Translation and Anthropology* (pp. 75–105). Oxford: Berg.

Soenen, R. (2006). An Anthropological Account of Ephemeral Relationships on Public Transport. A Contribution to the Reflection on Diversity. EURODIV PAPER 29.2006. Eurodiv Second Conference "Qualitative diversity research: Looking ahead," 19–20 September 2006. https://citeseerx.ist.psu.edu/viewdoc/download?doi=10.1.1.488.2161&rep=rep1&type=pdf

Tian, Z., & Link, H. (Eds.). (2019). Positive synergies: Translanguaging and critical theories in education. *Special Issue of Translation and Translanguaging in Multilingual Contexts*, 5(1), 93.

Tomić, V., Relja, R., & Popović, T. (2015). Ethnography of urban public transport: A tale of two cities in Croatia. *Anthropological Notebooks*, 21(1), 37–59.

Touquet, H., & Wets, J. (2013). *Context, drijfveren en opportuniteiten van Midden- en Oost-Europese immigratie: Een exploratief onderzoek met focus op Roma*. Leuven: KU Leuven – HIVA Onderzoeksinstituut voor Arbeid en Samenleving.

5   An Irish Pub

The site of this case is an Irish pub[1] situated in the centre of Ghent, a pub that has been frequented by the author on a regular basis over the years mainly to meet friends and to watch important events in the Irish and international sporting calendar. Irish pubs are a common feature in cities and went global some time ago (Hudson, 2019). In this respect, their more immediate links with the Irish diaspora (Bronwen, 2004; Popoviciu et al., 2006) have been transformed and redefined partly in keeping with the marketing of "Irishness" as a global commodity, more particularly in the form of the Irish pub, something that has been bemoaned by some (Forde, 2009; West, 2011), considered by others as a solid business model (Deller, 1996; Oram, 1996; Prystay, 1997; Grantham, 2009; Lennox, 2013). This was mainly before the financial crisis, and among other things, the main focus of these studies were on retailing hospitality (O'Mahoney et al., 2005) and hence fed into and instrumentalised a set of national stereotypes (Beller & Leerssen, 2007) in the global marketplace. In concluding his discussion of Irishness, Leerssen has the following to say:

> The image [of Irishness] is as current nowadays in postmodern and New Age literature and in post-colonial criticism as it was in Victorian *fin de siècle* (Leerssen 1996b). Indeed, this image, although it perpetuates clichés of (literarily) mediaeval vintage, has itself become one of Ireland's great assets and export products, winning them sympathy abroad, an eager audience for their writers and artists and a steady stream of visitors and tourists.
>
> (Leerssen in Beller and Leerssen, 2007, pp. 193–194)

And indeed, anyone who visits an Irish pub will notice, next to the mirrors and kegs advertising John Jameson whisky and the Celtic inlay designs from the Book of Kells, portraits of James Joyce, William Butler Yeats and Oscar Wilde jostling for position alongside pictures of famous rugby players, folk singers and rock stars, all Irish of course. The iconographic relations of those on display will shift across pubs in reflecting the owners' preferences but I wonder when gender issues will be raised in relation to the icons on display. Suffice to say that it is easier to find pictures of singers like Sinead O'Connor or Dolores O'Riordan than it is to find ones of writers like Lady Gregory

DOI: 10.4324/9781003363811-6

or Maeve Binchy. In each case, Irishness is articulated iconically in drawing customers to these pubs. The city of Brussels is home to a pub called the James Joyce, as is Lyon, Prague, Madrid, Patchogue and perhaps many more cities around the world, places that may play a role in new constellations of migration, not only of Irish people (Hudson, 2019). According to Graeme Lennox (2013) there were more than 6,000 Irish pubs in the world. Wikipedia now puts the figure at 7,000.[2] In the midst of all the globalisation and commodification of Irishness, there is certain irony to this, as Joyce, rejected during his lifetime in his own country, was someone who vaunted his exile and never held an Irish passport. But these considerations take us beyond the scope of this study, which is about natural translation and interpreting practices in an Irish pub in Ghent. It remains to be seen from what emerges from the data what types of translation and interpreting take place, how they are shaped by the setting and participants and, if it is the case, how the global and the local are possibly enacted through these practices.

Both as a locus and in terms of its language practices the pub provides a fitting example of what Pennycook and Otsuji would call 'metrolingualism,' precisely because of the shift in languages one would be likely to encounter in the course of any given day. Mundane metrolingualism is one of several concepts that serve well in encapsulating the language practices and forms of non-professional translation encountered in the pub (Pennycook & Otsuji, 2015, 2019) Metrolingualism

> describes the ways in which people of different and mixed backgrounds use, play with and negotiate identities through language… Rather than assuming connections between language and culture, ethnicity, nationality or geography, Metrolingualism 'seeks to explore how such relations are produced, resisted, defied or rearranged; its focus is not on language systems but on languages as emergent from contexts of interaction (p. 246)'.
> (Pennycook & Otsuji, 2015, p. 3)

They then go on to explain mundane in relation to their research:

> Alongside its slightly negative implications …, the term mundane carries (via its historical connections to contemporary le monde) a sense of worldliness, or terrestrial and material relations. It is these two senses that we wish to convey here: the quotidian and the worldly.
> (Pennycook & Otsuji, 2019, pp. 175–176)

The other concepts that will be used below are superdiversity and scale. Building on Vertovec's notion of superdiversity (Vertovec, 2007, 2010; see supra), Blommaert and Rampton have the following to say:

> Super-diversity is characterized by a tremendous increase in the categories of migrants, not only in terms of nationality, ethnicity,

language, and religion, but also in terms of motives, patterns and itineraries of migration, processes of insertion into the labour and housing markets of the host societies, and so on.

(Blommaert & Rampton, 2011, p. 3)

This view can certainly be transposed to the pub under discussion here, but this does not mean that we should not be cautious about the remit of the term, as will become clear later. The notion of scale is also important for our understanding of language practices in the pub. In discussion how the term has been used in the study of language practices, Slembrouck and Vandenbroucke note:

> At the heart have been analyses of both material and discursive processes, with variable emphasis on the circulation of, say, money, goods, commodities, labour and people, on how these entities are "talked into being," on attendant processes of reflexive engagement as well as, of course, on the scaled dimensions of communicative resources, languages, texts, media images and so on – thematic interconnections which are of particular interest to linguistic ethnographic enquiry.
>
> (Slembrouck & Vandenbroucke, 2020, pp. 71–72)

This proposes quite a programme of investigation that cannot be fully addressed in all its detail below. The term does shed light on a couple of the practices observed at the pub, however. These concepts will be brought into play in analysing the data presented in the following sections of this chapter and returned to in the conclusion of the chapter.

Contexts, People and Events

The "Irish Pub" is a locus of locally enacted global Irishness (among many other things) that is "talked into being" through a set of shifting situated language practices, including translation and interpreting. In our case, the dramatis personae of this and other enactments comprise staff and customers. The staff are mainly recruited in Ireland or from among Irish people already living in Belgium,[3] or from among local Flemish students and other students, often Spanish speaking.[4] The customers frequenting the pub first comprise staff from other Irish pubs in the city or region, who together form their own home-away-from-home networks. Then there are the locals, i.e. Flemish people who come to watch the games, and, as one of the staff remarked, "practise their English." Next are the "expats," people from far and wide who use the pub (loosely) as their local, the last group being tourists from Spain and other countries visiting the city. Who is present in the pub at any given time will certainly be influenced by the sports calendar in season ranging from horse racing in the early afternoons, soccer (mainly but not exclusively the

Premier League) in the late afternoons and evenings, European football on weekday evenings, and again at weekends, Six Nations and at times the World Cup rugby championship, club rugby, Irish (Gaelic) football and hurling, especially from the quarter finals on. This is not a complete list of events as they do not include the European Cup or the World Cup in soccer, Belgian championships, etc. A lot of these games are frequented by what you might call "expats" hailing from various parts of the English-speaking and partly French-speaking world from Australia, South and West Africa to Scotland and many other places in between. Next to these customers, the pub is particularly popular among Spanish tourists who visit Ghent in droves throughout the whole year.

Language practices will depend in part on who is watching which event and also on the staff members who are on duty at the time. For this reason, it is important to know what's on:

- A rugby game will attract customers for Great Britain and Ireland, France, Italy, South Africa, New Zealand and Australia along with local rugby supporters, mainly on weekend afternoons;
- A soccer game will attract locals, along with customers of Central and West African origin and "expats" from the UK and elsewhere on weekday evenings and weekend afternoons;
- A hurling or Gaelic football game will invariably attract county supporters, Irish people in general and the odd customer trying to make of these curious sports on Sunday afternoons;
- Racehorse punters, mainly of British and Irish extraction will be there on early afternoons during the weekend.

Each of these sports/games will come with its own shifting configuration of language use including and certainly not limited to varieties of English,[5] French,[6] Italian, Spanish and Dutch.

Particular Shapes of Multilingualism

A lot of the language practices are hidden by what I came to term "the (surface) ubiquity of English," an assumption many of the people entering the pub might consider as obvious. Why I use "surface," however, will also become obvious from extracts from interviews and observations at the pub:

INTERVIEWEE: I did five years of Dutch at school when I was 11 till 17 or 18 and then I went to Ireland, and I didn't speak a single word of it for 12 years. Then I came back and tried to dust off the old cobwebs and it made learning the basics okay but the colloquial was totally new.
INTERVIEWER: So, Ghent dialect, yeah, yeah

INTERVIEWEE: It was very difficult for me in the beginning trying to adapt. Between "Gents" and the classes there's a massive difference. If I hadn't had the classes I probably wouldn't have been able to get the hang of it. I find here – well I know we're running an Irish bar and the majority speak English, but I find myself speaking more Spanish than I do any other language.

This extract exposes a chink in the armour of English and highlights the distinction between Standard Dutch and Ghent dialect, something the staff become aware of and are confronted with from the outset. It also brings Spanish into play:

INTERVIEWER: Spanish? Is that because the people you're working with are Spanish people?
INTERVIEWEE: There are that many Spanish people coming round, customers or visitors or students here. Obviously, we show the football, Real Madrid and Barca, so I'm using more Spanish than I would necessarily Dutch (Really?), which is a strange phenomenon (Yeah).
INTERVIEWER: And what do the customers eh ....?
INTERVIEWEE: So the Spanish don't speak necessarily any other language so (Yeah, right) they just speak Spanish and that's it (Yeah) and a Flemish person will automatically speak English to you to give you a hand (yeah). They see you struggling in Dutch ...

The conversation then turns to language learning and attitudes towards language among the customers:

I find it hard to learn the Dutch because every time I struggled they automatically switched to English to help me out but actually in the long term it doesn't help you because you can't improve your language (right, yeah, yeah) but you struggle through a bad bout to get to where you need to be whereas the French won't speak any other language and the Spanish may not know any other language ... so you have to go through that pain barrier but because they are accommodating in the long run they don't help you. ...

INTERVIEWER: And does it ever happen that someone says no, you've got to speak Dutch?
INTERVIEWEE: Oh yeah, we get the odd customer I'd say about once a month or once every couple of months.

This is an interesting take on language learning and a polite recommendation to speakers of Dutch not to be too accommodating and refrain from "practising their English" and let the speaker "struggle" and "go through the pain barrier," something which speakers of French and Spanish will invariably do, according to the interviewee, even though they may be unaware of the fact.

Again drawing on observation and conversations with the staff the following can be proposed. Interactions between staff members and customers are usually initiated in English but have a number of possible outcomes as several competing language-ideological rationales (Woolard, 2020, inter alia) come into play:

- This is an Irish pub, so everyone speaks English;
- This is Flanders, so everyone should speak /speaks Dutch;
- Belgium is a multilingual country, so as a tourist I expect to be served in my own language;
- I want to practice my English, but I can't make out what you are saying. Is it English?
- I want to use Dutch, but I can't make out what you are saying. Is it Dutch?
- Etc.

So the surface ubiquity of English makes way for a number of practices in and across languages and forms of language negotiation and interpreting and translation (might) then kick in and these will be dealt with in the next section.

Pub Translation and Interpreting

Instances of Translation

We will first examine forms of translation found in signage and menus at the pub. These comprise language/translation features on the blackboard outside the pub (Figure 5.1).

On the blackboard below we can see the use of 'u' as time indication in Dutch. "Everyday Live Sports Televised" is an instance of a phrase that uses English words, and Dutch word order. Similar features can be found on the pub website, which are purposely not dealt with here.

We can be brief about the origin of the Dutch translation of the menu. According to the owner, it was the result of a friendly translational gesture by an acquaintance "for a few beers."

The menu contains several interesting (creative) translational features. In all there were 29 items on the menu. In terms of translation, we discovered seven instances of explicitation (Klaudy, 1998), as the following example illustrates:

Garlic Bread topped with Cheese – lookbrood met Cheddar

The reason why the type of cheese is explicitly mentioned in Dutch (Cheddar) is probably because other types of cheese are usually used as topping in Belgium, namely Emmental or Gruyère.

Figure 5.1 Pub Blackboard

There were 15 instances of Implicitation/Omission:

Grilled Goats Cheese and Honey Salad – Geitenkaas met Honing Salade

The reason for the Implicitation here is that goat's cheese is practically always grilled for such dishes in Belgium.

We also discovered an instance of 'creative' translation:

Traditional Fried Fish and Chips Served with Side Salad & Tartare Sauce & Lemon – Goud gefrituurde Kabeljauw met Tartaarsaus, Frietjes en Sla

The use of the Dutch word for golden in "goud gefrituurd kabeljauw" (literally golden deep-fried cod) enhances the dish and makes it sound more appetising, next to mentioning the fish explicitly as cod and not merely as fish.

There were six instances of close equivalents as the following example illustrates:

> Vegetarian Burger with Cheese, Salad and Fries – Vegetarische burger met Kaas, Sla en Frietjes (note the diminutive in frietjes again)

Words like homemade, classic, traditional, southern, champ, basket and platter were left untranslated. These words either belong to the lexicon of 'pub grub' (homemade, traditional) or tie a dish indexically to its country or region of origin (Southern to the USA, champ to Ireland). They may have been lost on the translator. Basket and platter can be considered obvious and hence dispensable, though the word platter is redolent in English of expensive seafood and other fine fare, which are nowhere near as expensive in continental Europe, thus rendering platter a non-item. Basket indexes simplicity and rurality in the UK and Ireland, whereas it is simply something they serve bread in Belgium, and certainly not sausages and chips. On the whole, the translation can be judged as useful,[7] and it could be argued that the large number of Implicitations and Omissions, by understating the obvious, might also enhance the element of surprise among the customers as to what they are being served. The Explicitations all had clear cultural justifications, as the example discussed above illustrates.

Instances of Interpreting

We will now turn to instances of interpreting at the pub. Forms of intra- and interlingual interpreting were observed both among staff and between staff and customers. Among staff, these first involved rewording or intralingual interpreting, i.e. rendering Irish (English) utterances in Standard English terms for a variety of purposes. For example, the meaning of utterances like "Watch out for yer man over there" and "Yer one down at the end still hasn't paid" are not immediately obvious to those unfamiliar with the pragmatic indexical load of "yer (your) man/ wan (one)." Though your is a possessive pronoun in Standard English, in Irish English it has indexical meaning in terms of the person being pointed or referred to in the immediate context or the person who is the topic of the conversation. In terms of gender, wan (one), is always female and may also have a slightly derogatory meaning, as in the example above. These understandings would not be part of repertoires of foreign learners of Standard English and hence would require translating, along with other features of Hiberno-English used by the Irish staff at the pub.

Ad-hoc interlingual interpreting also takes place between Spanish and English staff as a form of mutual language learning. This usually involves drawing up lists of words and phrases in English and Spanish on beer mats and exchanging them among each other.

In terms of interlingual interpreting between English and Dutch between customers and staff, a distinction can be made between discretionary and non-discretionary interpreting. Discretionary interpreting functions as an immediate aid and as an ad-hoc form of language learning for both the customers and the staff. It should be noted that the staff also follow Dutch classes and want to practice their Dutch at work.

There is also a mixture of intra- and interlingual translation in which a staff member will ask a customer to help interpret from a local dialect into Standard Dutch or into English. This is considered non-discretionary, in the sense that the locals expect to be served in their own language. It is also polite and sound business sense to do so.

One staff member organised Irish classes and there are a couple of Flemish customers who come to the pub to practice their Irish. People also frequent the pub to "practise their English." Among them are groups of secondary school students who might be tasked by their teachers to try out their English on a "native speaker.[8]" This invariably starts with one member of the group being designated to carry out the ice-breaking feat of ordering something in English. The staff usually enjoy these conversations and are willing to help the students out, but it must be added that such conversations seldom involve the niceties of Hiberno-English, though they may increasingly do as young people become familiar with Irish "accents" via YouTube and other social media.

Instances of Intersemiotic Translation/Interpreting

Another common translation/interpreting practice found at the pub involves commenting on, explaining and translating the commentary of televised Irish sports, in this instance a game of hurling (Figure 5.2).[9]

This usually involves staff or Irish customers on the one hand and other, often surprised, customers on the other hand who find themselves watching a sport they have never seen before. But how can we make translational sense of the practice? The practice can first be termed as intersemiotic (Jakobson, 1959) or intersystemic[10] (Marais, 2019) translation in the sense that we are clearly moving back and forth between various modes of audio-visual expression. We then have to trace the various elements of this instance of practice as it unfolds, though these elements will be similar to those that occur on other occasions. The first element comprises ad-hoc interpreting into Dutch, including answers to such questions as

> Wat zegt hij nu (What's he saying now)? Hoe doen zij dat, een pas geven met de hand (How do they do that, pass the ball with their hand)? Waar is de bal naar toe (Where has the ball gone)?

Figure 5.2 A hurler in action

Similar questions are asked and answered in English, also including "what did he just say[11]?" and "What do you mean there is no offside rule in hurling?" This interpreting is not constant and is interrupted by other forms of talk, during which the viewers continue to watch and comment on the game, one striking comment being: "it's like a wild type of hockey." This ad-hoc interpreting coincides with a second element that comprises at least two interwoven strands of discourse:

> Explaining what is happening in terms of action, play, moves, etc. - commentary;
> Explaining why it is happening in terms of rules, fair play, etc. – metacommentary.

So while interpreting, at the same time, the interpreters are explaining the former in terms of the latter and vice versa! This in turn coincides with a third element, i.e. that of gesturing, and pointing, drawing the viewers' attention to the ball (no mean feat[12]), or to certain typical moments to illustrate a rule or aspect of play, etc.

How then should we classify this complex (intersemiotic) translational activity, including its elements? Broadly speaking, it can be called ad-hoc audio-visual translation, but is that sufficient to cover all its elements? Perhaps ad-hoc multimodal translation might be a more appropriate term, but again this raises the question of whether we are addressing it as a multimodal object or as a multimodal process or both[13]? Regarding the match on TV, we can bring in such terms as ekphrasis and audio description to help us, but again subject to the time constraints framed by the turn-taking (Gavioli, 2015; Wadensjö, 2015) in the exchanges in the pub. This steers the discussion away from conceptualisations of audio-visual translation as normally practised by translators towards models of multimodal interpreting that use turn-taking as a framing element. Here the event on the TV would have to be incorporated into the multimodality among the participants in the pub.[14] Though ekphrasis and audio description may perhaps only cover what is happening on the field/screen, such exercises will certainly contain some form of metacommentary but perhaps not in terms of rules, fair play, etc., as provided by the interlocutors in this instance. Live "subtitling" might also be part of this ad-hoc translational practice, in the sense of translating in shorthand what the commentators are saying.[15] For indeed, some of the viewers may only partly understand the live commentary in English. This draws our attention to the added indexical nature of sports commentary and the importance of "local" or "regional" speech among sports commentators and panel members as a further sign of their "authenticity" (Coupland & Coupland, 2014). For important games, another person will invariably accompany a hurling commentator,[16] often a former player who speaks in a local register about the game "from within" as it were, in contrast to the official commentator who has a sound knowledge of the game but uses a register approaching the network standard. This is common practice in sports commentary and provides the answer to why, at any given game, at least one of the French rugby commentators have a Provencal accent.

Judging by the customers' comments and remarks – another persistent question arises:

In terms of "cultural" translation (Conway, 2012), what do the viewers, i.e. those watching the game for the first time, bring with them that helps make the interpreting more accessible? Here are a number of items that emerge from observation and conversation:

> Language skills, especially an indexical awareness (Lynch, 2019) that ties ways of speaking to given cultural and social contexts;
> Notions about ball games, rules, winning and losing, skill and chance, etc. – what Wittgenstein calls "family resemblances" (Wittgenstein, 2009, p. 36e);
> Longstanding widespread (partial) cultural images/stereotypes about (wild) Irishness that might help fit/build the picture.[17]

Indexicality, family resemblances, metonymy and cultural stereotypes seem to encapsulate the driving forces harnessed in creating an understanding in the situation. Appeals to "authenticity" emerge from a (partial or metonymic) recognition of what is "typical "about a form of speaking and playing. The question about why there is no off-side rule in hurling is an illustration of "family resemblances" as other field sports such as soccer and rugby do use the off-side rule. Remarks about hurling being "a wild type of hockey" can also be classed under "stereotyping" and "metonymy."

Taking Conceptual Stock

It is now time to take stock of the various types of (translational) interaction at the pub and return to the concepts discussed at the beginning of the chapter and tie them into the discussion. As has been demonstrated, natural intra- and interlingual translation and interpreting take place regularly within, are basic ingredients of or arise naturally from these multilingual configurations of language use in the pub. Intersemiotic translation also occurs on occasions, like the one illustrated above. Given the high number of nationalities, superdiversity is more than obvious in the city and is reflected in the pub but there is no complete overlap between city and pub as might be suggested in Blommaert (2013) or Pennycook and Otsuji (2015). In this sense, superdiversity can be used as a blanket term to cover its many manifestations but we still have to see how it becomes articulated in given situations in superdiverse cities. Like many other terms, we have to find out what superdiversity means and how it actually plays out. In this respect, superdiversity at the pub is just one of its many manifestations, which most likely differs in constellation and practices from its other forms. The types of sports and the particular type of drink culture involved would also have to be factored into the equation. This also means revisiting concepts such a "migrant" and "expat" to see what they mean in terms of activities and locations in the city, which requires bringing in the notion of scale. In the meantime, it is striking to note that "expat" is a common term at the pub, whereas migrant is seldom if ever used. The verb emigrate is often used however but, more often than not, to talk about those who left Ireland for the UK,[18] USA or Australia, in the past (mainly after WWII). The state of affairs underscoring such emigration painfully returned to Ireland following the global financial crisis in 2007, then forcing thousands of highly trained people to take to the road again.

As a term, mundane metrolingualism (Pennycook & Otsuji, 2015) allows us to conceptualise the ordinary worldly flows of language use and translation at the pub both daily, weekly and seasonally as is shown in the discussion of the data and observations above, particularly in relation to sporting events and in relation to the different types of customer, including tourists who frequent the pub at different hours of the day.

To return to scale, the notion is useful in delineating various stances on languages and the related affiliations that are invoked and get played out on a daily basis. Let us examine just one here: Irishness, as pertaining to (parts of) the island and/or as European or global cultural notion, also among immigrants with an Irish connection or story: this has far-reaching ramifications which often surface during televised rugby and Gaelic football and hurling games. By way of illustration, here is an interesting quote taken from the literature on scale referring to the author of this book:

> The following vignette is anecdotal but illustrates well the related point of "fractal recursivity" (Irvine and Gal, 2000). A former colleague, who grew up in Dublin but who has lived in Belgium for over 20 years, during a discussion of the concept of "scale" intimated how, when frequenting one and the same Irish pub in the centre of town, he embodied different units of reference for his interlocutors. This he said bore both on the topics attended to and the evaluative meanings exchanged on these:
>
> i 'Ireland' when he visited the pub with Flemish friends
> ii "Flanders" when meeting visitors from Dublin or the Irish Republic and
> iii The "guys from the other side we never talk to" when having a drink with a colleague from the UK who grew up in Ulster.
>
> Distinctions are applied recursively to a fraction of a unit, as meaningful distinctions are played out to constitute a smaller group or individual with presupposed ancestry in the larger scale unit."
>
> (Slembrouck, 2011)

This applies not just to the author but to many people frequenting the pub and comes together with similar sets of features. Take second generation Irish who grew up in England and work in Belgium, for example. During hurling or Gaelic football games, they will be noticed wearing jerseys of their Irish county of origin (an iconic articulation of scale). Inter-county rivalry will then surface in the form of banter and stereotypical remarks about supposed characteristics of people from a given county, which will invariably involve mocking their "accent.[19]" These second generation Irish are fully part of what could be called these "inward-looking" exchanges. Familiarity with the sport is a key factor, it must be noted. By way of contrast, Irishness would become exclusive and adversarial to some degree during soccer games against England. During a rugby game, people will then talk a more European or even global variety of Irishness into existence. This is either diaspora related and mainly involves people from Great Britain, South Africa, Australia and New Zealand talking about the Irish origins of family or relatives. It is also expressed in terms of affiliation to Irish culture[20] – a more European affair, it could be argued, that is articulated through an interest in music, literature, etc. and, particularly for Flemish people, in terms of sympathy for the struggle of a former colony against the might of the British empire.

As was mentioned already, scale would also help us understand the difference in the seeming hierarchy between expat, migrant, economic migrant, transmigrant, nomad, traveller and other delineations of the term.[21] Because of the range of items the term encapsulates (see the quote from Slembrouck and Vandenbroucke above) it would also help us understand the various articulations of superdiversity. Given its scope, scale can also be tied to translation and interpreting practices, as will be illustrated below.

Further Comments

Despite the literature on translanguaging, the instances of translation and interpreting discussed above remain largely under-theorised in sociolinguistics and studies in Multilingualism, where the added difficulty in communication and the time-gap involved (Cronin, 2008) is somehow side-stepped and becomes magically resolved. Given that not everyone translates, it could be factored in more tangibly if viewed as an aspect of repertoire and as a form of socially distributed communicative competence (Hymes, 1972). TS has only recently begun to take such instances of translation into consideration (Antonini et al., 2017) despite the long tradition of study outside of TS (Harris, 2013). But what about Toury's "Excursus C A Bilingual Speaker Becomes a Translator A Tentative Development Model," which takes us back to Toury (1995) or even earlier? This model is echoed in Cronin's three-phrase move towards fully autonomous translation (Cronin, 2008). Both models envisage a form of professionalism or full competence as the desired result. Angelelli (2016) comes closer to Hymes's notion of its distributed nature as a competence and to the realities of everyday translation in her discussion of family interpreters: "He gets to translate; I take out the trash" (personal correspondence). As early as 1978, Harris and Sherwood argued for "translating as an innate skill," which can also be viewed in terms of register and communicative competence. Toury (1984, 1986), in adopting the term natural translation, also proposed the very interesting notion of "native translator." Though it echoes the term "native speaker," it brings with it a whole different set of assumptions. The term contests the assumed underpinnings of a nation state and its often-asserted homogenism, whereby nation (space), language and culture are conflated into a single entity (Blommaert & Verschueren, 1991). "Native translator" assumes the existence of different "languages" next to each other in the same cultural spaces and not set off by borders and separate cultures. However, not everyone grows up translating or speaking the standard,[22] which is another argument in favour of repertoire, as it allows for shifts and changes, especially in these superdiverse times (Blommaert & Backus, 2013). But to turn once again to scale, I believe it would be useful to include translating in the broad sense of the term as part of "the scaled dimensions of communicative resources, languages, texts, media images and so on" (Slembrouck & Vandenbroucke, 2020, pp. 71–72). As has been demonstrated above, talking Irishness into being also involves intra- interlingual and intersemiotic translation.

Notes

1 I would like to thank the owner and staff of the pub who agreed to partici- pate in the study on condition that they remained anonymous.
2 https://en.wikipedia.org/wiki/Irish_pub#Around_the_world (27/10/2021).
3 This brings with it the notion of scaled migration or the idea that migration can be considered in terms of various degrees of permanence, which have to be considered empirically. In this sense, words like migrant or migration are true examples of Silverstein's 'shifters' (Silverstein, 1976).
4 On Erasmus exchange per semester or year.
5 It should be noted that this is the way people speak about languages and is in no way an attempt to circumvent such notions as metrolingualism or repertoire, as Chapter 3 clearly illustrates.
6 One of the Congolese customers told me he speaks five African languages next to French and English.
7 And not the object of mockery as translated menus often are.
8 A common term among teachers of English in Flanders.
9 https://en.wikipedia.org/wiki/Hurling.
10 As Marais correctly points out, language is also a semiotic system and hence proposes the term inter and intra-systemic to cover all types of translation (Marais, 2019, p. 57).
11 Indeed – some English speakers don't always understand the commentators.
12 The rimmed ball (sliotar) used in hurling is made of cork and leather and is about the same size as a tennis ball but is much harder. Its size makes it hard to spot during this very fast game but the camera crews filming these games have developed considerable skills over the years in tracing and showing the ball in flight.
13 For a comprehensive discussion, see Gambier and Gottlieb (2001).
14 For a comprehensive discussion, see Salaets and Brône (2020).
15 Viz. live captions on YouTube using voice-recognition technology.
16 These varieties of speech proved harder to grasp, not only by the Dutch- speaking locals at the pub.
17 See Tymoczko on the "Metonymics" of Translation (1999) and Leerssen on Imagology (Beller & Leerssen, 2007).
18 For an interesting take on the Irish diaspora in Britain see French, McCrory, and McKay (eds) (2019) (French, 2019).
19 YouTube is full of little videos on this topic: https://www.youtube.com/ watch?v=ee_N3g4ORLk.
20 To borrow a term from Ben Rampton.
21 For a detailed discussion of discourse on migration, see Taylor, Charlotte (2021). Metaphors of migration over time. Discourse & Society, 32(4), 463–481.
22 Another assumption regarding the "native speaker."

References

Antonini, R., Cirillo, L., & Rossato, L. (2017). *Non-professional Interpret- ing and Translation: State of the Art and Future of an Emerging Field of Research* (Benjamins Translation Library 129). Amsterdam: John Benjamins.

Beller, M., & Leerssen, J. (2007). *Imagology: The Cultural Construction and Literary Representation of National Characters: A Critical Survey* (Studia imagologica 13). Amsterdam: Rodopi.

Blommaert, J. (2013). *Ethnography, Superdiversity and Linguistic Landscapes. Chronicles of Complexity* (Critical Language and Literacy Studies, [18]). Bristol/Buffalo, NY: Multilingual Matters.

Blommaert, J., & Backus, A. (2013). Superdiverse Repertoires and the Individual. In I. de Saint-Georges & J. J. Weber (Eds.), *Multilingualism and Multimodality: Current Challenges for Educational Studies* (pp. 11–32). Rotterdam: Sense.

Blommaert, J., & Rampton, B. (2011). Language and superdiversity. *Diversities*, 13(2), ISSN 2079–6595, www.unesco.org/shs/diversities/vol13/issue2/art1 © UNESCO

Blommaert, J., & Verschueren, J. (1991). The Pragmatics of Minority Politics in Belgium. *Language in Society*, 20(4), 503–531. http://www.jstor.org/stable/4168280

Bronwen Walter. (2004). Irish women in the diaspora: Exclusions and inclusions. *Women's Studies International Forum*, 27(4), 369–384, ISSN 0277–5395, https://doi.org/10.1016/j.wsif.2004.10.006

Conway, K. (2012). Cultural translation. In Y. Gambier & L. van Doorslaer (Eds.), *Handbook of Translation Studies* (Vol. 3, pp. 21–25). Amsterdam/Philadelphia, PA: Benjamins.

Coupland, B., & Coupland, N. (2014). The authenticating discourses of mining heritage tourism in Cornwall and Wales. *Journal of Sociolinguistics*, 18, 495–517. doi:10.1111/josl.12081

Deller, G. (1996). Irish theme pubs power rise at Discovery Inns. *The Financial Times*, p. 27.

Forde, E. (2009). St Patrick's. 'Irish' pubs - the Disneyland of the Dipsomaniac; Day makes me ashamed of my homeland. (Editorial). *The Times* (London, England), p. 28.

Gambier, Y., & Gottlieb, H. (2001). *(Multi)Media Translation: Concepts, Practices, and Research* (Benjamins translation library, v. 34). Amsterdam; Philadelphia: J. Benjamins.

Gavioli, L. (2015). Turn-taking. In F. Pöchhacker (Ed.), *Routledge Encyclopaedia of Interpreting Studies* (pp. 428–430). London: Routledge.

Grantham, B. (2009). Craic in a box: Commodifying and exporting the Irish pub. *Continuum*, 23(2), 257–267. doi: 10.1080/10304310802710553

Harris, B. (2013). An Annotated Chronological Bibliography of Natural Translation Studies with Native Translation and Language Brokering 1913–2012. https://www.academia.edu/ 5855596/Bibliography_of_natural_translation (last accessed 25/10/2020).

Harris, B., & Sherwood, B. (1978). Translating as an innate skill. In D. Gerver & W. H. Sinaiko (Eds.), *Language Interpretation and Communication* (Proceedings of the NATO Symposium on Language Interpretation and Communication, Giorgio Cini Foundation, Venice, 1977), NATO Conference Series, Series III (Human Factors), 6, pp. 155–170. Oxford/York: Plenum. Available digitised from BH.

Hudson, C. (2019). The 'Craic' goes global: Irish pubs and the global imaginary. In C. Hudson & E. K. Wilson (Eds.), *Revisiting the Global Imaginary Theories, Ideologies, Subjectivities: Essays in Honor of Manfred Steger* (pp. 155–173). Cham: Springer International Publishing.

Hymes, D. H. (1972). On communicative competence. In J. B. Pride & J. Holmes (Eds.), *Sociolinguistics. Selected Readings* (pp. 269–293). Harmondsworth: Penguin.

Irvine, J. T., & Gal, S. (2000). Language ideology and linguistic differentiation. In P. V. Kroskrity (Ed.), *Regimes of Language: Ideologies, Polities and Identities* (pp. 35–83). Santa Fe, NM: School of American Research Press.

Jakobson, R. (2000 [1959]). On linguistics aspects of translation. In L. Venuti (Ed.), *The Translation Studies Reader* (pp. 113–118). London/New York: Routledge.

Klaudy, K. (1998). Explicitation. In M. Baker (Ed.), *Encyclopaedia of Translation Studies* (pp. 80–85). London: Routledge.

Lennox, G. (July 28, 2013, Sunday). THE GLOBAL CRAIC HEADS; There are more than 6,000 Irish pubs all around the world. Graeme Lennox meets some of the pioneers behind a phenomenon worth (EURO)4bn a year. *The Sunday Times* (London). Retrieved from Nexis Uni.

Lynch, M. (2019). Indexicality. In P. Atkinson, S. Delamont, A. Cernat, J. W. Sakshaug, & R. A. Williams (Eds.), *SAGE Research Methods Foundations* (pp. 1–15). London: Sage Publications Ltd. https://dx.doi.org/10.41 35/9781526421036818823

O'Mahoney, G. B., Hall, J., & Binney, W. (2005). A situational model development in hospitality retailing: The case of Irish pubs. *Journal of Services Research*, 5(2), 77–95.

Oram, R. (1996). Making stout profits: In black and white. (Marketing of Guinness as a cold drink with Irish theme pubs). *The Financial Times*, p. 11.

Marais, K. (2019). *A (Bio)Semiotic Theory of Translation: The Emergence of Social-Cultural Reality*. London & New York: Routledge.

Pennycook, A., & Otsuji, E. (2015). *Metrolingualism: Language in the City*. London/New York: Routledge.

Pennycook, A., & Otsuji, E. (2019). Mundane metrolingualism. *International Journal of Multilingualism*, 16(2), 175–186. doi:10.1080/14790718.2019.15 75836

Popoviciu, L., Haywood, C., & Mac an Ghaill, M. (2006). Migrating masculinities. *Irish Studies Review*, 14(2), 169–187. doi:10.1080/09670880600603794

Prystay, C. (1997). Betting on the luck of the Irish. *Asian Business*, 33(7), 34–36.

Salaets, H., & Brône, G. (Eds.). (2020). *Linking Up with Video: Perspectives on Interpreting Practice and Research* (Benjamins Translation Library 149). Amsterdam: John Benjamins.

Silverstein, M. (1976). Shifters, linguistic categories and cultural description. In K. H. Basso & H. A. Selby (Eds.), *Meaning in Anthropology* (pp. 11–55). Albuquerque: University of New Mexico Press.

Slembrouck, S., & Vandenbroucke, M. (2017) Scale. In K. Tusting (Ed.) *The Routledge Handbook of Linguistic Ethnography* (pp. 70–83). London/New York: Routledge.

Taylor, C. (2021). Metaphors of migration over time. *Discourse & Society*, 32(4), 463–481. doi:10.1177/0957926521992156

Toury, G. (1984). The notion of 'native translator' and translation teaching. In W. Wilss & G. Thome (Eds.), *Die Theorie des Übersetzens und ihr Aufschusswert für die Übersetzungs- und Dolmetschdidaktik* (pp. 186–195). Tübingen: Narr.

Toury, G. (1986). Natural translation and the making of a native translator. *TEXTconTEXT*, 1, 11–29.

Vertovec, S. (2007). The emergence of super-diversity in Britain (Working Paper No. 25). Centre on Migration, Policy and Society. Oxford: University of Oxford.

Vertovec, S. (2010). Towards post-multiculturalism? Changing communities, conditions and contexts of diversity. *International Social Science Journal*, 61(199), 83–95. doi:10.1111/j.1468-2451.2010.01749.x

Wadensjö, C. (2015). Discourse management. In F. Pöchhacker (Ed.), *Routledge Encyclopaedia of Interpreting Studies* (pp. 116–118). London: Routledge.

West, P. (2001). Last orders down at MacFoney's. *New Statesman*, 130(4552), 14.

Wittgenstein, L. (2009). *Philosophical Investigations* (Revised 4th ed., G. Anscombe, Trans.). Chichester: Wiley-Blackwell.

Woolard, K. (2020). "You have to be against bilingualism!" sociolinguistic theory and controversies over bilingualism in Catalonia. *Word (Worcester)*, 66(4), 255–281. doi:10.1080/00437956.2020.1827501

6   An Italian Restaurant

The site of the case is an Italian restaurant situated in the centre of Ghent and includes a network of other locations and people connected to the restaurant. The popularity of Italian food and the number of other Italian eateries in the city should go a long way towards maintaining the anonymity of the participants in this study. The more astute reader with a knowledge of Ghent might be able to identify some of those concerned however, but this should only add to their good reputation. The main actors in the case belong to what could be called a newer generation of Italian migrants who, though they have contacts with earlier migrants, have set up newer networks that reflect their own concerns and worldview, aspects of which will become apparent in the discussion below. As will become visible from the data presented below, the Italy they come from and how it is represented in their work and discourse, including the menus they serve, is very much regional and slightly at odds with mainly unitarily national representations and menus presented in more traditional Italian restaurants set up by members of earlier waves of Italian migrants. Such a regional view of Italy has a strong pedigree, as Manfred Beller argues:

> Despite political unification in the nineteenth century, the image of Italy remains strongly differentiated by region (Venice, Tuscany, Rome, Naples, Sicily, etc.) The Italian auto-image stresses socio-economic differences between North and South in a country that stretches from the Alps to Africa. From a central or North-European perspective as expressed in traditional travel literature and rh clichés of tourism, Italy as a whole is the land of Mediterranean Southerners.
> (Beller in Beller & Leerssen, 2007, pp. 194–195)

But, as always, it is important to understand how such images are shaped in and by the increasingly multicultural settings in which the participants in this study live. More specifically, given the focus of the book, the chapter explores how the participants approach translation and multilingualism in practical terms, i.e. translating cookbooks, and how all this reflects their positions on their origins and on the multicultural society they live in and help create.

DOI: 10.4324/9781003363811-7

Cookbooks

Cookbooks are a hugely popular genre, and their translation is plagued by all sorts of difficulties, many of which are cultural in nature. This goes without saying but of course it also raises numerous questions about how to go about studying such translations, which also have to be viewed within the remit of publishing houses' sales strategies and their impact on the translated book market, a vast undertaking by all means. Studying translations of cookbooks is a favourite topic among MA students and translation scholars have paid some degree of attention to the topic (Teixeira, 2008; Chiaro & Rossato, 2015). There are no publishing houses involved in this case however as the first book discussed below was self-published. The constraints exerted by publishing houses can hence be mainly set aside, which will allow us to focus on other contextual, language and translational constraints that will emerge in the process, and constraints there certainly are as will become obvious from the discussion that follows.

Book (1) – Text and Paratexts

The materials analysed and discussed in this subsection comprise a cookbook first self-published by the restaurant owners in 2001, material for a new cookbook (as yet unpublished), interviews with the restaurant owners and the editor of the new cookbook and observations made during my many encounters with those concerned. The purpose while analysing the data is to lay bare elements that were instrumental in creating and translating the first cookbook and also inform the second, yet unpublished second cookbook and its translation by grounding the works in the multilingual sociocultural context from which they emerged.

The 2001 cookbook will first be examined from the point of view of its framing paratexts (Genette, 1997) that consist of the *Forward* written by an Italian from the same region as one of the restaurant owners and the *Introduction* written by the "coordinator."

The brief *Forward* is as follows:

> A restaurant can be a magical place that transports you to another world. I would like to tell you a wonderful story about a restaurant I discovered while out for a walk...
>
> It was a sun-drenched afternoon, one of those glorious unpredictable late summer afternoons in Flanders. I had just moved to Ghent and was living close to the famous Friday Market and headed off to discover my new city.
>
> As an Italian, I have an inbred interest in everything that is beautiful and good in life and so while rambling along the river Leie, I arrived at the superb Minnemeers Bridge just across from the Museum of Industrial Archaeology. The to and fro of seagulls invoked visions of the sea.

When I crossed the street, I noticed a light shining in what looked like a café or a restaurant. On arriving closer, I saw the warm terracotta colours of an ancient eatery where people sat drinking coffee. I stopped before the door and took in the whole scene. 'Il XXXXXXXXXX - cucina Siciliana' was written in large letters on the window; I felt like I'd found the very place for me! Just imagine, a Sicilian restaurant close to where I live! My mouth began to water...

Stepping into il XXXXXXXXXX was like my first visit to the opera where I heard Cavalleria Rusticana. 'XXXXXXXXXX' means midday, but it was evening time when I tasted my first Girelle and Couscous alla Trapanese and met my new friends XXXXXXX and XXXXX.

It seemed as if I was back on the Mediterranean. Ever since then, each time I wish to spoil my pallet, I know there's an island of delight, warmth and friendship on the banks of the Leie not far from home.

XXXXXXXX XXXX (my translation from the Dutch)

In helping to frame the cookbook, the forward and its writer fulfil two major tasks:

1 They create a sense of 'authenticity': an Italian with a refined sense of taste writing about the food at his new friend's restaurant. As he is from the same region, he is in a position to judge.
2 They create as a sense of 'home away from home' (new home/old home) in which the island of Sicily is transported metaphorically to an island "of delight, warmth and friendship" on the banks of the river running through Ghent, thereby encapsulating a shared sense both of being an emigrant and being from the same region/nation.

It must also be noted that key words remain untranslated in the Dutch text, which were also left untranslated in the English. These untranslated terms draw attention to themselves and serve to heighten the 'authenticity' of the text as is also the case in the *Introduction* and the recipe (see below). Given its essentialist leanings, the notion of authenticity mentioned above and also present in the discourse of the second project warrants further comment as to how it should be understood here. In their concluding remarks to the study of the discourse of heritage tourism in Wales, Coupland, Garrett and Bishop note the following:

But we do not need to read Goffman as debunking authenticity, *tout court,* in favour of pervasive performance. Analysing discourses of authenticity forces us to be circumspect about authenticity and performance alike. Social actors *do* seek out and value authenticity, often behind complicated layers of communicative strategies, norms and representations. Constructivism has banished simplistic assumptions about 'natural behaviour' and ideology-free social categories, that critical battle is won. Authenticity is only clearly approachable as a felt or an attributed or negotiated quality of social experience. It is certainly not a pre-discursive phenomenon offering itself for inspection, even if its main device is to imply that this is precisely the case.

(Coupland et al., 2005, p. 219)

In a similar way, both the *Foreword* and the *Introduction* tie the text and the whole translation enterprise indexically (Silverstein, 2003) to its "Sicilianness." As the following excerpt illustrates, the *Introduction* sets up an implicit contrast with the rest of Italy and in doing so relies on a historical evocation of the island of Sicily that itself draws on stereotypical images (Beller & Leerssen, 2007) of the Arabs and its other invaders[1] in relation to food:

One of Sicily's best kept secrets is its old exquisite gastronomic tradition. Only a few Sicilian dishes, such as 'caponata' (sweet and sour Mediterranean vegetables) and 'cannoli' (pancakes with ricotta cheese) have become known on the other side of the Straits of Messina. Even Sicilians are sometimes unaware of how their favourite dishes are spiced with history. The many foreign powers who once conquered the island left their mark on the culture and not in the least on the way they eat and cook.

The contrast between spicy hot and sweet and sour in the region around Palermo reminds us of the Arabs and in the provinces of Ragusa and Sircusa, vegetables are cooked with the same simplicity that takes us back to the days of the ancient Greece empire. They learned to spice their pastry from the Saracens and from the French the use of herbs and sauces. The Normans and Spanish were fond of sumptuous banquets that contrasted strongly with the much simpler "cucina povera" of the local workers.

One the hand, Sicilians created complex dishes to tickle the fancy of the spoiled (mainly foreign) elite. On the other hand, the poor farmers and fishermen were able to conjure up delicious meals from as good as nothing. So, Sicilian cuisine is essentially flexible: extravagant in its festive meals and no-nonsense in its daily fare but still dedicated to the exceptional tastes the island has to offer.

The Coordinator (my translation from the Dutch)

This short text establishes a set of connections between various aspects of taste and food and the various cultures that left their mark on the island of Sicily, which are indexed as follows: Arabs = hot; Saracens = spicy; Greeks = simplicity; French = aromatic; Normans and Spanish = opulent, to the point of being gluttonous (as in spoiled (mainly foreign) elite). The author also relies on the trope of hiddenness[2] (even to Sicilians) of aspects of Sicilian culture and cuisine, thereby invoking a sense of mystery[3] and the exotic. Much like authenticity, exoticism has been seriously challenged in the literature, Edward Said's Orientalism being a major case in point. The exoticism invoked in the *Introduction* above seems quite harmless in comparison, as it is couched in intriguing culinary terms and glibly glosses over the destruction of successive invasions. As Leerssen remarks on the exotic:

> Foreign lands and cultures may inspire incomprehension, apprehension, fear and loathing, but in some cases they can also elicit admiration and delight. This positive appreciation of the exotic is in some respects the very opposite of ethnocentrism, the foreign country is positively valorised and in many case seen as a preferable alternative to one's domestic culture.
>
> (Leerssen in Beller & Leerssen, 2007, p. 325)

This positive appreciation is clearly visible in the paratext and in the description of the recipes in the cookbook. Even though they were written by Sicilians themselves, they were written and transmitted to us from the point of view of the emigrant looking homeward. This point of view is equidistant geographically to Sicily as any person reading the book in Belgium, which might comprise its attraction. But if we recognise it as a trope, does it mean we should dispense with the exotic as a possible marker of positive difference? Exoticism has been heavily criticised in anthropology as well (Kapferer, 2013) but the struggle with the term has resulted not in its rejection but in the following:

> Here, I think, Dumont's comparative method and approach to the exotic achieve potential significance. Dumont articulates a methodological perspective that could conceivably start from any point whatever on the globe without necessarily privileging one logic of practice over another. Anything and everything is possibly exotic to any other. This includes that which is within the domains or fields of commanding political centres and their theories as well as that which is marginalized or peripheralized. What Dumont offers is a method for determining the exotic as an authentic difference.
>
> (Dumont as commented on by Kapferer in Kapferer, 2013, p. 827)

So much like authenticity, the exotic can also be considered as "only clearly approachable as a felt or an attributed or negotiated quality of social experience" (Coupland et al., 2005, p. 219). This will allow us to see how it is negotiated and constructed in any given situation and not take it as an a priori given.

The 2001 book further comprises a list of *Essential Ingredients* containing matter-of-fact descriptions of typical produce followed the *Recipes* proper, an example of which will be discussed below.

The *Index* contains a list of recipes per page. The translator (non-professional) is also mentioned along with another assistant translator (also non-professional).

Here is some basic translation information relating to the list of recipes. The book contains 61 recipes in total, the names of which are all partially translated, i.e. at least one Italian term remains untranslated, as the following example illustrates: *Crostine con pomodori e mozzarella - crostini met tomaat en mozzarella*.

Of the 61 translated recipe titles, 15 adhere to the Italian word order, as the following example illustrates: *Tagliatelle con calamari - tagliatelle met inktvis*

This is not always the case: *Involtini di pesce spada - zwardvisrolletjes*

Another 15 contain forms of implicitation (Klaudy, 1998) (including Italian dialect words that are left untranslated) as the following example illustrates: *Spaghetti al pesto con mandorle e pistacchi - spaghetti met Siciliaanse pesto* – almond and pistachio pesto becomes Sicilian pesto.

Another 12 of the translations use explicitation (Klaudy, 1998), as the following example illustrates: *Tonno saporito – gestoofde tonijn met Mediterrane groenten* – Mediterranean vegetables added in translation.

Fifteen of the translations are what can be termed 'equivalent' word-level translations (Koller, 1995) that adhere to the Italian word order and make use of non-standard Dutch, as the following example illustrates: *Insalata di arance e finocchi - salade van appelsien en venkel*

None of the desserts in the book (four in total) were translated.

The following is an example of a recipe that remains untranslated into English as this is not necessary for the purposes of the analysis.

Extract 1: recipe from the first translated cookbook

Pasta e ricotta - pasta met verse ricottakaas

Kinderen vinden dit gerecht heerlijk maar ook volwassenen smullen ervan! **Ik maak het graag voor mezelf in een melancholische bui, als ik behoefte heb aan 'troostend' voedsel.**

320 g korte, geribbelde pasta, zoals **penne rigate** of **conchiglioni rigati**

300 g verse **ricotta**;

I eetlepel rode **pesto**, gemaakt van zongedroogde tomaten; zie de recepten bij **crostini**

I courgette, in fijne lucifertjes of blokjes gesneden

5 eetlepels olijfolie **extra vergine**

3 eetlepels melk

2 eetlepels versgeraspte **pecorino**

10 muntblaadjes,

grof gehakt en een paar muntblaadjes om te versieren

een handvol licht geroosterde en grof gehakte amandelen

2 eetlepels geroosterd broodkruim, zie "essentiële ingrediënten", peper en zout

Breng een voldoende grote pan gezouten water aan de kook en doe er de pasta in.

In een grote kom meng je de **ricotta** met de melk, de rode **pesto**, de olijfolie en de munt. Kruid met zout en versgemalen peper. Zet even weg.

Verhit wat olijfolie in een goede braadpan en sauteer de courgette tot die mooi kleurt. Haal van het vuur en meng de courgette onder het **ricotta**mengsel.

Giet de pasta af als ze **'al dente'** gekookt is -zo'n 2 minuten voor het einde van de kooktijd- en meng ze goed, onder de **ricotta**.

Warm de oven voor op 180°. Doe de pasta met **ricotta** in een passende ovenschotel, bestrooi met de **pecorino** en het broodkruim en laat in een hete oven gratineren tot er zich een knapperig goudbruin korstje vormt.

Bestrooi met de gehakte amandelen en versier met nog wat muntblaadjes...

Mmmmmmmmmmammma mia!!!!!!!!!!!!!!!!

Certain items have been highlighted in the recipe and its title that will be commented on here. First, with regard to the single items in bold, a lot has changed in the world in relation to Italian cuisine and its ingredients since this translation was published in 2001. This has been caused by the boom in cooking programmes on TV and online and related cookbook sales. Since (then) young TV chefs like Jamie Oliver introduced a new generation of globalised viewers to the delights of Italian and Mediterranean cuisine. This meant that people became familiar with lesser-known ingredients and dishes next to that already global Italian duo pizza and pasta and a few other sundry articles. Such and other related changes have led translation scholars to reconsider and challenge the boundedness of cultural items not only in cooking. In 2007, Jan Pedersen in his study of subtitling put forward the notion of shared transcultural extralinguistic cultural references (ECRs[4]). Almost all the ingredients marked in bold in the recipe above could by now be considered ECRs. They can be bought at most supermarkets, and you do not need to go especially to an Italian shop to find them. But whether they had attained the status of ECRs back in 2001 we can only guess. Left untranslated or un-explicated in translation, they remain as indexes (Silverstein, 2003, p. 202) of "Sicilianness" along with the images they might invoke and perhaps also as indexes of belonging to a circle of Sicilian cooking enthusiasts who bought and use the book and frequent the restaurant from time to time. This includes the language ideological evocations these lexical items might generate in the process (Kroskrity, 2000). The exclamation 'mama mia' at the end of the recipe takes us beyond the Italian cliché back to the cook's childhood and the comfort ("troost") he finds in cooking and eating this dish when in a "bout of melancholy." Framing the recipe in terms of childhood memory and as comfort food seems to create a sense of homesickness that any migrant could relate to and somehow curiously grounds its narrator in the target rather than in the source culture in the way he addresses his local audience. Otherwise, all the other important information required (amounts, weights, measures and other more common, hence accessible ingredients) to use the recipe was translated into Dutch.

This analysis of the text and paratext of the cookbook has revealed a focus on Sicilianness and the "authenticity" and exoticism of the cooking. It is argued here that this focus is strengthened by the consistent presence of untranslated Italian and Sicilian terms, and a general adherence to Italian word order in Dutch translation of the recipes. It is nonetheless true that translating such and other terms is a problem all translators of cookbooks face. There is a huge body of literature on the topic of translating "realia" that covers a whole range of genres. This has engendered considerable debate and the proposal of various by now classical models of analysis for categorising and studying realia or other related terms (Newmark, 1988; Nedergaard-Larsen, 1993; Leppihalme, 2001; Pedersen, 2011, inter alia). These models are designed to help us understand what happens to realia in translation. In this case, the non-translation of certain items, in contrast to the translation of others, is understood as being part of an overall (translation) strategy (Gambier, 2016) to maintain their indexical connection with Sicily and by extension Italy thereby also foregrounding their authenticity and to a lesser extent their exoticism.

Book Project (2) – Transcripts and Emergent Conceptualisations

The role of paratext served by the *Forward* and the *Introduction* in the 2001 cookbook is replaced in the new cookbook project + translation by more ambitious regional framing narratives within which menus are juxtaposed with other important elements such as music, childhood memories and other sociocultural practices relating to each cook who was called on to write the regional menu (see below). So, the project became inter-regionally Italian rather than Sicilian in the positions/perspectives taken by the various authors/cooks involved, as the following excerpt from one of the framing narratives illustrates:

> So, parmesan, how do you get parmesan? Yes, with cows and milk.... In the other regions of Italy, you have mountains, a lot of sea, and then suddenly there you have it, the flat plain of the Po, with fruit, grass, cows, pigs but that's mainly for prosciutto. So, we have a region full of prosciutto, parmesan and fruit... So, the Gallic influence in Northern Italy. We're in the world of butter and cream, while in the south you have oils. People in the south found

other solutions: ricotta, buffalo mozzarella, just put some mozzarella on it and off you go... But the Lombardian, the guy from the
North still has his cow, yeah, no he IS a cow – butter and cream....
in Piemonte too, in Veneto of course, Friuli, all in the Greater Po
region because it goes from region to region. The Mediterranean is
still a long way off. That crossover with the Arab all the way down
south, but the Po region is the border between the continental and
the Mediterranean... you can draw the line at Tuscany.

(my translation from the Dutch)

The narrator of this piece attempts to divide up Italy in terms of its
produce and culinary traditions: north, continental – butter; south,
Mediterranean – oil; far south Arab culinary influences. We can see
from the outset that the book is planned on a much larger scale and this
scale is linked directly to the growth of the Italian community in the city,
which will be further commented on below. First, it contains a number
of menus, each of which was conceived of and written by a cook from a
different region of Italy. Each menu has its own framing narrative, like
the one above, in which the cook tells his or her own culinary story. In
this way the book/translation would be pan- or incrementally Italian
rather than simply Italian by default, the emphasis being on the regions
rather than the country. The project is consciously multi-authored. And
if anything, their shared 'Italianness' is enhanced by their common bond
in that they are migrants (among other migrants who have found a home
away from home) living in a foreign city with varying degrees of attach-
ment to their native regions.

The cookbook proper would then be further framed by narratives
contributed by other members of the Italian migrant community in the
city, not only in the restaurant business, the details of which cannot be
discussed here for copyright reasons.

The project underwent a slow experimentation and 'entextualisation'
process (Silverstein & Urban, 1996), which was described by S in an
interview:

We started with "the circle of friends" and located them on a map
of Italy ... so various regions in the north, south and islands. Then
we held experimental cooking sessions to try out menus which were
photographed by the group. ..., the next thing was to write down
the menu from each region.[5] ... The cooks were also interviewed by
other members of the circle of friends (not cooks) and the interviews
transcribed ... as each was an essential part and told us something
about the background of each cook and his or her menu.

(My translation from the Dutch)

The whole book / translation project would then be further inserted
into another overarching framing device that I cannot mention here for

copyright reasons except to mention that it draws on a classic of Italian literature. The translation process then began with much multilingual comment (Dutch, English, French, Italian).

This happened in two different ways:

- Some texts were translated directly into Dutch by native speakers of Dutch;
- Others were explained/translated in Dutch by Italians who know Dutch (recorded on Dictaphones and transcribed).

S makes a distinction here between what they call a "vertaling (translation) and a "vertelling" ("telling" or story/tale/(re)verbalisation). S points to their reliance on S's understanding of Italian when it came to their "vertellingen" or "tellings" stories/tales. The result is a multi-layered document mainly in Italian and Dutch but with a hybrid overlay of various Italian dialects, Flemish, English and French. They all share a commitment to keeping the "layeredness" in some form in the finished product and to the importance of the creative process and the friendship from which it arose. The rationale for keeping the "layeredness" is commented on in the following extracts from an interview with the restaurant owners, during which several related themes also emerge, as illustrated in Figure 6.1 below.

The themes listed in the column are illustrated by the extracts in the column next to them. These will be discussed as we proceed. First, the general norm expressed by the makers of the prospective work was that it had to keep its (cultural and linguistic) authenticity[6] in translation (extract to theme 5) For this reason, there was a shared reluctance to hand the project over to a professional translator. This stemmed from their fear that the various voices and the language use particular to those voices (extract to theme 4) found in the project would become homogenised as a result. The editor even used colour coding in the transcripts to keep track of these voices in the interaction, to make initial notes on translation, and further comments by others on the project.

So, the phase of experimentation and complex colour-coded entextualisation mentioned above resulted in complex textual trajectories that mirror a desire to recreate in the 'layers' of the cookbook the very sociolinguistic reality it emerged from (Pennycook & Otsuji, 2015). It can be asserted therefore that, as far as the authors of the project are concerned, authenticity becomes tangible/visible in the way they wish to tell their story and this ambition is also articulated in their discourse on the project + translation, which is the point that Coupland, Garrett and Bishop are making (2005, p. 219). The struggle to maintain 'authenticity' not only involves a reluctance to use professional translation but also a reluctance to use standard forms of language.

Translation is viewed by the participants as an integral part of the multilingual and multicultural circle they belong to (extract to theme

	Theme	Content (extract Interview with YY and XX – my translation from the Dutch)
1	Immigration and language change/loss	YY: I immigrate; say I live for 30 years in Germany, **language evolves in Sicily too**; it's not like it stops there and you, you've been here in Belgium for 30 years and you speak Sicilian to your children and then I myself I go to Sicily **and my Sicilian is old because I speak Sicilian like thirty years ago. I haven't evolved with it so when I go there I sound like an old man of 80 years old...**
2	Shifting language affiliations and awareness	I: But you have done that, you've learned Dutch... YY: We've learned Dutch, followed courses but not XX, he just picked it up. I did take a few courses in the beginning. Yes, **most Italians living here in Belgium speak French, yes those of the previous generation, so...** I: But you are a new, more recent generation... YY: Yes, the generation before us only spoke French... I come from Italy, and I go to Leuven. It's not that I studied it all. I started working in a restaurant and people spoke French there. I had no idea that you had to speak Dutch in Flanders... XX: A lot of Italians still don't know that...
3	Language and 'integration'	... XX: **So, I live in this country and that's the language they speak here so that's what integration is about**...
4	Different voices/Friendship	.... YY: In the beginning we wanted to get as many people as possible involved in the project; **we were in a kind eh of period of friendship at the time**, yes something like that
5	Translation Vs Story or tale	**Translation was the weakest part for us; a story that isn't in perfect Dutch that when you read it, you know it was done by Italians ... told by Italians, a home tale**.......
6	Another type of integration	I: An encounter in fact? YY: Yes, that was the idea, we're all here from all different regions; that's the way it is and it's a kind of integration in a way; **there are different ways of becoming integrated plus the fact that we rediscover each other here**; We're more Italian here than we are in Italy...
7	Language and cultural diversity	YY: Nowadays the place is full of people from everywhere... **I find that mixing of language and cultures very important.**

Figure 6.1 Themes in discourse

7), which is further mirrored in the society around them (Arnaut et al., 2016). Therefore, the persons designated by the participants to translate the work also came from within their circle, people who, following Harris (2013), could be called 'natural' translators. Given the purpose of the translation set out above, these young bilinguals were considered to have had the right credentials and hence were the first to be called on. But it must also be noted that not all bilinguals translate. Translation is a socially distributed communicative competence: not everyone gets to or is "appointed" to do so (Hymes, 1972; Angelelli, 2016). Generally speaking, in this case those appointed to do the work grew up and went to school in Flanders and come from immigrant backgrounds.

The complexity of the project can be further predicated onto the scope of the migrant network and its complex set of relations both with Italy and with Flanders (extract to theme 6). As can be noted from the extracts above, these migrants also show an awareness of language change and loss (extract to theme 1) along with the importance of acquiring the local language for 'integration' – an important term in the Flemish government's policy discourse on migration (extract to theme 3). They are also aware of the increasing levels of multilingualism and multiculturalism in the broader society around them, something they view positively (extract to theme 7), a view that may not be shared by all migrants, however. In discussing the materials given to me by the participants, I have attempted to follow Geertz's recommendations by allowing the findings in relation to translation in this context to "be cast in terms of the constructions we imagine [they] place upon what they live through and the formulae they use to define what happens to them" (Geertz, 1973, p. 15).

The 2001 book and the second book project + translation are presented as (non-professional) translations but can also be considered as "hybrid" language projects to the extent that they purposely mix Italian, Dutch and other languages. It would be erroneous, however, to assert that the books manifests "interference" for the source language (Toury, 1995, p. 62) or to consider the frequency of these Italian lexical items in the book as a "terminological issue" that needs fixing and hence lays bare the translator's incompetence. The 'mixing' was conscious and became an even more conscious strategy in the second book/translation project. It is curious yet important to note then that the book wasn't translated for a foreign Dutch-speaking market but for the local Dutch or even Flemish market, as data discussed above indicate. The book and the new project + translation were conceived within and for the target culture by migrants living in that "target culture" It was designed for themselves and others and for themselves as others.

The focus on the various regions in Italy in the project + translation can also be understood in two ways, first in terms of the degree of 'settledness' in Flanders of the people involved: each belongs here to a certain extent and somehow represented his or her region at the same time in a shared but less foregrounded Italian context. Second, it could be understood more tentatively in terms of a former type of discourse within a larger European context, i.e. that of a Europe of the Regions. In this discourse, the regions had regained a more prominent status in "Europe" at the time, during which the nation states somehow faded briefly into the background. This seems very hard to imagine against the backdrop of Euroscepticism and Brexit but ways of talking about things hold sway at given moments and fade equally into the background or are swept away by such sea changes as the Brexit for example.

Furthermore, the mention in the data of various generations of migrants (extracts to themes 2, 3 and 6) should allow us to view migration and mobility not as a temporary but as a permanent aspect of any society (both for host and donor) within which each generation on the move has its own demographics, reasons for moving, different networks, etc.

So-called settled people also have different experiences of migration /
encounters with migrants which again raises the issue of mobility, something we will expand on in the next section.

Mobility as a Permanent State

The idea of mobility being a permanent feature of any society is taken up
by Lelièvre and Marshall (2015). In their proposal to set up an anthropology of mobility, they identify the following three challenges:

1 conceptualising subjects as mobile in both the past and the present,
2 observing mobility simultaneously at the level of the individual and
   the collective, and
3 overcoming through contextual analysis the enduring problem of
   mobility as a marked or 'Othered' category.

In the conceptual framework that they set out, mobility is understood
"as a mediator between political subjects and political institutions, thus
making it possible to examine how subjects and institutions are continuously remade in relation to each other through their practices, perceptions, and conceptions of movement."

   The idea of institutions being continually remade in relation to the
subjects they encounter is in no small measure evidenced by changes to
the city's website in accommodating newcomers but also by the practices
observed at city office for migration. This has been happening over time
(see Chapters 8 and 9). This does not constitute a major political sea
change but rather a more pragmatic approach to the everyday realities of
increasing superdiversity. As Fitzgerald notes:

> The major flaw in the notion of a "deterritorialized" world is the
> assumption that social life was "territorialized" at an earlier point.
> Rather, the putative coupling of locality and culture is an artefact
> of the social scientific imagining of exotic container villages and na-
> tional container societies, which naturalises efforts by states to cre-
> ate containers out of a world interlaced with the movement of goods,
> people, and ideas.
>
> (Fitzgerald, 2006, p. 10)

The power of our imaginings of migration continues to linger, however.
In the meantime, the participants in this study have all encountered the
institutions Lelièvre and Marshall mention over time, ranging initially
from immigration offices, then (language) schools, training centres, to
social security and tax offices, and at a later stage, schools and other centres their children attend and visit, etc. This means that the encounters
with political institutions are staggered, though perhaps more frequent

and intense initially. Each of these institutions approaches the genre of belonging to or participating in some area of public affairs (in civil society) from a different angle, in compliance with appropriate legislation on the area concerned. Each of these institutions also generates discourse and documents on its respective area of competence while also addressing newcomers to the society (see Chapter 9). These discourses feed into and co-construct the public debate, in this case on migration, and are also engaged with by (short- or long-term) migrants at the various points of encounter. This is clear from the data discussed above in which, among other things, the notion of 'integration' (theme 3) is prominent.

The newer generation mentioned in this chapter arrived in Belgium in part following the disaster caused by the 2007–2008 financial crisis. Some had planned other careers that were then denied to them and found themselves delving deeper into the local and regional cuisine to find a means of survival that might prove global and that would go beyond the already globalised but limiting clichés of pizza and pasta. Their migratory trajectories resulted in their living abroad in multilingual communities. Since then the discourse of Europe of the Regions, which is also echoed in the concept of Italy of the Regions framing the cookbook project + translation had all but disappeared. It has now been replaced by the competing discourses on globalisation and multilingual multicultural cities/societies, something that is viewed positively in the data discussed in this chapter but heavily contested by a growing number of voices that people the political institutions that migrants encounter. The cookbooks and their translations are ultimately a precipitate of the multilingual and cultural environment their makers find themselves in and also help create, along with types of mobility they have managed to negotiate over time. This is an environment in which translation is an everyday element and the types of translation and textual practices they use also help contextualise the type of authenticity[7] they seek and wish to adhere to. Understandings of mobility can further be tied to how people on the move are designated: expat, migrant, economic migrant, transmigrant, nomad, traveller and other delineations of the term and these designations also place the designated at a given level within a social order of mobility (see Chapter 9 for a more detailed discussion).

Further Comments

The book and the project + translation reported on in this chapter belong outside publishing officialdom as such and hence have come with their own set of language, aesthetic and translational constraints. It could be argued nonetheless that the sense of authenticity and/or the exotic that they adhere to still remain strong selling points in other guises for a lot of cookbooks and cooking programmes. How often have we not seen famous chefs travelling abroad to get a sense of real cooking somewhere and bringing it back to a local audience by providing their own take on a given dish or recipe? This process can be described in various ways, the most negative being cultural appropriation. But isn't one's own take rather a form of translation or transfer in itself as it can never really be the same as the local dish – that old chestnut in translational reasoning? Next to that nowadays the chef's local audiences comprise people who come from that authentic/exotic somewhere else he or she has been attempting to emulate. In this case, we witness the chefs themselves coming from that other authentic/exotic somewhere else, which in itself is nothing new either. Migration and mobility are also generational, something which the increased movement brought about by globalisation and superdiversity tends to obscure. When it comes to cooking, all this movement has resulted in realia or culture specific items becoming increasingly shared "transcultural extralinguistic cultural references" (Pedersen, 2007). As was mentioned above, the sense of authenticity and/or the exotic to which the participants in this study adhere finds its expression in the set of aesthetic, language and translational choices in the book and in the project + translation. This chapter comprises an attempt to uncover the factors informing those choices and the context in which they were made. All of this is also predicated upon the act of cooking as a constant goal and the authenticity it instantiates.

Notes

1 For more information on stereotypical features of these peoples and cultures see Beller and Leerssen, 2007: Arabs, p. 94; Saracens, p. 58; French, p 154; Greeks, p. 166; Spaniards, p.242; Normans, p. 47.
2 For a discussion of "secret" and other cognates in Italian tourist discourse on Flemish cities see Sambre (2009, pp. 119–120).
3 For a discussion of the exotic in literature, see Beller and Leerssen (2007, pp. 325–326). For a discussion of the role of the exotic in anthropology, see Kapferer (2013).
4 ECRs are expressions that refer to entities "outside" of language, such as names of people, places, institutions, food, customs etc., which a person may not know, even if s/he knows the language, Pedersen (2007, p. 30). For a fuller definition, see Pedersen (2005).
5 For obvious reasons, neither the photographs nor the recipes were made available to the researcher.
6 See the discussion of authenticity in the previous subsection.
7 For a study of authenticity in relation to an Italian restaurant in the USA, see Lie et al. (2018).

References

Angelelli, C. V. (2016). Looking back: A study of (ad-hoc) family interpreters. *European Journal of Applied Linguistics*, 4(1), 5–31.
Arnaut, K., Blommaert, J., Rampton, B., & Spotti, M. (Eds.). (2016). *Language and Superdiversity*. London: Routledge.

Beller, M., & Leerssen, J. (2007). *Imagology: The Cultural Construction and Literary Representation of National Characters: A Critical Survey* (Studia imagologica 13). Amsterdam: Rodopi.

Chiaro, D., & Rossato, L. (Eds.). (2015). Food and translation, translation and food. *Special Issue of The Translator*, 21(3) http://tandfonline.com. kuleuven.e-bronnen.be/toc/RTRN/21/3

Coupland, N., Garrett, P., & Bishop, H. (2005). Wales underground: Discursive frames and authenticities in Welsh Ming heritage tourism events. In A. Jaworski & A. Pritchard (Eds.), *Discourse, Communication and Tourism* (Tourism and Cultural Change 5). Clevedon: Channel View Publications, 2005. Print.

Fitzgerald, D. (2006). Towards a theoretical ethnography of migration. *Qualitative Sociology*, 29(1), 1–24. doi:10.1007/s11133-005-9005-6

Gambier, Y. (2016). Translation strategies and tactics. In Y. Gambier & L. van Doorslaer (Eds.), *The Handbook of Translation Studies Volume 1 (2010)* (pp. 412–418). Current revision: 2016. Amsterdam/Philadelphia, PA: John Benjamins.

Genette, G. (1997). *Paratexts: Thresholds of Interpretation* (Literature, Culture, Theory 20). Cambridge: Cambridge University Press.

Harris, B. (2013). An Annotated Chronological Bibliography of Natural Translation Studies with Native Translation and Language Brokering 1913–2012. https://www.academia.edu/5855596/Bibliography_of_natural_translation (last accessed 25/10/2020).

Hymes, D. H. (1972). On communicative competence. In J. B. Pride & J. Holmes (Eds.), *Sociolinguistics. Selected Readings* (pp. 269–293). Harmondsworth: Penguin.

Kapferer, B. (2013). How anthropologists think. *Journal of the Royal Anthropological Institute*, 19, 813–836. doi:10.1111/1467-9655.12066

Klaudy, K. (1998). Explicitation. In M. Baker (Ed.), *Encyclopaedia of Translation Studies* (pp. 80–85). London: Routledge.

Koller, W. (1995). The concept of equivalence and the object of translation studies. *Target*, 7(2), 191–222. doi:10.1075/target.7.2.02kol

Kroskrity, P. (2000). *Regimes of Language: Ideologies, Polities, and Identities* (School of American Research Advanced Seminar). Santa Fe, NM: School of American Research Press.

Lelièvre, M. A., & Marshall, M. E. (2015). 'Because life it selfe is but motion': Toward an anthropology of mobility. *Anthropological Theory*, 15(4), 434–471.

Leppihalme, R. (2001). Translation strategies for realia. In P. K. Kouvola & R. Hartama-Heinonen (Eds.), *Mission, Vision, Strategies, Values: A Celebration of Translator Training and Translation Studies* (pp. 139–146). Helsinki: Helsinki University Press.

Liu, H., Li, H., DiPietro, R. B., & Alexander Levitt, J. A. (2018). The role of authenticity in mainstream ethnic restaurants: Evidence from an independent full-service Italian restaurant. *International Journal of Contemporary Hospitality Management*, 30(2), 1035–1053.

Nedergaard-Larsen, B. (1993). Culture-bound problems in subtitling. *Perspectives: Studies in Translatology*, 2, 207–241.

Newmark, P. (1988). *Textbook of Translation*. Oxford: Pergamon Press.

Pedersen, J. (2007). Cultural interchangeability: The effects of substituting cultural references in subtitling. *Perspectives, Studies in Translatology*, 15(1), 30–48. doi:10.2167/pst003.0

Pedersen, J. (2011). *Subtitling Norms for Television. An Exploration Focussing on Extralinguistic Cultural References*. Amsterdam/Philadelphia, PA: John Benjamins.

Sambre, P. (2009). Il vettore spazio-temporale nel reportage marketing: una prospettiva cognitive-discorsiva italo-belga. *Civiltà Italiana*, 2009, 115–128.

Silverstein, M. (2003). Indexical order and the dialectics of sociolinguistic life. *Language & Communication*, 23, 193–229. doi:10.1016/S0271-5309(03)00013-2

Teixeira, E. D. (2008). Tradução culinária e ensino: um exemplo de metodologia de avaliação utilizando etiquetagem e o WordSmith Tools [Cookery translation and translator training: a methodology of assessment using manual tagging and WordSmith Tools]. *Domínios de Linguagem*, 4. http://www.dominiosdelinguagem.org.br/pdf/09-07-09/Texto%202.pdf

7   A Block of Flats

Figure 7.1 Demolition of block of flat at Rabot

DOI: 10.4324/9781003363811-8

The site of this case study was the Rabot housing complex in Ghent. The complex is situated just outside the city's ring road and was built back in the 1960s on the grounds of an old shunting station on the north-west side of the city. The new complex was meant to house inner city dwellers from the working-class Patershol neighbourhood. Following a process of gentrification, Patershol is now an up-market neighbourhood with restaurants and galleries. The Rabot housing complex is undergoing the fate of many such high-rise projects across Europe. It is currently being demolished[1] to make way for more amenable low-rise social housing and its inhabitants and the communities they formed over the decades have been displaced and scattered (see Figure 7.1 above). Before the dwellers left the block, it had been a home not only to local people from Ghent but people from all over the world, much like many high-rise social housing complexes in European cities.[2]

On first seeing the documentary and performance by the artist Simon Allemeersch (Allemeersch et al., 2014) on the Rabot project, it was clear to me from the outset that there was a considerable amount of translation going on in the housing block. This was confirmed during the interview but something else emerged that shed light on spatial and social mobility and laid bare related and less obvious forms of translation in the building. Next to translation from Dutch to Turkish, Romanian Albanian etc., there were other forms of translation rooted in the dynamics of the building and the surrounding city. The analysis will address one particular but less obvious form of translation, i.e. intralingual translation.

A Letter #2 – By Design

The analysis presented in this case study will address and discuss what is known as intralingual translation (Jakobson, 2000 [1959], p. 114) with a view to grounding it and placing it socially and sociolinguistically. The materials drawn on for the analysis comprise an in-depth interview with an artist/leader of a self-help project, observation, documentation, the book and documentary issued by the group and the group's website.[3] The focus lies in the translation of letters received by people living in the block of flats. The transcriptions are field note transcriptions and do not use the usual CA conventions. The purpose of the transcripts is to illustrate and highlight themes touched on in relation to translation and the framing devices used by the respondent to discuss translation practices in the block of flats. The data also comprises a description of the "writing system" developed by one of the flat dwellers, something which is also partly explained by the respondent in the interview. The extracts have been translated from Dutch into English for the readers of this book:

Interview Extract 1

S: And this belongs together with an abysmal poverty – and I cannot express it any other way – a poverty of text. So, it is not because people get a monthly allowance, have running water and electricity and a roof over their heads – that is not enough. No, sometimes it is not even about that; "taligheid" (having/possessing language/ being articulate) is also part of it, knowledge of who we are, of what is going on in the neighbourhood, of the circumstances we live in, in order to make sure that those people can stay out of trouble. Many problems come about because people in fact have a sort of non-understanding of what is going on around them, a non-understanding of why decisions are taken in the city about their own buildings; and this brings about terrible dissatisfaction and friction and often it is us in society who fail in what we provide in terms of social services. We fail miserably, because the idea probably is 'they probably know that already' or 'that's not important' or 'we can always send them a letter when it gets that far or something like that" ... People... the language with which people are approached passes completely above their heads. This is not a single ..., for example, people who wrote letters daily to people living in social housing, they fell over backwards when they discovered the literacy issues in the building.

I: Yes, so they are what used to be called underprivileged?

S: Yes, yes! There is this textual poverty. And by textual I mean cultural text. This ranges from not being able to read what is hung up in the hall, because they cannot read or because they are not used to reading to ... that they would rather believe what the neighbour says about why they are demolishing the housing blocks rather than have access to decent media and get the right information themselves.

The whole issue of literacy brought with it adjacent translation practices that would otherwise have remained invisible, and which probably need to be examined at other sites and in other countries. The obvious question was how do people cope with the everyday, even in what is considered to be "their own" language? The interviewee pointed out that such literacy issues did not prevent flat dwellers from communicating with each other across a variety of languages. One major threshold in understanding, however, constituted official discourse written in Dutch that arrived in through their letterboxes on a regular basis. To solve the problems in understanding that this discourse brought with it, people had to rely on those living in the building who could help. According to the interviewee, the ad-hoc translation work belonged within and was resolved through a set of checks and balances in the building's economic exchanges. These exchanges were dictated by a sense of individual equality that had to be respected at all times: no one should be beholden to another for too long, if at all and there was always something someone could do in return, some skill or know-how that someone possessed that could be put to good use. The interviewee encountered many instances of this during his stay in the block, one of the most poignant being an exchange between him and a man who had been living in the flats for a long time:

Interview Extract 2

S: I had no idea what he was talking about: "it's those constructions that you use." He says, "I usually never hear them and here I do, and I have the impression that they make me smarter." And the next time we met he tried to pay me 5 Euro for it, which is typical of the place…. The very fact that he tried to pay for it is really typical. It (his offer) said everything about how the place works, in fact. Yes, yes they want it to be recognised, no matter how little is given, that they can pay for it and in that way we all belong and work within the same equal economy. That really struck me each time …

In this respect, as Mauss points out, "[t]he unreciprocated gift still makes the person who has accepted it inferior, particularly when it has been accepted with no thought of returning it" (Mauss, 2002, p. 83). In their brief exchange, the flat dweller is reminding Simon of the gift of his language he has been the beneficiary of. He wishes to both acknowledge it and return the favour, a common practice in the block of flats. So, this short extract gives us an insight into the checks and balances that constitute the economy mentioned above. It is also important to note that "language services" are recognised as being a valuable part of that economic system.

How this translation work was done is explained in the following extract, which narrates the story of one of the flat dwellers. This flat dweller had developed his own "writing system," which allowed him to a certain degree to deal with the official letters he receives through the post:

Interview Extract 3

S: Yes that is me [He shows his symbol, invented by Freddy[4] a camera on a stand]. So, if he found a letter [with my symbol] in his letterbox, then he would know that I wanted to remind him that we had an appointment on a given day. And the other way around too and … he keeps his system going, but he can only do that with the help of the neighbours; for example, his post: he opens his post with his neighbours. In any case, that is the usual ritual during which the people open their post, when they meet each other. They wait for the post man in fact and a neighbour then reads his letters out loud and he notes the information straight away on the envelope in his own writing (system) the way he wants. So that is literal translation, literally 'the service' [needed] to get it translated. Sometimes, if he has a message that is too extensive to transpose into his hieroglyphs, for we call them hieroglyphs because actually are ... If it were too extensive to note in his system, then he would go to the woman next door, who can write well according to him but according to my norms she can only write a little bit, and she would write out the complete content so that he could then bring that letter to me and put it in my letter-box. So that means literally transforming information into language; that is the most basic form of translation you can find... (6:40)

Freddy's story is special because it also involves his own sign system, but it is not the only example of non-professional translation in the building. In relation to these regular translation events, the main lines of Simon's narrative are the following:

- Flat dwellers meet at the letterboxes in the hall when the post man/ woman arrives;
- Letters are opened and read by a non-professional translator or letters are brought to a flat where they are opened and read by a non-professional translator;
- A non-professional translator then tells the dweller in Ghent dialect what the letter is about and what course of action to take.

This type of translation is mainly intralingual (Jakobson, 2000 [1959], p. 114). The codes involved are Standard written Dutch and oral Ghent dialect. The source text can be anything from a gas or electricity bill / letter from the police/ insurance company or other forms of official written discourse in Standard Dutch. The medium involves spoken interpretation of written discourse. It is important to note that this translation work is carried out in the multilingual context of the building, which also involves translation and interpreting from other languages such as Turkish and Romanian for example.

Literacy issues and "textual poverty" are instrumental in creating and framing these intralingual translation events. It is not always easy to find and document or to trace their textual or discursive dynamics. A short description of Freddy's writing system may help illustrate this, however. He uses the envelope of the bill or letter he receives to note basic elements of information. The first element, which is usually situated at the top left of the envelope, if the space is available, is a weekly "calendar." This calendar comprises seven vertical strokes parallel to each other to indicate the days of the week. These strokes are divided by a horizontal line in order to make a distinction between a.m. and p.m. A circumflex cap on the top or underneath any given line will indicate the day and approximate time at which something has to be paid or some action has to be taken. The items to be paid or the actions to be taken will then be further specified on the envelope in the following fashion: the first vowel or consonant sound of the word will be approximated in writing in keeping with the phonological rules of Ghent dialect. This will be followed by a drawing [of an icon indicating the object involved], e.g. a tap for water [water bill] or light bulb for electricity [electricity bill]. The amount to be paid will also be marked on the envelope. Though Freddy's code is limited, it is a code nonetheless, next to which he can also count and manage sums of money.

Other forms of intralingual translation that take place in the building mainly involve various forms of "explicitation[5]" and explanation, which are needed to make the official Dutch discourse clear to a challenged reader or writer. Curiously enough, this closely resembles Vermeer's notion of translation as "offer of information" within Skopos theory (in Nord, 1997, p. 32). Hence, this may involve taking simplified notes in more or less the same code and may not involve transfer to another code, as in Freddy's case.

Intralingual Translation as an Element in an Economy of Exchanges

In her analysis and discussion of intralingual translation Karen Korning Zethsen identifies a number of key elements: Knowledge differential, Time, Culture and Space (Korning Zethsen, 2009). These elements can be clearly used to further explain intralingual translation practices in the building under discussion.

The notion of knowledge differential is usually cast in terms of expert-to-lay translating and interpreting as in the popularisation of scientific literature in newspapers and magazines, for example. This too stems from the unequal social distribution of repertoires (Gumperz, 1964; Hymes, 1972) but in this case is more striking because of the lack of access to basic repertoires pointed out in the interview extracts.

Time also plays a role in interlingual translation; this is usually understood in the literature as longitudinal, as in when readers no longer have access to older varieties of their language. In our case we can add two related concepts namely (time)span (between the arrival of a letter and the final date on which some form of action is required) and consequently the degree of urgency involved in paying bills, keeping appointments with social services, the police, and keeping out of debt.

Like repertoire, culture can also be cast in terms of degree of access to, unequal distribution of, and the distance from "normalised" forms of everyday culture that marginalisation brings with it.

Space is usually cast in terms of constraint, i.e. the limited number of pages/words allowed by a publisher to carry out an interlingual translation. In this case, given the urgency mentioned above, such notions as 'brevity,' 'conciseness,' take on a heightened social and personal relevance (Blommaert, 2001). The limited space on the page becomes the limited space of encounter and interaction near the letterboxes or in someone's flat and the subsequent immediacy and brevity of the message: the former more public space for more easily transferable messages, the latter for transferring more complex or sensitive matters. Viewed in de Certeau's terms of space "as the effect produced by the operations that orient it, situate it, temporalize it" (de Certeau, 1988, p. 117), the operations in either case remain largely translational but of a different order. The shift in imagined space in the model (typically from scientific to shortened popularised article) is predicated on reading practices; that at the letterboxes precisely on a lack in reading practices. Each comprises a form of compressed re-entextualisation in another form of the language, each with different contextual purpose.

This ultimately leads to genre and the breaking of its conventions. Here, this involves letters containing bills, insurance policies, etc. The letter is considered a primary genre by Bakhtin (1986, pp. 61–62). It is addressed to one person by another or by a representative of an institution to an individual. It is personal, which means that it is illegal to open another person's post without his or her consent. Such agreements are (partly) breached in (intralingual) translation in the building. The letter enters a new communicative trajectory involving translation and mediation. This means that, though the addressee remains the same, the message is reformulated (Jakobson, 1959) to make it accessible. This also means that other (unintended[6]) addressees who are also present at the letterboxes may get involved, as they may find themselves in a similar (bureaucratic) situation, etc. There is a tacit understanding among those involved first about the purpose of this communicative event and second about some form of compensation at some stage which is never mentioned (Mauss, 2002), which may consist of running errands, doing odd jobs and giving short-term loans among other things. In professional translation situations, all of these factors would fall under codes of secrecy and professional behaviour that also belong in a perhaps more explicit economy of remuneration and exchanges. To return again to Hanks (Hanks, 1987, p. 135), genre is conventionally understood as a set of discourse features, but when we take into account "orienting frameworks, interpretive procedures and sets of expectations" in intralingual translation, these factors have a huge impact on what the 'set of discourse features' will ultimately look like.[7]

Further Comments

Rather than "siting translation" in the larger orders of empire and state (Niranjana, 1992), the focus here has been on locating (less obvious forms of) translation that accompany enmeshed local and migrant flows and their related translation spaces. In other words, it is a matter of finding and "placing" translation in the sense of trying to understand translation as it happens in this and similar sites. As these translations are seldom documented in the archives, they often remain ephemeral and invisible. This does not mean that they do not exist, however. As was pointed out above, the meeting at the letterboxes in the hall or at kitchen tables in flats are all part of a system of exchanges that belongs to a larger dynamic of relations among people in the building. It is within this system that particular forms of translation and other language practices can be located. The translation work done will be compensated for in some way or other within the local economy. As a result, tallies will be kept and discretion maintained in compliance with the system and perhaps in a way that might seem challenging or even appalling to those living outside the system, given the literacy issues involved. This also means that this delicate set of checks and balances helps mitigate possible stigma. To conclude, placing (intralingual) translation, i.e. trying to find translation and understand the (often invisible) social contexts in which it takes place, also means trying to understand the nature of the economy of exchanges involved in each case. This leaves us with the following open question: What would the economy of exchanges tell us about what gets done intralingually in other situations? And subsequently, what forms of compensation/remuneration are used, etc.?

Notes

1 Views of Rabot: http://erwinacke.blogspot.be/2014/04/gent-rabot-torens.html.
2 For more details on the demographics in the neighbourhood see: https://stad.gent/rabot-blaisantvest/over-de-wijk/cijfers-over-rabot-blaisantvest.
3 For copyright reasons, some parts of the data cannot be shown here but can be viewed at the group's website http://www.rabotatelier.be/ or on YouTube at http://www.youtube.com/watch?v=LOY6WX1FvT8#t=35.
4 Names have been changed to maintain anonymity.
5 For a useful overview of the literature on explicitation and related phenomena in translation, see Zufferey and Cartoni (2014).
6 Viz. Goffman's notion of the unratified hearer (bystanders, eavesdroppers and overhearer) (Goffman, 1981).
7 Viz. the notion of translatum in Skopos Theory (Nord, 1998).

References

Allemeersch, S., Capelle, B., & Debaene, M. (2014). *Rabot 4–358* (1st ed. 1 volume). Gent: Rabot Atelier & Kunstencentrum Vooruit vzw.

Bakhtin, M. M. (1986). *Speech Genres and Other Late Essays* (C. Emerson & M. Holquist, Eds. and V. W. McGee, Trans.). Austin: University of Texas Press.

Blommaert, J. (2001). Context is/as critique. *Critique of Anthropology*, 21(1), 13–32.

de Certeau, M. (1984). *The Practice of Everyday Life*. Berkeley/London: University of California Press.

Goffman, E. (1981). *Forms of Talk*. Oxford: Blackwell.

Gumperz, J. J. (1964). Linguistic and social interaction in two communities. *American Anthropologist*, 66(6/2), 137–153.

Hymes, D. H. (1972). On communicative competence. In J. B. Pride and J. Holmes (Eds.), *Sociolinguistics. Selected Readings* (pp. 269–293). Harmondsworth: Penguin.

Jakobson, R. (2000 [1959]). On linguistics aspects of translation. In L. Venuti (Ed.), *The Translation Studies Reader* (pp. 113–118). London/New York: Routledge.

Korning Zethsen, K. (2009). Intralingual translation: An attempt at description. *Meta*, 54(4), 795–812.

Mauss, M., Halls, W., & Douglas, M. (2002). *The gift: The Form and Reason for Exchange in Archaic Societies/(Routledge Classics)*. London: Routledge.

Niranjana, T. (1992). *Siting Translation. History, Post-structuralism, and the Colonial Context*. Berkeley: University of California Press.

Nord, C. (1997). *Translation as a Purposeful Activity: Functionalist Approaches Explained*. (Translation Theories Explained, 1). Manchester: St Jerome Press.

Zufferey, S., & Cartoni, B. (2014). A multifactorial analysis of explicitation in translation. *Target*, 26(3), 361–384. doi:10.1075/target.26.3.02zuf

8   An Inner-City School

This chapter provides a humble addendum, again from a translational perspective to the huge body of work being done by Professor Piet Van Avermaet and his team in relation to inner-city schools in Ghent among many other things. The data discussed in this chapter stem from observations at the school and an interview in Dutch conducted at the very beginning of this research project. The interview was with the school principal and two teachers, one of whom is of migrant origin. Again the point of inquiry was translation, which was not the main focus of the other scholars who had done research[1] at this and other schools in the city. The questions the interviewer brought to the meeting were designed first to gain some background information on multilingualism and possible translation practices at the school, second to inquire into these practices and thirdly to get a sense of their importance (evaluation) for those concerned. A full seven years later I returned to the school to talk to the principal and teachers again. The purpose was to see whether any major changes had taken place over such a long period of time. An analysis and discussion of the first interview are presented in the body of this chapter and completed by a separate section on the second interview.

Talking to the Teachers

Having got permission to visit the school and talk to the principal and staff, I sent ahead a questionnaire related to the main topic I wished to discuss with them, namely translation.

Nominally speaking, the interview was structured (Fontana, 2007, pp. 1–2). The questionnaire was divided into three sections, the questions falling under and relating to background, practices and evaluation.

The following questions were asked in relation to background:

> a 1. How many different languages, next to Dutch, are spoken by the children at the school?
> a 2. What has been their experience as staff regarding their different language policy?
> a.3 Do you also have a translation/interpreting policy, and if so for which languages?

DOI: 10.4324/9781003363811-9

The following questions were asked in relation to practices:

> *b 1. Do you use interpreters all the time?*
> *b 2. Who interprets for whom, when and where?*
> *b 3. Do you also translate and if so how and what type of document:*
> *school exercises, messages to parents, non-sensitive documents?*

In terms of evaluation, the participants were asked the following:

> *c 1. How important is this interpreting and translation work?*
> *c 2. Does it benefit the pupils, parents and teachers?*

On the face of it, these seem like rather straightforward questions, but keeping Briggs's insights in mind, I was not expecting straightforward answers:

> Interviews are cooperative products of interactions between two or more persons who assume different roles and who frequently come from contrasting social, cultural, and/or linguistic backgrounds. A mode of analysis that envisions interview data as, even ideally, a direct outpouring of the interviewees' thoughts or attitudes obscures the nature of the interview as a social interaction and a communicative event. Such a perspective also misses the point that the interview situation itself is a rich source of data if it is viewed as an object of analysis as well as a research tool.
>
> (Briggs, 1986, p. 102)

Another thing to keep in mind was the difference between an answer and response.[2] An interviewer is often too busy to notice the difference and may wonder, both during the interview and while transcribing it afterwards, why someone often fails to give a "straight" answer. Briggs draws our attention to the "imaginings" of those involved in the interview:

> Interview researchers … imagine the social worlds depicted in the content of responses,… But interview materials simultaneously imagine an interpsychic world for the interviewee…, interviews are saturated by images of the social dynamics of the interview itself… But a fourth sphere is being constructed, that of the imagined texts that will be created through the use of interview data.
>
> (Briggs, 2002, p. 914)

Answers are seldom if ever straight and if they are, they may perhaps coincide narrowly with the interviewer's expectations, especially with regard to Briggs's fourth sphere. Responses are a broader category, however, replete with a whole range of imaginings. It's the interviewer's job to try to identify and disentangle them and not shove them aside in haste. It is important to note here that even structured interviews, despite their research focus and design, will also contain expressions of these imaginings. Given this the order of the questions was not kept too strictly, also because answers often anticipate and contain responses to questions further on in a questionnaire. The respondents had already read the questions beforehand.

Indeed, as will be noticed below, the responses reveal just how complex the situation was at the school in relation to translation and interpreting and the sensitivities involved. In what follows, I will provide relevant quotes[3] from their responses to each of the questions and make brief comments on them. I will then pinpoint and discuss a few of themes emerging from the interaction and attempt to tie these themes to literature[4] on the topic.

Background

School Languages

The teachers did not provide a complete list of all the languages spoken by those attending the school, but they did list a number of languages such as Turkish, Arabic, Spanish, Greek, Bulgarian and other languages from eastern Europe. However, they also remarked that it wasn't always clear what a child's home languages were, as the following extracts[5] illustrate:

8. I. And next to Turkish are there other languages?
9. D: There are quite a number of languages. But if you ask, ehm.
10. L1 & L2: other languages for sure.
11. I: Yes
12–13. L1: And someone came and said, did you know that little one and that little one, they're speaking their own language too. And we didn't know [inaudible] – a language.
14. I: And where are they from?
15. L1 From Ghana, it was G speaking to someone else in a Ghanian language.
16. I: Yes.
17. L1 But whether that's their home language, I can't say?
18. I: Yes, but yes.
19–27. L1: We have many children whose home language is Bulgarian who also master Turkish and for example, at the moment, because I teach children who are newly arrived in the country who speak other languages and this happens more and more often, children who have lived in another country and have been to school there, where Dutch is a school language and other Bulgarian children, but mamma speaks Bulgarian but then a lot Spanish. And a boy who has

been to school in Spain and speaks Spanish and another Bulgarian child who speaks Greek and has been to school and has received literacy training in another language and Greek has a different alphabet.

28. I: Yes.

29–31. L1: It's so complex. And the children can, as you were saying, have learned a whole load of languages in a society before they arrive here. And it's up to us, and it's a real quest, to find out which language they master best or their home language, so to speak.

...

53–54. D: There is a whole range of different languages (yes) with a few large ones (yes).

L1: Yes, Turkish is the largest.

Next to the obvious multilingualism in the school, it is important to note, in terms of literacy training and language policy, that the school gives a lot of importance and consideration to the home language or languages a child might speak. This explains the "quest" mentioned by L1 and brings us to the next question which requires some prior explanation before delving into the responses.

School Language Policy

Not long before this interview took place, the school had just completed an important project with the University of Ghent involving literacy training in the home language alongside training in Dutch, which is the official language of instruction[6] in schools in Flanders. Almost seven years have elapsed since this interview. The project, though successful, continues to be a source of irritation,[7] particularly among Flemish nationalist politicians and city councillors. Despite the protest, the policy of allowing multilingual practices in the classroom as a tool to improve learning skills is becoming increasingly popular and gaining in strength, as the lesson plan and materials[8] on the Ghent Centre for Education website illustrate. At the time of the interview, the project was still fresh in the minds of the interviewees and the benefits of allowing for interaction with home languages in the classroom were clear from their discourse from the outset:

3–7. D: ...We continue to work on that project, in the spirit of that project. The only difference is that we no longer give literacy training in Turkish to first year pupils. On condition that Turkish is the language they master best. That's the only difference. But we continue to remain positive towards the home languages and we will always do so.

61–64. D: Certainly in the context of Ghent, I believe, the home-language multilingual project has meant a lot (yes). In quite a number of schools in Ghent. As a result, a radical ban on using a home language at school has considerably diminished and people have become a lot more nuanced about it in Ghent schools.

66–69. D: But they are perfectly welcome here to use their home language as they like, especially for learning purposes. They can use their home language as a step towards learning (yes). Thirdly, there is a richness to including all these languages; it allows us to think about languages, of differences and similarities and this creates debate.

137–142. D: What I find wonderful for all the children who come here: it's not a problem. (Laughs). There are schools kids go to and these kids don't speak Dutch and that is a problem, because they don't understand anything, the can't do anything, they can't follow and lots of other things they can't do, whereas xxx's view, the view at our school is that children arriving here bring a lot with them. Let's first see what they know, and are able to do and use that and start from there to help the children get ahead.

This multilingual language policy is clearly at odds with official policy but, as mentioned above, it is gaining ground in the schools in Ghent. The policy is individual, in the sense that it takes into consideration the various language and learning needs teachers encounter among the pupils in their class (see the subsection on Practices below). It is schoolwide in the sense that it also takes into account all those working in the school including cleaning staff, etc. This became amply clear following an incident that took place soon after this interview, which will be reported on further on in this chapter. Accepting multilingualism also means accepting language barriers and using various means to get around them, including translation. As Meylaerts and González Núñez remarked, there is "no language policy without translation policy" (2018), which brings us to the next question.

School Translation/Interpreting Policy

This question was asked in a general sense but was understood narrowly by the participants as comprising official forms of translation and interpreting services provided by the city for the school, as the following extracts illustrate:

159–161. L2: And sometimes we work with interpreters and then they have to keep to the rules, and they have to communicate that too at the beginning of such an exercise.
I: So, their code of ethics (that's it)
170–171. D: If an interpreter comes (yes) from the interpreting and translation service he has his code of ethics and...
L2: and then that's purely translating.

174–203. I: But the importance of shared community communication is central?

L1: Understanding each other, making everything clear why you do something. And if the messages are difficult ones, we then opt for an interpreter. That's more or less the line we take in (yes, yes) our policy.

L2 We also have an interpreter telephone (yes) for urgent cases...

L1: But that doesn't always work because the people can't see anyone.

L2: It's not always easy, eh. The most difficult messages are transmitted through an interpreter. ...

L1: Before, we used to have a permanent service: people from the Ghent translation and interpreting services used to come here on a weekly basis and they sat in the parents' room, and we could ask them to translate for us (yes). ...

L1: But we don't have them anymore.

D: What we don't do is translate letters, not anymore (not anymore). In the past that used to be almost exclusively into Turkish, a lot of letters were translated into Turkish. In the meantime, there are so many other languages that it's simply not feasible to translate these letters (yes). And Dutch is the official language, so. But we do try to contact parents individually through staff at the school gate, so to speak.

The connection between degree of communicative difficulty and the presence of / need for an official interpreter is well known in the literature. The connection between the presence then further absence of "official" interpreters and translators (including cuts in funding for such services) and narrow interpretations of language policy by politicians is also well documented and will be discussed further below. Superdiversity has also had an impact on translation policy, as the piece of the extract illustrates. Other aspects of "policy" also emerge in everyday practices, which will become apparent in the next section.

Practices

Translators/Interpreters at School

The school staff make a distinction between official interpreters sent to them by the Ghent translation and interpreter service and others, including themselves, who are involved in everyday interpreting and translation as part of a larger positive communication strategy. The importance of this strategy will become apparent in the subsection on evaluation. Translation and interpreting is an everyday practice at the school and happens in class among and between pupils and teachers. It is also present among staff, in the schoolyard, at the school gate, during parent-teacher meetings, etc. In-class translation was formerly and continues to be part of a buddy system in which a pupil or pupils with a better command of Dutch helped a newcomer through the home language to express him- or herself in class:

263–275. B: They do translate; for example, children translate for each other in class, so yes so the home language can find a place in class. Why are the children in class? To learn, and if they can learn better by using their home language then of course they should use their home language. So children translate for each other in class in the same way parents do for each other (so yes).

L2: That happens during reading lessons too or for things you want them to do at home, and one pupil who speaks Dutch well and who also speaks Turkish and Bulgarian, he can tell the new kid who only speaks Bulgarian what he has to do (yes) but you can't be entirely sure (or check) what they say. It's really difficult, eh. But it's really nice to see how they do try (yes, yes) to get it across as well as possible.

L1: The newcomers in my class as well, yes, yes; each child is different and acquires a language differently and for some it can take only two months and others only pick it up after six months and when they're busy in the group and they want to say something or add something, they start straight away among themselves in Bulgarian to gain confidence and then they say it in Dutch – really nice, eh (yes).

Translation is also part of everyday communication outside of class, ranging from solving disputes in the playground to helping parents understand the letters they get from the school, for example.

110–125. L1: It's not always all that obvious … sometimes you end up in a confrontation with a group of children who all speak the same home language and then it's sometimes difficult to make clear that Dutch should also be part of the communication and that not everybody, a newcomer who speaks another language, understands … it's so important that children feel at home and safe and that they can use their own language as well, of course they can, and that they can express themselves when there is a conflict in the playground, that this should be translated into Dutch, and if you don't allow that to happen, things might become physical and surely that's not the idea… It's important that the children understand this and that you tell them so. Fortunately, one of the teachers speaks Turkish and Bulgarian and can translate at moments like these – it's essential that the children understand why we should speak Dutch, if one of the other children doesn't speak their language; it's important that the child can participate too (yes, yes) otherwise it's "this is no use to me, they don't understand me. I don't speak the language and can't speak to them." It's not, it's not about speaking a language, it's about communicating with each other even outside verbal language (eh, yes). It's important that they realise this.

It is interesting to note in this excerpt how Dutch, rather than being the official language of instruction, takes on the role of a mediating language in solving schoolyard disputes. Mediation through translation is also important in other situations:

> 204–217. L2: Being "low threshold", the people know who they can get in touch with or who can help them.
>
> L1: People have found their way, eh. At this school, we've come from a time when translating meant into one language, but now there are so many languages and what happens now is people ask each other, with a letter in hand, "what does this mean?" Or "can you help me?" Or it's the "brugfiguur[9]" they know or through a teacher or the teacher who speaks Turkish from another class, like "could you tell me," but also make sure that communication doesn't only happen on paper and that you can tell them (yes) or perhaps show them, yes, show them. I'm thinking now of those from first and second class who will soon be going on "countryside classes," that they have to bring a case with them full of different things. I thought it was nice because you could put all that in the letter, drawings that you could show them, shampoo, this and that, a towel (yes) that's the way we do it, kind of automatically but perhaps that's not so obvious for them as it is in other schools, I'd imagine, (yes) what needs to be done, that we can show that as well, (yes) and let them know in different ways and that's very important too.

Next to keeping things as "low threshold" as possible and keeping the channels of communication open, teachers are aware of the impact superdiversity has on the amount of work the official interpreters are expected to do in the school (and other schools) at crucial moments in the year:

> 190–193. L1: But it is not all that obvious in the interpreting services to find the right person and the right translation, and we notice that they are very limited in what they can do during those very busy moments, like parent-teacher moments, everyone arrives here at the same time at school and it's hard to find the right interpreters at such moments and get them to show (yes). It's no easy matter...

The responses to question b 1 also provide answers to question b 2 and b 3. In reply to b 2. Who interprets for whom, when and where?, we note the distinction made between "official" interpreting carried out by trained interpreters working for the city services and ad-hoc interpreting and translation done throughout the school by teachers and other members of the school staff. In response to b 3. Do you also translate and if so how and what type of document: school exercises, messages to parents, non-sensitive documents?, we note that the translation of letters to parents had stopped as a result of the growing number of languages to translate letters and other official announcements into. This resulted in a redistribution of the translation workload in a manner indicated especially in lines 204–217 above. One major element of translation policy that emerges from translation practices is encapsulated in the term "low threshold." In very classical terms, translation and interpreting serves the purpose, perhaps not of removing barriers to communication, but at least of lowering them, which given the level of superdiversity at the school is a very realistic stance. We also note the mainly positive terms used to describe interpreting and translation, which need to be looked at in more detail in terms of function and position, as shall become clear in the following subsection.

Evaluation

Importance of Translation/Interpreting Work

The reasons for including questions on evaluation were twofold. First, I was already aware that schools can rely on the translation and interpreting services provided by the city and was interested in how this played out in real terms in the school. Second, I was interested in evaluation from a theoretical perspective, as evaluative discourse provides insights into how people experience events and what their positions are regarding such events (Vološinov, 1986, p. 10). The extracts discussed in the previous two subsections have already revealed instances of evaluation in relation to multilingualism and translation/interpreting. The extracts also answer *c 2 Does it benefit the pupils, parents and teachers?* and illustrate the importance of translation and interpreting in all areas of school activity. We will now examine instances of evaluation of multilingual and translational activities a little more closely in order to tease out their implications.

In relation to multilingualism and translation, obvious indicators of evaluation[10] such as adjectives (important, wonderful, beautiful), adverbs (always, very, purely), modal verbs (should, have to) and, perhaps less obviously, nouns (problem, interpreter) also provide clues of stances regarding language use, parent-pupil and parent-teacher relations:

137. D: What I find **wonderful** for all the children who come here: **it's not a problem**. (Laughs) There are schools kids go to and these kids don't speak Dutch and **that is a problem**...
151–153. Li: I find it **very important** that you explain to them in a very simple way, what you are doing and why you are doing it, place it all **nicely** for them and get them involved.

274–275. L1: when they want to add something and can't make themselves clear they start off straight away amongst themselves in Bulgarian and then they say it in Dutch – **really nice**, eh (yes)

212–213. L1: I find this **wonderful** because you can put all that in a letter, you can draw things and show them.

They use the same Dutch word ("mooi") to describe each instance and how they feel about it. For pragmatic reasons, I had to resort to different translations (wonderful, nicely, nice) of the word. All of these utterances are best understood against the backdrop of multilingualism and the barriers it creates. The first is about recognising multilingualism and making it part of the school policy, which has an immediate impact of lowering the barrier for the children who come to the school: "it's not a problem." This is in sharp contrast with other schools that follow a monolingual Dutch track: "and that is a problem" for all concerned, not only the children with other home languages who go to these schools.

The next two utterances are about the benefits, first, of teaching methods that are shaped to fit the multilingualism in the class and, second, of multilingual interaction in the class and the educational results achieved. The last excerpt is about reaching parents and optimising communication by using multimodal formats in school letters to bridge language and cultural gaps.

Next to the instance alongside "nicely" above, the evaluatory term "belangrijk" (important) occurs a further 16 times in the interview. Here are a few more examples:

243–245. L1: It's **very important** that people feel good and that's not only a matter of language, but a feeling also that they are welcome (L2 that they're welcome) a feeling of equality.

294–299. L1: but they can be language buddies and that's **important** for children who know no Dutch at all, because they don't understand or speak it, it's important to have a language buddy in the class who can sit beside them for that very reason when they have to do an exercise and they can participate a little bit more in the activity thanks to the language buddy and **that's super, that's very important**, because we have lots of language buddies; I don't like the term interpreter because that puts too much pressure on the kids.

358–360. D: The **most important** thing is communication, and if you have to use the home language for that, then we use the home-language for that very reason; **even more important** is learning, that the children learn by using their home-language, which is why we use that home-language. (OK)

The first excerpt is about parent-teacher relations and how parents should feel welcome at the school. The other two are about the obvious importance to them of multilingual policy and related teaching and learning methods.

Evaluation also means making distinctions (Bourdieu, 1979) and this is clear in the distinction staff make between "official" and ad-hoc interpreting. Distinctions are also made in terms of preference, as is clear in excerpt 294–99 above in which L1 says the following: "because we have lots of language buddies; I don't like the term interpreter because that puts too much pressure on the kids." Here is another striking example of distinction:

> 162–171. L2: We also have translations to do between times and go-betweens who speak other languages and that's a different thing. Then you're not really an interpreter but a colleague within the school and then it's a matter of trying to find out how best to go about it (yes, yes). So then you **won't be purely** interpreting, eh. Then you're sharing the school's view ("vision"), if you've been working there for a number of years, and are able to make things fit and then you'll start to mediate, **there's much more to it than** interpreting, (yes).
>
> I: So if you ask for an interpreter, he or she will be more removed from what's happening here?
>
> D: D: If an interpreter comes (yes) from the interpreting and translation service he has his code of ethics and...
>
> L2: And then that's **purely** translating.

In this extract, a distinction is made between being an interpreter and being a colleague and subsequently between translating (interpreter) and mediating (colleague). This is further strengthened by the evaluation visible in "you won't be purely," "there's much more to it than" and "purely." Here, we are given a clear indication of positioning and identification as colleagues, which, in fact, also changes (perceptions of) the type of activity involved.

To return to the initial purpose of inquiring about evaluation, it is clear from the discourse that the school staff have a lot of respect for the interpreters from the city service and recognise the pressure they are under and the difficulties they face catering for all the languages at such a super-diverse school. From a theoretical perspective, we have pointed to other things emerging from the evaluative language. First, we note how the school staff position themselves positively towards their pupils, parents and colleagues. Second, we note how they also evaluate by making distinctions, the most striking being the distinction between being a colleague and being an interpreter and hence between mediating and translating. There doesn't seem to be anything new in this as the term cultural mediator is used a lot in the sector and discussed at large in the literature but as always it is important to discover what people mean by a term in a given situation and not be immediately content with a definition from the literature. The distinction is still worth revisiting therefore by examining it together with other themes emerging from the interview to which we will now turn in the following subsection.

Further Emergent Themes and Connections

The various aspects of multilingualism, and translation/interpreting in the school have been dealt with in detail in the discussion of the responses to the interview questions in the previous three subsections. These responses also contained other themes which we will examine below, also in an attempt to understand more fully the distinction the staff made between colleague and interpreter. The first set of questions in the interview addressed multilingualism, language policy and translation policy. The school is multilingual *de facto*; having a multilingual language policy is another matter, particularly given the Flemish region's *de jure* monolingual Dutch policy. As the school embraced multilingualism and the use of home languages, this has had a major impact on teaching models and communication practices both within and outside the school.

In a more recent article on language policy, Spolsky (2019) first identifies its three basic "independent but interconnected components, language practices, language beliefs or ideologies and language management," and then goes on to suggest some modifications, especially to the third component:

> In earlier studies (Spolsky, 2006, 2019), I suggested that a probable cause of the general failure to develop and implement wise and effective national language policies was the result of ignoring the existence at other levels (family, education, work, ethnic or religious group, region) of competing management goals and activities.
>
> (Spolsky, 2019, p. 324)

> Language policy in a speech community in any domain or level depends on three components, language practices, language beliefs or ideologies, and language management; in the latter, I now recognize the distinction between advocates without power and managers with authority.
>
> (Spolsky, 2019, p. 335)

The multilingual language policy (and related practices and beliefs) at the school can be considered as lying at the intersection of competing stances on language use (language ideologies) in the Flemish community as discussed above. It also lies at the interface of education, work and family. In terms of management, it involves advocates without power[11] (to use Spolsky's terms) that support the multilingual policy through their daily multilingual teaching practices at the school and through communication with parents and other members of staff. It also involves "managers with authority" spread across the community who are in favour of working with a multilingual policy in schools. Among them are the school principal, but also colleagues from the Ghent Education

Centre and from Ghent University with whom the principal has worked closely. Elements of language belief or ideology are visible in the school's language practices and overall communication strategy, which also involve translating and interpreting, as will become clear from the following excerpts from the interview data:

> 180–182. L2: It's not always easy, eh. The most difficult messages are transmitted through an interpreter. ...
>   I: But that's after a while (yes); that doesn't happen straight away?
>   L2: Yes but "in-between communication" is through all and sundry, to be honest (yes).
>   209–210. L1. But also make sure that communication doesn't only happen on paper and that you can tell them (yes) or perhaps show them, yes, show them.
>   326–332. I: So to sum up, you value translation work but official interpreting and translation work that's eh...
>   L2 In fact you can't really do that, eh for kids (yes)
>   I: So it's part of everyday communication?
>   L2 In fact this happens in a playful way at child level.
>   D: If now and then a document needs to be officially translated then we can send it through to the translation and interpreting service (service)...
>   356–357. L1: You reduce the gap between school and home (yes), eh through understanding things, through communication and through translating as well.

Multilingual communication is a key element in all these extracts. Again in practice, we can distinguish two poles of communication ranging from "official" and "difficult" communication that requires the help of the translation and interpreting service to "in-between communication," in which everyone is involved. The purpose of the latter is to address pupils in a playful way or to bridge the gap between school and home. Bringing an interpreter into the classroom is not considered appropriate, nor is appointing pupils as (permanent) interpreters in the class (see extract 29–299 above). These forms of multilingual communication can be considered as language-ideologically construed and designed to achieve certain goals. Here too we can see how the distinct roles of interpreter and colleague are played out (see also previous subsection).

Aspects of (multilingual) language policy are also evident in reflections on language use made by the principal, which tread a line between language management and language ideology:

> 58. D: The children are welcome, and they are entirely welcome (yes) so the home language they speak as well.

61–64. D: Certainly in the Ghent context, I think, this project of home-language multilingualism has indeed meant something (yes). In many Ghent schools, I believe. As a result, the radical ban on home languages in school has diminished sharply and people are a lot more nuanced about the matter in many schools in Ghent, I think.

97–98. D: But here, there has always been an atmosphere here from the early 1980's, that the home language should be given a place. But thanks to the project we've got arguments.

126–130. D: We postpone that, but how we deal with languages consciously versus unconsciously and getting (them) involved versus regulating, we always say regulate, that's what we always say, we can always regulate: it's allowed here and not there and that's the end of it. But reflecting on why it is appropriate or not to use the home language at a particular moment, reflecting on that and making it discussible (em, hem) that makes it a lot stronger.

In the first quote, the idea of children being entirely welcome also means accepting and taking their home languages into account. This is an interesting way of looking at multilingual education, as it starts with the child and not with the regional language policy the child is obliged to comply with on attending school in Flanders. The child has something to offer in terms of already acquired language skills and is not a "problem" in terms of having to comply with language policy. This view is further developed in lines 123–130, in which the advantages of involvement and open reflection on multilingual practices in school are weighed off against the limited scope and impact of regulation. In lines 97–98, the principle remarks on an historical awareness in the school of the need to include home languages and in lines 61–64 he points to the growing consensus in Ghent schools on home-language multilingualism.

It is clear from the responses that language policy also intersects with translation policy. Embracing multilingualism also means allowing for translation, be it official or ad-hoc. Present-day understandings of translation policy[12] are based directly on Spolsky's language policy model: "that which is the result of translation management, practice, and belief" (González Núñez, 2014, p. 22). In keeping with Spolsky's remarks on "the existence at other levels (family, education, work, ethnic or religious group, region) of competing management goals and activities" (Spolsky, 2019, p. 324), it seems obvious that these levels must also be taken into account in translation policy. This brings us back again to the distinctions in type and role made by the school staff:

- "official" translation carried out by interpreters/translators in "difficult" situations (translators/interpreters);
- ad-hoc translation carried out by the staff in general in everyday situations (mediators).

As all concerned are clearly involved in translation, is there any real difference, whatever you wish to call it? I would like to suggest that there is a difference and that it is of an indexical rather than denotational nature in terms of what is being transferred. Because of their code of ethics, interpreters are expected to remain neutral and maintain a certain distance from the other interlocutors in the interest of fairness, among other things. All this indexes officialdom, but it takes nothing away from the tact and skill needed to transfer a difficult message. Because of some notion of shared indexical grounding (the school and its activities), school staff (mediators) can dispense with certain preliminaries that might estrange a pupil or a parent. In the meantime, they are involved in something akin to "transduction,[13]" whereby elements of involvement and belonging are transferred alongside the message translated from a letter, for example. Here too we witness what has been regulated (code of ethics/professional training) and what is unfolding in terms of what the school principal calls involvement and appropriate language use.[14] These modes of translation co-occur and are not considered as being diametrically opposed to one another. They remind us once again that there is more to translation than information transfer in another language.[15]

The care with which school letters are drawn up also shows language ideological underpinnings of the school communication strategy. At the same time, they also show an awareness of the sensitivities involved in addressing certain groups in society, as well as an awareness of shifting demographics in the neighbourhood of the school:

> 222–232. D: We also limit the number of letters we hand out. (yes, yes). We also pay close attention to the language in those letters, and that's a quest as well; we've got three schools, this one and one in xxxx and the other in xxxx and those two other schools are receiving more and more pupils from privileged parents whose home language is Dutch and it is quest to communicate well with each parent, particularly given the diversity of the population.
>
> L1 I have a feeling that people with another home language[16] or of another origin feel less than others and that remains a very sensitive issue. You have to motivate them an awful lot to get them involved in school.
>
> L2: But I don't think it's only a matter of the home language but their social contacts (contacts); I'm thinking now of disadvantaged Belgians who are experiencing exactly the same thing.
>
> L1: But I think for speakers of other languages that it's doubly (doubly, yes) the case.

Depending on who is being addressed, a letter might be understood as condescending, on the one hand or as the voice of officialdom, on the other. This raises issues of literacy similar to those discussed in the previous chapter. It also gives us an insight into soaring house prices in Ghent, and how young well-educated couples are moving into work-ing-class/migrant neighbourhoods[17] where housing is still affordable. This is an interesting dynamic, as it is often the case that people of mi-grant origin have been living in these neighbourhoods much longer than the newly arrived who would most probably self identify as Flemish.

Viewed outside of language and translation policy, the data also con-tains other emergent themes, one of which is "indexical biography," which provides in this case an insight into "the social and cultural itin-eraries" (Blommaert & Backus, 2013, p. 28) children have already been on before arriving at the school:

> 19–27. L1: We have many children whose home language is Bulgarian who also master Turkish and for example, at the moment, because I teach children who are newly arrived in the country who speak other languages and this happens more and more often, children who have lived in another country and have been to school there, where Dutch is a school language and other Bulgarian children, but mamma speaks Bulgarian but then a lot Spanish. And a boy who has been to school in Spain and speaks Spanish and another Bulgarian child who speaks Greek and has been to school and has received literacy train-ing in another language and Greek has a different alphabet.

An awareness of the presence of these "indexical biographies" at such a young age has prompted the teachers to seek further positive outcomes in the classroom:

> 83–89. L1: And I think that we must do, in schools and also in other institutions and services, that it's important in education, when you work with children that you don't only look at what the teacher can get into their heads but look at all the things that a child has brought with him/her and do something with that; get out what's already there inside (yes) and when you work with children like we do at this school, children who have a rich variety of home languages, you have to, as a teacher, do your best to help them get that out there. Eh, you don't just have to pack them full of stuff during the lessons but help them get that stuff out and that's what I find so powerful here, that's our strength.

The question then is, if such an approach to multilingual instruction were to be regulated and streamlined, would it survive. I believed it would at the time of the interview and, judging from the Ghent City and other websites, there is much evidence to show that it has.[18] And it must be noted that we practically always tend to think of language and trans-lation policy in terms of regulating the availability/acceptance of given languages and translation/interpreting services and all the professional training that issues from such regulation. What we do to a much lesser extent is what the school principal suggests, i.e. to make room for openness and reflection that is much needed when it comes to multilingual teaching for the simple reason that it's probably not all that common. The theme that encapsulates this openness in and outside the classroom is that of a "quest" (lines 29–31 and 222–232 above).

Another theme that emerged in the interview is the loneliness children feel when no one in the school speaks their home language:

> 361–371. L2: So most kids can always turn to someone who speaks their (home) language; it seldom happens, but it does happen at times, but very seldom there are children who have (no one) to turn to, and that's a different matter altogether (unclear) but the parents could speak English and that worked out but that child in second year kindergarten, it must have been very hard for the child (yes, yes) if you can't turn to someone who speaks your language.
>
> L1: In fact, they looked for each other, a little sister from second kindergarten and her brother who was in the one of the higher classes; they meet each in the schoolyard and I see them saying things to each other for a quarter of an hour, a little bit of English, but not enough in fact (yes, eh).
>
> L2: Not enough but he could say a word here and there, but she couldn't (it was another language)
>
> L1: For some kids there's a huge gap, not just language-wise but also in terms of school culture, eh (yes, yes). That's a threshold too.

This point hit home quite hard and cast me back in time to all those years ago when I first arrived in France. Though I had learned French in secondary school, it was all bookish learning (school culture?), and I couldn't even hold a simple conversation or order something in a shop or café. It took a while before I could put that learning to use and begin to speak with some degree of confidence. In the meantime, I realised that no one around me spoke the variety of English I grew up in – Dublin vernacular. The feeling of isolation that brings with it is literally dumbfounding and it is probably something that most migrants experience at some stage on their journey.

Seven Years On

I returned to the school seven years later to speak to the principal again. He is still working at the school and is just as committed as he was when I spoke to him and his colleagues for the first time all those years ago. The principal confirmed that they were still involved in the same or, allowing for shifts in the demographics of the school, similar multilingual and translation practices observed all those years ago. He then sketched a couple of more recent developments, like increased diversity and precarity, for example, which were already nascent or unfolding and have been re-ported on to some degree above. These will be returned to and addressed again below. Multilingual and translation policy featured strongly in the discussion so far in this chapter but now it is time to examine the foun-dations of these policies further by focusing on the main theme to emerge from the conversation with the school principal seven years on: ethos.

From Practices and Policy to Ethos

On the whole, our conversation could best be termed as an exploration of various elements of an ethos underlying the multilingual and translational practices discussed in detail so far. The notion of a multilingual ethos has already been proposed by McCracken et al. (2020). This perspective on a multilingual (teaching) ethos is indeed a response to the multilingual real-ities we are increasingly faced with, and their article is about developing such an ethos and taking steps to do so. However, they do not discuss the notion of ethos as such. Ethos (from the Greek) is usually understood in two main ways, first as character (of a person/speaker) and by extension the character of a person or group, community, culture, era, etc. (OED), so in this case that of the school. In rhetoric, ethos is further understood as the credibility of the speaker, which is part of "la presentation de soi[19]" [the presentation of self] in public life (Amossy, 2010). As Amossy notes, "l'ethos, ou l'image de l'orateur, n'a rien à voir avec l'acceptabilité du dis-cours : l'essentiel est que celui-ci réponde à des critères de validité logiques" [ethos, or the image of the orator, has nothing to do with the acceptability of speech/discourse: what matters is that it complies with logical criteria of validity[20] (Amossy, 2010, p. 8). It is clear that much is at stake in deter-mining a person's character, let alone that of a group, community or era. This is also the case in determining the credibility of a speaker.

In what follows we hope to trace elements of a possible ethos based on the idea that the character and credibility of the speaker (in this case the school principal and those involved in running the school) is reflected in their discourse on commitment to and propagation of the practices re-ported on above. This discourse points outwards towards their practices and has to take the element of time or duration into account. Their char-acter and credibility are enhanced by the persistence of these practices over a long period, which are the result of years of conscious effort, and did not come about by themselves. To recapitulate, the principle points out three vital elements to using home languages at school:

> Their importance for the wellbeing of the children (17–18; 32–33);
>   Their importance as a steppingstone in learning in general and also in learning Dutch (45–49);
>   Their importance as part of a rich diversity of languages children come into contact with from an early age (48–49).

The multilingual and translation practices reported above stem from and build on these three elements. Maintaining these priorities and practices indeed requires long-term investment and this also involves facing pressures, both internal and external, that might curtail these practices or cause them to fall into disuse and be replaced by others. Clear indications of these pressures emerge from the principal's discourse, which will be discussed in the remaining part of this chapter.

External pressure is twofold but still mainly consists in the (legal) insistence on the sole use of monolingual Dutch in teaching and communication, but this has changed over time despite the legal obligation. Resisting this pressure over the years has certainly paid off in broader social terms. The principle points to a clear shift in attitudes outside the school:

> 14–18: D:... I think, back in the time of the first interview, that it was a highly polarised debate (yes, yes, yes). Luckily, I believe that we've moved away from that polarisation. Well, I hope so (yes, yes) and that everyone, that it's become more kind of common sense that the home language has its value (yes, yes) and that still remains so here among us at the school.
> 31–32: D: Yes, but in school circles and in most schools, I believe, and in the "pedagogische begeleiding[21]," (ah) people are much more positive about it [i.e. home languages] (yes, yes).

External pressure can be exerted from less obvious corners, as the following quotes illustrates:

> 195–196: D: The one thing that does bother me a little is the number of people who come and tell us how we should do it (yes?).
> 202–203: D: ... but the number of people who come and tell us how we should approach it all, and that makes me think "just join in."

The principal is full of praise for the work done at colleges and in research projects, which he calls "very exciting eh very interesting" (206) but insists that they could learn a lot from and come to appreciate the wealth of knowledge, knowhow and experience they have built up over the years by spending some time at the school (205–212). This point is echoed albeit from a prospective angle in the following quote:

> The important question we have to ask ourselves as knowledge generators in diverse schools is how we can not only translate multilingual research and theory into practice, but also enable our practice to extend our understanding of the possibilities of multilingual instruction.
> (McCracken et al., 2020, pp. 6–7)

"Joining in," as the principle puts it, would form a healthy corrective when "translating" theory into practice.

Aspects of internal pressure also emerged from the conversation. Such pressure is again dealt with in a routine manner by drawing on the school's experience and knowhow. One less obvious form of pressure arises from new (teaching) staff who might compare the situation at the school to that of schools in the Brussels Capital Region where Dutch is sometimes perceived as being under threat and has to be "defended" and "protected" from falling into disuse (Janssens, 2018). This is a very different somewhat entrenched view that has to be addressed as it might skew perceptions of the school from the outset: (172–173): "D: people bring these things with them to school; its a challenge to have do to that [i.e. tackle such views] again and again."

The other more routine form of pressure consists in the arrival of new children and parents:

> (160–163): D: It's always, here are always new people who arrive at all times (yes); that part of school culture it's in the very walls of the school[22] but how do you take people along with you in the story of the school (ah em)? It's a challenge from time to time, like explaining about the use of the home language, for example.

As was pointed out and discussed in detail in the previous sections of this chapter, multilingual and translational practices are part and parcel of the school's teaching and communication practices. Their persistence and resistance to pressure serves as evidence of an ethos.

Another element of ethos to emerge from the discussion as an integral part of learning at school is what the principle calls "learning how to live together" at school:

> (85–88) D: … You don't only learn at school, you also live at school, absolutely (laughter) (ah ha) and learning how to live together, yes that's part of it, that's a learning process as well, and we absolutely have to learn that. So I see the school as a learning place for society …

The implications of living together at school extend far beyond teaching the children how to do so and hence how to live in society. The whole school is involved in some form or other. For example, members of the cleaning staff are recruited from the diverse local community and fulfil an important function as mentors and persons of respect who speak the children's home languages. Establishing relations and respect are key elements in all of this, as this long extract illustrates:

> (108–119) D: Or about policy that works better (policy, yes) when there's a connection (when it's more small scale? Yes?) when there is a relation, "no performance without relation," that what we say

(OK) and that's what we tell the children (yes, yes) as well, because we find it important for them to learn this (yes): no relation, no performance, and I believe this applies to all our staff, that there is no performance without relation, but if it all happens anonymously through inspectors who check if everything is ok (yes). And imagine if I arrive at school and see that it hasn't been well cleaned and I call up the service that's done the job and they then address the person who's done it. Isn't it much nicer when our staff feel co-responsible for how the school looks (yes) and that it is clear that the cleaning staff can talk to the other members of staff or to the children and ask to be respected. I will only be respected if I respect others. How can you respect others if you don't see each other, if everything happens separately at different times (yes).

The Dutch word "prestatie" (performance) is mainly used in this context in terms of performing a task, doing work, making an effort, etc. The slogan-like expression ("geen prestatie zonder relatie") is enhanced by the rhyme created by the -tie at end of each noun (relatie, prestatie) but gains its strength from the way it links work to relations in which

> (95–96) D: Connection is important, connection with the whole school team and everyone who works at the school can be somebody of significance for it.

It is argued here that the elements of ethos apparent in these extracts stretch beyond teaching proper and involve creating and maintaining an atmosphere that is conducive to multicultural and multilingual learning in a broader sense. Creating and maintaining such an atmosphere means recognising the multicultural and multilingual realities in society and trying to deal with them in a consistent way over a sustained period of time. This in itself is surely conducive to creating an ethos. Viewed as character and the credibility of the speaker, the notion of ethos has to be examined in context however, to see what such a character might consist of and whether the speaker is actually credible in terms of "logical criteria of validity" (Amossy, 2010, p. 8) both in discourse and action. Lest the discussion so far should paint too idyllic a picture, it is important to return to the increased diversity the precarity it brings with it.

The School as Mirror of the Neighbourhood

The heading of this subsection is taken from something the school principal said:

> (240:)D: It remains an exciting context to work in and our ambitions remain the same, like a mirror of/for? the neighbourhood (yes?)

I suppose there is nothing unusual about this remark but perhaps it applies to some schools more than others. Being a mirror of and for the neighbourhood is both an ambition for the school, i.e. something the neighbourhood can see itself in and recognise. But it is also a statement of fact. The school indeed reflects the neighbourhood both in terms of its demographics but also in terms of its dynamics:

> (253–257) D: This is a neighbourhood a lot of people still keep arriving in (yes?) disadvantaged people, a large concentration of underprivileged people (yes) but who sometimes do better over the years and then often leave the area too (ah ok); a lot of children come and go here in our school but that's often because people have been able to improve themselves (ah).

Though people leave the neighbourhood and others move in, parents who have left might still send their children to the school:

> (258–260) D: and what's nice is that some parents still send their children to school here (ah!) because of the welcome, because they are welcome here, which is very pleasant.

The neighbourhood dynamics is also reflected in the precarity the principle mentioned at the beginning of our conversation:

> (56–62) D: We continue to invest in this. I think the social context children grow up in that that's also a very important factor (yeah, yeh). How you deal with language, what type of language they use in whatever language and how they communicate with the children; a culture of books and storytelling, a culture of communicating. Throughout the years, there have always been children who have grown up in precarious conditions, but their numbers have increased, and we see that here at school (yes, yes?) and that certainly plays a role I believe, in the sense that multilingualism functions as a plus (yeah, yeh).

It is worth noting how he links precarity to (levels of) literacy in this extract and how multilingualism (esp. the use of the home language) can act as a positive force.

The neighbourhood demographics and dynamics mirrored in the school and pointed to in this short subsection are also reflections of larger sociocultural and economic forces. The school tries to tackle these forces in the way they know best, as the account given in this chapter hopefully has made clear. The types of translation and interpreting practices discussed above are hence best understood in and through the school as a mirror of the neighbourhood.

Further Comments

The elements of ethos to emerge from the analysis of the conversation with the school principal chime with the list of perhaps more ambitious "lenses" proposed by McCracken, Rikers and Cummins in promoting a multilingual ethos by reflecting on their teaching practices:

> Scaffold comprehension and production of language;
> Reinforce academic language across the curriculum;
> Engage students' multilingual repertoires;
> Maximise literacy engagement;
> Connect with students' lives and the knowledge, culture and language of their communities;
> Affirm students' identities by enabling them to use their language and literacy skills to carry out powerful intellectual and creative academic work.
>
> (McCracken et al., 2020, p. 8)

All of these lenses are nonetheless present in some form in the school's practices, along with years of experience that has allowed them to consolidate their (multilingual) ethos. This also includes the ways they use translation and interpreting in the interests of the children and their parents, among others.

Notes

1 For a full overview of the research, see https://www.ugent.be/cessmir/nl/over-cessmir/promotoren/piet-van-avermaet and other related websites.
2 On the distinction between reply and response, see Goffman (1976).
3 The translations of these excerpts are my own.
4 This will also include language policy and translation policy, which are mentioned and dealt with in plain terms in the discussion of the interview data.
5 The line numbering is from the original Dutch document and may vary slightly in translation.
6 Belgium comprises four language areas. The Dutch language area is monolingual Dutch. Though you can speak any language you wish in private or address a customer in any language you wish, "language freedom" is restricted to Dutch in the Flemish region in a number of areas including government and legal affairs, and education. See https://www.vlaanderen.be/uw-overheid/over-vlaanderen/de-taalwetgeving-in-vlaanderen.
7 See article in the Brussels Times (26/09/2019): https://www.brusselstimes.com/70239/ghents-push-for-multilingual-classrooms-sparks-outrage-among-local-politicians.
8 Lesson plan and materials: https://stad.gent/nl/onderwijscentrum-gent/meertaligheid-en-talensensibilisering/functioneel-meertalig-leren-het-secundair-onderwijs/werkvormen-en-lesvoorbeelden.
9 Literally "bridge person or character": liaison officer.
10 This is loosely based on appraisal in Systemic Functional Linguistics: https://www.grammatics.com/appraisal/.

11 This is perhaps true in terms of regional language policy but not in real terms of language use in the school.
12 For a historical overview of how the term has been used in Translation Studies, see Meylaerts (2011).
13 See Chapter 2 for a discussion and illustration of the term·
14 This obvious difference has resulted in calls for closer involvement by interpreters and translators in daily school affairs in countries like South Africa where interpreters are used in class (Brewis, 2017). In a related vein, see also Aguilar-Solano (2015) on a study of volunteer interpreters at two hospitals in Spain.
15 For a discussion of professional codes of ethics and non-professional translation, see Drugan (2011).
16 Than Dutch.
17 See Chapter 3.
18 See https://meertaligheid.be/materiaal/je-spreekt-thuis-verschillende-talen-dat-is-goed-voor-je-kind.
      See also https://stad.gent/nl/onderwijscentrum-gent/diversiteit/taal-en-meertaligheid.
19 Viz. The Presentation of Self in Everyday Life (Goffman, 1959).
20 My translation.
21 Literarily "pedagogical guidance" – a Flemish government body in charge of school/pedagogical services.
22 This is a Flemish expression which means that things happen naturally, more or less.

References

Aguilar-Solano, M. (2015). Non-professional volunteer interpreting as an institutionalized practice in healthcare: a study on interpreters' personal narratives. *Translation & Interpreting.org*, 7(3), 132–148.

Amossy, R. (2010). *La présentation de soi: Ethos et identité verbale* (L'interrogation philosophique). Paris : PUF.

Bourdieu, P. (1979). *La distinction: Critique sociale du jugement* (Le sens commun). Paris: Ed. de Minuit.

Briggs, C. (1986). *Learning How to Ask: A Sociolinguistic Appraisal of the Role of the Interview in Social Science Research* (Studies in the Social and Cultural Foundations of Language). Cambridge: Cambridge University Press. doi:10.1017/CBO9781139165990

Briggs, C. L. (2002). Interviewing, power/knowledge, and social inequality. In F. Jaber, J. Gubrium, & A. Holstein (Eds.), *Handbook of Interview Research Context & Method* (pp. 910–921). Thousand Oaks, CA: Sage Publications.

Drugan, J. (2011). Translation ethics wikified: How far do professional codes of ethics and practice apply to non-professionally produced translation? In O'Hagan, Minako, ed. Translation as a social activity. Community translation 2.0. *Special Issue of Linguistica Antverpiensia: New Series*, 10, 111–127.

Fontana, A. (2007). Interviewing, structured, unstructured, and postmodern. *Blackwell Encyclopedia of Sociology*, 5, 2407–2411.

Goffman, E. (1959). *The Presentation of Self in Everyday Life*. New York: Doubleday.

Goffman, E. (1976). Replies and responses. *Language in Society*, 5(3), 257–313. http://www.jstor.org/stable/4166887

Gonzalez Núñez, G. (2014). *Translating for Linguistic Minorities: Translation Policy in the United Kingdom*. Leuven: KU Leuven. Faculty of Arts.

Janssens, R. (2018). *Meertaligheid als opdracht. Een analyse van de Brusselse taalsituatie op basis van taalbarometer 4*. Brussel: VUB Press.

McCracken, M., Rikers, L., & Cummins, J. (2020, Summer). Developing a multilingual ethos to foster student and teacher agency. *International School*, 22, 6–8.   https://www.proquest.com/magazines/developing-multilingual-ethos-foster-student/docview/2414425192/se-2

Meylaerts, R. (2011). *Translation Policy in Handbook of Translation Studies* (Vol. 2, pp. 163–168). Amsterdam: John Benjamins Publishing Company.

Meylaerts, R., & Gonzalez Núñez, G. (2018). No language policy without translation policy: A comparison of Flanders and Wales. *Language Problems & Language Planning*, 42(2), 196–219.

Spolsky, B. (2006). *Language Policy*. Cambridge: Cambridge University Press.

Spolsky, B. (2019). A modified and enriched theory of language policy (and management). *Language Policy*, 18(3), 323–338. doi: 10.1007/s10993-018-9489-z

Vološinov, V. N. (1973). *Marxism and the Philosophy of Language* (Studies in Language, L. Matejka & I. R. Titunik and M. Silverstein, Ed.). New York/London: Seminar Press.

9   A City Registration Office

The city registration office is a poor translation of the Dutch term "bev-olkingsdienst" (literally population service), which is what the locals call it. The translation focuses on registration, which is a key element in this chapter. Its official name is Dienst Burgerzaken (Civil Affairs Service). It's the place you go to for all types of official documents concerning your or a family member's person: birth, marriage and death certificates, drivers and other sorts of licences, identity cards and proof of abode, etc., etc. It is also the place all people arriving in Ghent (including migrants) have to go to, to register. It's the service that provides official proof in the form of various documents of your civil existence and aspects of your civil status at various times in your life. And you can go there to let them know if anything should change in that status or if you've lost an official document of some sort. The Dienst Burgerzaken is where the events reported in this chapter took place.

Renewing My Residence Permit

This chapter comprises a personal narrative and a set of observations that link translation and migration as witnessed during the process of renewing my residence permit. This narrative and related observations belong within the general remit of an auto-ethnography as they attempt to describe the process of renewing my residence permit while placing it alongside similar attempts to acquire documentation by others in the same situation and linking it to the broader social dynamics involved (Butz & Besio, 2009).

Despite the fact that I have been living in Belgium longer than I have ever lived in Ireland, I am still an Irish citizen and hold an Irish passport. My two sons have double nationality, something which for obvious reasons, I am not allowed to have: neither of my parents were born in Belgium or are Belgian nationals. So, I had to make a choice and, before doing so, agonised over it for a while. I will trace the basic reasons here as they are of some relevance for the case I wish to discuss further on in this chapter.

I had left Ireland on what some people might call a whim, though there was nothing whimsical about how it felt at the time. I had some vague plan about heading east and, in retrospect and for lack of a better word, a type

DOI: 10.4324/9781003363811-10

of curiosity or hunger that I could not yet articulate or that could be satisfied by the job I had at the time or by the future or 'life' that seemed set out for me then, all of which made me effectively leave. What type of emigrant I was, was unclear to me then and I argue here that clarity on this issue is seldom sought among emigrants and is more often found in trenchant and usually ill-formed statements made by non-emigrants with a political agenda. An attempt will be made below to frame this issue more cogently.

I had left my country (Ireland) like hundreds of thousands of others before me, very often but not always out of economic necessity, who left their friends and family behind and headed off, mainly to places where people 'speak English,' which is a factor that should not be underestimated. This fact (or given) only occurred to me much later. There was a certain logic and historical precedent to it (see French et al., 2019, for example), which had managed to escape me for ages. What I was doing was nothing special, even though it was extremely important and life changing. Speaking and hearing a variety of English wherever you arrived helped cushion the blow of homesickness and a sense of alienation. English had long been the language of empire and colonisation (Mufwene, 2001) before its American variety helped kick-start a new round of globalisation (Pennycook, 2007). We had a shared past in and through English and, at moments of trial and difficulty, even a shared enemy, the one from whom we had learned the language in the first place. Arriving somewhere where English was not the default was a whole different matter, however. Nor can I speak for those who left Ireland with no English. My parents, like most of the people in my neighbourhood, did not speak Irish and hence were out of step with or were unaware of the beliefs associated with the language that were inculcated into us from an early age at school. They had little in common with the dominant discourse on Irish language and culture at that time, which did not stop them from feeling very much a part of the relatively new country they lived in.

Much has changed since, but back then we had the Irish language drilled into us much like Latin, which wasn't conducive to cultivating skill, let alone a fondness for what was considered our native tongue, which strictly speaking in my case it wasn't, though there is room for people like me in Rampton's model (Rampton, 1990). I am not offering this as an excuse but rather pointing to a state of affairs at a given time. The sense of belonging that comes with speaking a language from childhood was somehow missing, though not entirely. My brother used to say mockingly: "I'm not from Ireland, I'm from Dublin." And there was a certain truth to it back when we were adolescents, as his remark reflected or rather lingered in the shadow of official discourse about Irishness (Kiberd, 1996, p. 615). There was something about us young Dubliners then that could not be redeemed and hence had to be abandoned. We could never be entirely au fait 'as Gaeilge.' Happily, all this changed for the better (O'Toole, 1998, pp. 143–156). The question was:

what remained of this antagonistic yet playful stance on being Irish, which after all is a form of belonging once I moved away? What became of the instant indexical understandings and nod-and-wink collusion that go together with belonging somewhere? Are they replaced by others elsewhere? How would one's awareness of local gatekeeping help gain an understanding of it in another culture and related languages? This is very much an open question that has to do with gaining access to less obvious aspects of the languages of the country you arrive in. Before achieving such degrees of understanding, more basic levels of competence are expected, even demanded. In the documentation on language policy and "integration into Flemish society," a knowledge of Standard Dutch is set out almost as a prerequisite.

This requirement fits into a larger logic of contra-distinction, of how nations set themselves off from each other through language; but it also functions inwardly in setting out another set of social contra-distinctions that can be operationalised when needed (Bourdieu, 1979). So in its purpose, the standard is not unlike that of the roman god Terminus[1]; he guards the borders. However, we tend to forget that a border functions in both directions. In this respect, learning Standard Dutch is really only a starting point, and the same applies to learning any standard language. It should be noted, however, that, in the documentation[2] provided by the city of Ghent, learning the standard is couched in a discourse on equal opportunity and not one of social or ethnic difference. This also functions bi-directionally. However, knowing the standard can be a barrier or even counterproductive in certain (work) situations, as it will result in a person being indexed socially and perhaps not immediately in terms of his or her foreignness (Silverstein, 2003) – see Chapters 5 and 7. In this way, a sense of belonging is dialogic and as argued above, also involves understanding certain tropes along with what is *not* being said exactly and what is being said in addition to the actual words spoken.

As far as 'discrete' languages are concerned, being an emigrant allowed me to hear other emigrants' tales, one from an expert in European law who grew up speaking Irish in Chicago. Another was from a young commander of a tank regiment in the Iran-Iraq War whose parents insisted on his learning English, then largely the language of the enemy. He came from a family of musicians, which proved disastrous under the new regime. One evening, I let him listen to the Chieftains. "Ah, he said, 'that's where it comes from."

"What?" I asked.

"The Chieftain tank," he said, "a tank that doesn't have to stop to fire."

These and many other stories, along with my own reflections on my situation, put the whole notion of speaking any given language into a very sharp perspective and helped me understand that my case was relatively anodyne by comparison and far from unique. Learning from experience, long before my studies, I not only came to realise that there were different languages, language varieties and dialects, but also that words meant different things even in the same language, as the Chieftain story indicates. I had long been familiar at home with curt allusions to my origins by those who found my speech improper, but this took on a new form when I left Ireland: the gold standard of RP pronunciation and its accompanying rules of grammar were often brandished at me with a certain degree of venom by those who had learned this supposedly 'accentless' accent. So for as far back as I can remember, language use has always been an index of place and class (Hymes, 1972; Bourdieu, 1980; Silverstein, 2003). All of this did not prevent me from agonising about which passport to carry, though. I had learned Dutch and French in the meantime and could have easily applied for Belgian citizenship and passed the language test without too much difficulty. Didn't I have a school friend who had become an American citizen? Why didn't I take the step? I simply could not. I had left my country but could not manage to leave it behind altogether. So, I told myself I had a European passport and that we were all Europeans and that was that.

Whether this was a cop out or not I will leave to you to judge but it explains why I, like everyone else of foreign extraction, have to queue up at the "bevolkingsdienst." Sitting there waiting for my number to come up, which can take an awful long time, brought all these thoughts back to me. They provide a material explanation as to why I was sitting there but also a backdrop against which I might try to understand the events and observations that are described below. As Butz and Basio:

> We find it useful to imagine autoethnographies as emerging practically from between two poles on a continuum. At one pole, the accustomed agents of signification (academics) strive self-consciously to understand themselves as an important part of what they are signifying; at the other, the accustomed objects of signification (research subjects) involve themselves as authors in public acts of self-representation.
>
> (Butz & Basio, 2009)

This report belongs somewhere along the continuum. Before this attempt to renew my residence permit, my visits to the service had become less frequent over the years, which does not mean I had become unfamiliar with how things were done. Before I managed to get in, get a number and find a seat, I had to stand in a queue that stretched out through the main door. I am convinced that all of the people queuing up with me would have tales to tell similar to mine about their immediate or more distant pasts that were causal in their being in the queue. I had to go through this waiting game[3] a number of times before I could eventually renew my residence permit.

In fact, I could have spared myself the trouble of all these visits and waiting, had I managed to renew the thing on time. Because of my absent-mindedness – nothing unusual among academics, it seems – I now had to assemble proof for the administration that I was indeed who I said I was (my expired permit served this purpose) and was indeed working where I claimed I was working (payslips, bank statements, proof of payment of utility bills, etc.) and had not inadvertently left the country at any stage between the expiry date of my permit and the actual time I requested renewal. This took time but the response took much longer. I was told they were being extra careful these days because of all that had happened.[4] The lady at the desk even referred to "Brussels" at one stage and rolled her eyes. Brussels was indeed the place they'd sent my file to and were expecting a reply from. The allusions were not lost on me nor or on them for that matter, but the Brussels[5] they refer to is of a different hue to the one rejected by the Brexiteers. Then again, this chapter would not have been written, as I would have had no notes or on-site observations to make it possible.

I am no different from the hundreds of people who visit this office every day. Like me, they are faced with the task of getting their papers in order or to paraphrase Brian Friel[6] on the relation between personal identity and being able to "produce" related personal documents, etc. They too have to queue up and wait and negotiate language barriers in whatever way feasible, ranging from the use of the odd word and gesture to language brokering (Hall, 2004; Hall & Sham, 2007) or ad-hoc interpreting to knowing the official language enough to get things done. If you go there, you will witness people jumping the queue to see if they can get a number from the machine near the desks. When they realise the machine does not dispense tickets for the hatches and desks but is a machine to pay your permit fees with, they return disappointed to the back of the queue.

Language-wise, things have changed since my early visits, however. Then, they used to have signs up in a number of European languages as well as in Turkish and Arabic; now the languages are too numerous to account for in signage. Back then, there was an insistence on using Dutch; now this insistence has been set aside for purely practical reasons and civil servants often switch to a variety of English that is clear enough for the purposes at hand. This use of a lingua franca or French (an older lingua franca), which I witnessed on a couple of occasions, is obviously against language policy in Flanders but what else, given the burden of work and the sheer number of applicants and the variety of languages, can these civil servants do?

I was reminded of my familiarity with the place by a man sitting next to me during one of my visits:

– You've been coming here for a long time.
– Indeed, I have.
– Yeah, I know you from around and from here of course. English, right?
– No, Irish and you're Dutch, right?

- Yeah. Getting your permit renewed?
- Yes, but it's complicated.
- Same here. Mine ran out and then you realise you're still a foreigner.
- Tell me about it.[7]

He had been waiting much longer than I had and when his number appeared on the screen, he gave me a knowing nod and wished me luck.

This encounter led to reflection on degrees or types of emigration, their duration and possible termination, if at all. This was linked to thoughts I had earlier on what it means to be an expat, a recent far from innocent euphemism that can be found on the city website. As Lefleur and Marfouk argue

> [m]oreover, some immigrants manage to shake off the label of immigrant. This is the case for those people who call themselves (or are called) "expats" to emphasize that they are probably better educated or trained or are from a better social class or come from a richer country than other immigrants. In this way an American engineer who works for a Belgian company will be called an expat, whereas his colleague, a Senegalese worker will be more quickly considered a migrant. This arbitrary labelling of a person as an "expat" or an "immigrant" thus creates an artificial hierarchy between migrant flows who are either considered desirable for the host country and migrant flows whose contributions to the host country are constantly put into question.
>
> (Lafleur & Marfouk,[8] 2018, p. 22 – my translation from the Dutch)

This is how we/they are addressed on the "civil affairs – migration" page and on the international section of the Ghent city website,[9] which interestingly is only in English, next to Dutch of course. In the documentation, "expat" is used as a shorthand for those planning to move to the city to work or to explore new job opportunities. The term is couched in a positive yet serious and informative message about what to do and the benefits of being an expat in Ghent.

As a former colleague[10] of mine noted, once a word or expression crosses into another language it takes on another meaning. Though the source document may have been drafted in English, it was drafted by Flemish users in consultation with "expats" and addresses other expats. So, much like Chieftain, it most likely has taken on another local meaning in the meantime. It should be noted in passing that in terms of frequency "expat" (28 occurrences) is close to Dutch (32 occurrences) The "expat" is addressed directly 23 times in the headings and running text throughout the document. The five other occurrences relate to Twitter (1), Facebook (1) and websites (3). Dutch is mentioned directly on seven occasions throughout the text when informing the reader of the medium of education in schools and language learning requirements and opportunities. The reader is also informed of the relatedness of Dutch, English, and Scandinavian languages, something which few expats may be aware of. The remaining 25 occurrences are found between brackets next to web links informing the reader that the documents, etc. are in Dutch. They serve as a sotto-voce reminder not that a lot of translation work still needs to be done, but of the understandable language realities facing "expats" who plan to "relocate" to Ghent. Though this word ("relocated") only occurs once, its more explicit cognates like emigrate, immigrate and migrate are all conspicuously absent in the document. Relocating contains overtones of moving from one neighbourhood to another and relieves one of the stigma of leaving home or country, whatever the reasons may be. It is not the purpose, however, to criticise the city authorities for their willingness to accommodate newcomers. The purpose is to point to sociocultural and language realities that remain hidden in such a document, realities that the authorities are also very much aware of: see the following word cloud in Figure 9.1 below.

Nevertheless, it seems hard to be an expat if you are not an English speaker or someone with professional qualifications. As a blanket term, it sits uncomfortably with most of the émigrés I have met in my life. Perhaps it's because of the commonly held view that an expat never really arrives, in the sense of becoming a member of a local community and hence never really leaves home, that he or she lives in a state of postponed involvement in all sorts of different ways. One important way is a willingness or capacity to acquire the local language, the term expat seemingly dispensing you

Figure 9.1 Word cloud
Source: Welcome to Ghent

of the obligation or allowing you to deal with the language as an object of curiosity. It is tied to monolingual views on communication and commerce – in the older sense of the term – with our fellow human beings. In this respect, perhaps the term 'relocate' is more appropriate than initially believed. This view of the expat has a long pedigree and at the same time is something to be challenged: "A final challenge is to overcome the implicit understanding of the mobile subject as an enduring political 'Other' in anthropological thought" (Lelièvre & Marshall, 2015, p. 5). Such a description of expat, though alive in the minds of many, can easily be debunked, as much depends on definitions of emigrant and immigrant and on classifications of the same and how the term expat is used in relation to them (Lefleur & Mafouk, 2017). For example, if people are considered 'merely' economic migrants when they are not, they will experience considerable difficulty trying to prove otherwise (Maryns, 2006). Such people would hardly be considered, let alone welcomed as "expats." If they are seeking work, their treatment will very much depend on where they come from, either inside or outside the EU. The term economic migrant is also subject to fluctuations and shifts in how we understand and interpret the four freedoms[11] enshrined in European Treaties, among other treaties. In European terms, the 'freedom of movement of workers,' for example, was once considered something to be advocated and pursued; now it is viewed as the main cause for social dumping, something which paradoxically requires collaboration across the member states to be effective. Such freedom of movement was also one of the main reasons for Brexit and present anti-immigrant sentiment in such countries as Hungary. The financial crisis that hit the world in 2007–2008 and made itself felt with varying degrees of pain and hardship in Europe also created a huge pool of 'economic' migrants who were far from happy with the term or with the prospect of leaving home, particularly those who had invested so much in their studies. Irish economic migrants found themselves once again in Australia, Canada and the USA, where some now live illegally and may run afoul of policies on migrants. Hence 'economic migrant' can hide deeper forms of social unrest that either stem from negative effects of globalisation (Burawoy et al., 2000) or from an opportunity to flee more longstanding forms of prejudice and discrimination at home. In this respect, the Ghent authorities were acutely aware in the past of the prejudice underlying the huge influx of Bulgarian migrants seeking work in the city, the then lord mayor taking the initiative to visit his colleagues in the region with a view to redressing the situation. These initiatives were informed by a sense of fairness for all and are far removed from the fear mongering stances of populist politicians.

The definitions discussed so far tell us more about ourselves, about our stances and resultant policies and funding than those we are trying to define and subsequently classify. So rather than putting forward contesting definitions, we would be better served by conducting (linguistic) ethnographic studies of what immigration[12] means to immigrants as well and what it looks like in a given society (Heller, 2006). It is not the purpose here to engage fully in this debate but to focus on how it plays out in terms of language use and more particularly translation.

All the factors outlined above come into play in various ways and to varying degrees each time a person enters the civil affairs – migration office in Ghent. They are embodied and articulated to varying degrees in the people standing in the queue. Viewed from an auto-ethnographic perspective, these factors are both mine and shared by many:

> Auto-ethnographers must not only use their methodological tools and research literature to analyze experience, but also must consider ways others may experience similar epiphanies; they must use personal experience to illustrate facets of cultural experience, and, in so doing, make characteristics of a culture familiar for insiders and outsiders.
>
> (Ellis et al., 2010, p. 4)

They are instantiations of or concomitant with broader social and global dynamics. They are both real concerns, the stuff of political agendas and statistics on paper: figures can be helpful and have a chastening effect in this respect. They are causes of vexation, real strife, political upheaval and so forth. And the civil affairs office is both a channel and a buffer for all of the above. It is a locus where more immediate concerns stemming from these processes are negotiated through the medium of language and gesture. Whatever your status is and whatever needs to be done will become visible to you and them in the process.

If there was one thing that emerged from an observation of interactions during my visits to the office, however, it was the critical flexibility with which the people working there use language and other resources at their disposal to solve the mass of daily problems with which they are confronted. What follows is a description of a complex set of interactions involving translation into Dutch (from 'Bulgarian') and exchanges in English and French among other languages including the context in which they occurred.

A Typology of Exchanges at the Office

In order to frame an interpreted interaction discussed below, I would first like to provide a concise typology of basic forms of interaction observed between the civil servants and the visitors during the course of my various visits to the office, all of which were determined by degrees of access to (shared) language resources:

1 The person seeking assistance with documentation is accompanied by a person (often his or her senior) who speaks Dutch, addresses the person at the desk directly and liaises with the applicant in his

or her language or in a shared language. Such interactions include triadic sight translation/interpreting turns followed by dyadic turns in Dutch and another language.

2 The person seeking assistance with documentation is accompanied by a person (not necessarily his/her senior) who speaks a mixture of basic Dutch and possibly English, addresses the person at the desk directly in this way and liaises with the applicant in his or her language or in a shared language.

3 The person seeking assistance with documentation addresses the person at the desk directly through basic salutation and gesture. After brief negotiation during which it becomes apparent that the person seeking assistance does not speak Dutch, the person at the desk tries a couple of other languages or simply continues directly in English.

4 The person seeking assistance with documentation addresses the person at the desk directly in Dutch and the event is then conducted in Dutch. This involves possible degrees of competence in Dutch, ranging from what could be called fluent exchanges, which does not mean they are not problematic, to minimal exchanges strongly relying on the documents used in and essential to the exchange. Depending on the degree of competence, he or she may be accompanied by one person or even more who may not address the person at the desk but may interact with the applicant. It would seem that the higher the degree of competence the higher the likelihood that the applicant will be alone.

5 Persons (of a certain age) seeking assistance with documentation address the person at the desk initially in Dutch then switch to French and are addressed in Dutch and French.

6 Persons seeking assistance with documentation are accompanied by a young person who acts as an interpreter for the accompanying adults or peers.

These are all recognisable types of exchanges that have been discussed in the literature, mainly from a professional perspective (Bistra, 1997) but it is interesting to note that these instances all occur at this particular site, possibly alongside others that I failed to notice.

A Description of an Interpreting Event in Group 6

Group 6 contains the only instance of what can be termed overt[13] translation/interpreting (House, 1981), were it only for the fact that the person at the desk addressed the young speaker in the following way: "so you're the interpreter, I take it?" This metapragmatic move made by the woman at the desk framed the event as such. The exchange that followed can hence be considered an interpreting event, though not entirely so as there was more to it than interpreting. Here is a brief description in English, drawn from notes made after the event of what happened along with a paraphrase and the odd quote (all in English translation) of what was said in Dutch. Unfortunately, I was unable to note the elements of this conversation that took place in Turkish as I do not speak Turkish but can assure the reader that it was Turkish from the remarks made in this regard by the interlocutors. Which variety of Turkish it was I cannot say either.

When her number appears on the screen, a young girl shows up at one of the desks with two adult women who obviously cannot speak Dutch. The lady behind the desk asks her what her business is, to which she replies that she would like to help the two women with their papers. She said they wanted to apply for work permits and had all the papers to prove they were/would be legally employed. The woman behind the desk then said the following: "So you're the interpreter, I take it?" to which the young girl said 'yes.' The girl then handed in the papers that were subsequently examined by the woman. Before doing so, the women inquired as to the young girl's age and wondered why she wasn't at school at this hour of the day. The young girl informed her that she had already finished secondary school and was happily employed by the same person who wished to employ the other two women she was interpreting and acting as a go-between for. After perusing the documents briefly, the women behind the desk began to comment on the rates of pay mentioned on the forms, stating that they were extremely low, to the extent that she wondered whether they were legal. She advised the girl to inform the women that they should ask for more money for their work. In the meantime, the young girl continued to interpret all of this to the two women applicants, who seemed a bit dismayed at this turn of events.

During her conversation with the young girl, the woman was also involved in backchannel with a colleague sitting at the desk next to her, from which it became clear that she was highly suspicious of what was going on and feared that the young girl was being used to no good end by her employer/ future employer of the two women applicants. She asked them to wait while she checked the forms thoroughly and retired to the back of the office where she liaised with another colleague.

In the meantime, the young girl moved to another desk where she began chatting with a boy approximately the same age as she and helping him with his exchanges with the person behind the desk. It was obvious from this that her command of Dutch was better than that of the teenage boy. When the woman returned she asked where "the interpreter" was, upon which one of the women applicants went and fetched her from the other desk. The woman behind the desk then addressed the girl directly, stating that unfortunately the forms were incomplete, that another form was also needed, that the employer would have to come here himself and provide more information otherwise she would be unable to proceed or help the two applicants. The girl interpreted this to the two women. The woman behind the desk returned the forms to the girl and the company retired to a seat to wait very briefly for the teenage boy to finish his business at the other desk, after which they all left. When they left, the lady behind the desk turned to her colleague and shook her head. Obviously, this was not the first time she had been involved in such an encounter.

There are few things worth noting from an interpreting point of view about how the woman conducted the encounter. She knew full well that the girl was not a trained interpreter but asked the perfunctory opening question nonetheless, as if she were complying to protocol. She broke frame on at least four occasions (Goffman, 1981), first to inquire about the girl's age and why she wasn't at school, second to comment on the content of/ rates of pay on the forms, thirdly to conduct asides with her colleague voicing her suspicions and fourthly to address the girl directly and not as an interpreter at the end to inform her about the future course of action. All of these incursions would have resulted in friction, if a professional interpreter had been present. However, they do indicate one salient point: that the woman overstepped bounds of professionalism to voice her concern about the well-being of her interlocutors, given the girl's age and level of education and the low wages the applicants would receive. The institutional gatekeeping, on the other hand, manifested itself in shortcomings in the forms. What might have happened if the paperwork had been in order? There is ample literature to show that there is nothing unusual about such forms of non-professional interpreting or the central concern they lay bare, that of a young person being obliged to act and make decisions that are clearly beyond his or her remit or responsibility – for a brief discussion of the positive and negative outcomes involved see Angelelli (2016, pp. 9–11). But as Angelelli further indicates, young people acting as interpreters often feel they have no choice but to do so (Angelelli, 2010, p. 100). She also points out that

> [i]n the presence of linguistic diversity, monolingual interlocutors have no choice but to resort to interpreting for their communicative needs. Many times professional interpreters are not available to meet these needs, and bilinguals (whether adults or youngsters) step up to the plate with varying degrees of success.
>
> (Angelelli, 2010, p. 101)

Though the young girl was no professional interpreter, she clearly came to the office to interpret, which allows us to assume that this wasn't her first time. In this respect, Angelelli's study points to how young bilinguals can become "linguistic advocates for their immediate families and communities" (Angelelli, 2010, p. 100). This is worth reflecting on further in relation to the language practices found in the other groups.

Key Emergent Factors in Groups 1–6

The typology provided above is by no means exhaustive, but it already allows us to realise just how complex these exchanges can be and gives us an understanding of the burden of work facing the people at the desks each day. On the whole, we can identify at least three key factors that play a role in these exchanges.

Competence in Dutch

The first is degree of competence in Dutch. It will also prove apt here to apply Rampton's notions of language expertise, inheritance and affiliation to further delineate the various relations of the applicants to and competence in the Dutch language (Rampton, 1990) and to point to how these relations impact on the multilingual exchanges, including translation and interpreting, which take place at this particular site. The reason for using Rampton's tripartite delineation is because the official discourse on Dutch is still cast in terms of learning the standard language and not some local variety. The lessons immigrants follow are in the standard and competence in the standard is expected in job applications and at work. So, the concept of native speaker still remains the yardstick against which other speakers are judged, despite the fact that the city openly welcomes "expats" and continues to chart minorities and where they live in the city and in the whole of Flanders,[14] a clear recognition of the growing plurality of our societies. As Monica Heller points out in her discussion of the transformation of linguistic minorities in Canada:

> Nevertheless, we will see here the beginnings of the construction of a new basis for legitimacy, one founded not on authenticity and tradition, but rather on pluralism, on the extensiveness of the minorities' social networks and on the quality of the linguistic resources the minority possesses. These values emerge as important because of the nature of the new economy, in which the ability to cross boundaries is important, but so is the construction of new global international norms. Languages are still seen as autonomous systems; what is valued is multilingualism as a set of parallel monolingualisms, not as a hybrid system. What is valued also is a mastery of a standard language, shared across boundaries and a marker of social status.
>
> (Heller, 2006, p. 5)

Heller wrote this in the revised edition of her book just before the enthusiasm for the seeming benefits of globalisation were washed away by the 2007–2008 financial crisis, a crisis it must be pointed out, that set off a new intensified wave of emigration. I am not arguing that Flanders is following the same policy towards migrants as Canada, but Heller's remarks on language are equally applicable to Flanders and can be found in its policy documents.[15]

To return to Rampton and the three delineations of native speakerism (language expertise, inheritance and affiliation), the persons most likely to fall under inheritance can be found in groups 1 and 6, respectively. In the main, the Dutch speakers in group 1 are of Flemish extraction and have more than likely grown up speaking a variety of Dutch and will have learned standard Dutch if not at home then at school. The girl in group 6 may not speak Dutch at home but certainly will have learned it at school and spoken it along with the local variety with some of her peers. When it comes to Dutch, she will probably be appreciated for her expertise by the two Turkish applicants but will be 'kept close' in terms of inheritance when it comes to Turkish. Given her comments, the woman behind the desk clearly places her on the side of inheritance in Dutch and expects an appropriate degree of expertise in conducting the exchange (see further on 'fractal recursivity' and scale in chapter 5 (Slembrouck, 2011, p. 159)). This would seem to indicate various degrees if not types of inheritance. The people in group 1 comply with the norm of parallel monolingualisms (Heller, 2006, p. 5), whereas the girl in group 6, albeit innocently, draws attention to the sociolinguistic reality of the city by presenting herself as an interpreter, or to be more precise, by being willing to take on the role of interpreter attributed to her by the woman behind the desk.

None of the persons in groups 2–5 (including the applicants in group 1) were brought up or were schooled from an early age in Dutch, except for those in group 4 who are from the Netherlands (and are required to renew their residence permits from time to time). So, the people brought together in groups 2–5 can be considered as possessing varying degrees of expertise in Dutch and may or may not consider themselves as having some form of affiliation with the language. But it must be noted too that duration of stay may not necessarily imply an increase in degree of affiliation.

The older French-speaking persons in group 5 are very often Belgian citizens with seemingly lower levels of competence in Dutch but this is not always the case, and it is not the purpose here to generalise. Their competence in and possible affiliation to Dutch is further complicated by other (sociolinguistic) allegiances within the broader Belgian context. It is important to note that despite sociolinguistic realities – multilingualism and the daily use of Flemish varieties of Dutch in public spaces – the discourse on (competence in) the standard remains omnipresent and applies both to newcomers and to Flemings from all walks of life (viz. the reference to Terminus above).

Importance of / Reliance on Documents

The second factor is the degree of importance of or reliance on the documents themselves in conducting the exchange. In groups 2–4, we can clearly see the importance of the documents themselves and the trajectory involved, including possible multiple visits to the office and consultations at home and elsewhere with others who help complete the process of complying with the formalities involved, also through translation. These documents form an aid in collaborative meaning making during encounters between staff and applicants. In this way they are constantly pointed and referred to and drawn on during the interactions. To return once again to Hanks (1987) and genre, the documents do not merely comprise textual features but form the documentary component of "orientation frameworks," "interpretive procedures" and "sets of expectations" that will be understood differently and negotiated accordingly by the actors involved. Hence, the documentation process is completed incrementally, which further demonstrates the material nature of these exchanges, how the documents themselves are vital to the process of carrying out the task 'correctly' as they will again be referred and gestured to at various stages of completion up to the point that they can be handed in or sent off – see Maryns (2006, pp. 14–198) for her meticulous description of text trajectories.

Overt/Covert Translation and Interpreting

Most importantly for the purposes of the overall argument in this case, the third factor is the presence of overt or covert translation / interpreting throughout the exchanges. As is the case with all the other translation practices mentioned so far, they are framed by forms of multilingualism that are often dressed up as serial or parallel monolingualism (Heller, 2006; Piller, 2016), which makes them harder to spot and hence theorise the nature of the translation involved. All the exchanges, except for those in group 6, comprise some form of covert translation (House, 1981), the types of interaction falling under group 1 being the most obvious. The exchanges in group 1 seem at first glance forms of serial or parallel monolingualism mediated by the Dutch speaker accompanying the applicant, as the person at the desk and the applicant do not share a language. But perhaps more importantly for reasons of expediency, the interlocutors are not allowed by the ad-hoc rules of exchange set up at the beginning of the event to discover if they actually do speak Dutch. It can thus be argued that the default interactional order in such exchanges is monolingual until negotiated or accepted as being otherwise. These exchanges can also be clearly cast in terms of covert translation and interpreting during which the Dutch speaker resorts to 'un-explicated' consecutive interpreting strategies to relate the official's discourse to the applicant and the applicant's to the official or alternately by using paraphrase in both languages of exchange to convey instructions in both directions. Here, as in many multilingual exchanges, the problem of translation is magically resolved by segmenting and sequencing language use, thus giving it the semblance of separate events, which is belied by the overall purpose of the communicative event.[16]

So, it is worth noting that the Dutch speaker did not present him- or herself as an interpreter in the instances I noticed, as the young girl clearly did or at least accepted. This can certainly be also linked to the language ideologies mentioned in Heller (2006) and set out above. The Dutch speaker presents himself as such to the person at the desk and is tacitly acknowledged as such by the applicant for the purposes of acquiring the right papers. In contrast, the young girl explicitly presents herself as bilingual, which brings with it a different set of interactional rules and procedures, and which, it must also be noted, the woman behind the desk initiated and was willing to comply with, to a degree.

To return to the interpreting event in group 6 from a more general perspective, one can rightly ask whether the stance taken by the woman behind the desk (see the previous subsection) is the result of the increased pressure she and her colleagues are under in dealing with such an influx of migrants or whether there are other factors involved as well: for example, exposing forms of potential exploitation masked as positive employment strategies she could not help but notice. Another thing is also clear: such encounters are not envisaged in the positive discourse addressed to "expats." It would be a mistake, however, to equate the woman's stance as being that of the whole office but then again, I did note a certain sense of frustration during my various visits when it came to balancing front-office workload and psychological strain with what can be loosely termed as policy demands, i.e. sticking to Dutch in all encounters being one of them.

To return to my own predicament as part of the general discussion, the contrast between front-office coping practices and the slow-turning mill of bureaucracy in "Brussels" also became apparent when I was finally informed I could go and collect my renewed residence permit. As the person at the desk had said "they are being extra careful about everyone these days after all that had happened," which may explain the delay, but raises questions about whether bona-fide residents had also become suspicious, something clearly voiced in right-wing discourse on migration. So, I went through the same procedure again: waited in the queue at the door, when I got there, showed the woman at reception the letter stating I could come and collect my permit, was issued a number, took a seat and waited once again for my number to appear on the screen next to the desk number. When my number appeared, I went to the desk, showed the woman the letter and told her I was coming to pick up my residence permit, that all (document) formalities had been complied with, etc. She looked at me in disbelief. Surely it could not be that simple; she then looked back along the row of desks to someone who was clearly her superior and inquired about my case. The man approached her and recognised me: I had already spoken to him on a few occasions before in straightening out my documents and making sure they were complete and filled in correctly. He then addressed his colleague in Ghent dialect, which I assume he thought I did not understand[17]: "Och Heere, diene mens, 't is al de zoveelste keer, is 't nog altijd nie in orde" (Oh God, the poor man; it must be the umpteenth time, has not that been sorted yet) upon which the woman produced the permit, which I was very relieved to sign and also pay the surcharge for.

The typology of exchanges and the three factors that play a signifi-cant role in defining these interactions all emerged from being part of, observing and reflecting on the tedious process of getting my papers in order much like all the other people who visit the office. They underlie or are adjacent to the multilingual and hence translation and interpreting practices experienced at the city office. Ostensibly these practices are part and parcel of getting your papers sorted and what it means to do so but they also reveal other elements of a broader social canvas, including the hidden agenda of an employer with seemingly good intentions.

Further Comments

Acquiring the right papers can be a real struggle for some or simply a source of (prolonged) annoyance for others. Along the continuum be-tween struggle and annoyance, one can find people with various degrees and types of (language and cultural) competence (see typology above). We mustn't forget, however, that the people mentioned in the typology – more pertinently groups 2 and 3, for they remain less linguistically visible in this discussion – clearly have sets of language competences but perhaps not those set out in policy documents. This means that such vague no-tions as multilingualism have to be contextualised and determined be-forehand if possible, as they have a bearing on the genre of activity and related "papers" involved. To return to Friel, the struggle to acquire/pro-duce "documents, and images is very much the business of those working at the office and at the same time the goal of the thousands of people that frequent the office daily, including me. The difference is that you are reminded of, or rather, that you are confirmed in the fact, not that you are an individual that somehow belongs to a nation (as Friel mentions) but that you are clearly a foreign national residing in a foreign country, no matter whether you have embraced the Dutch language in terms of expertise or affiliation, which, though off-putting, I suppose is only fair.

Notes

1 Thanks to Prof. Andrew Chesterman. See his inspiring keynote lecture at EST 2016 in Aarhus: http://bcom.au.dk/research/conferencesandlectures/est-congress-2016/stream/ (09/12/2016) see also Seamus Heaney's equally inspiring discussion of Terminus (Heaney, 1998).
2 https://www.in-gent.be/voor-jou/nederlands (13/09/2022).
3 A game in Wittgenstein's sense of the term: "One can say that the concept of a game is a concept with blurred edges" (Wittgenstein, 2007, p. 71e).
4 This was an oblique reference to the terrorist attacks in Zaventem and Maalbeek (Brussels) in 2016. I felt rather uneasy about the prospect of being numbered among those who do something of the sort.
5 Brussels sets off its own complex inward- (Belgian) and outward-moving (European, global) chain-lightning of indexicalities: Jacques Brel, pralines, regulations on the shape of bananas, Donald Trump's hell hole, etc., etc.

6 RTE Documentary on Brian Friel (2000) (3:09–3:27) https://www.youtube.com/watch?v=L5-Mj6RMB2E&t=175s.
7 This brief exchange was translated from Dutch.
8 For a discussion of the terms immigrant, emigrant, expat and foreigner and for a full debate on immigration in Belgium see Lafleur & Marfouk 2017 – Dutch translation 2018.
9 https://stad.gent/en/expats-ghent (13/09/2022).
10 Personal correspondence with Jim O'Driscoll, University of Huddersfield, https://pure.hud.ac.uk/en/persons/jim-odriscoll (13/09/2022).
11 The 'acquis' in this area is based on the Treaty on the Functioning of the European Union, in particular Articles 63–66. Annex I of Directive 88/361/EEC provides the definition of the different types of capital movements. Additional interpretation of the above Articles is provided by relevant case-law of the European Court of Justice and Commission Communications 97/C220/06 and 2005/C293/02.
12 For a theoretical ethnography of migration see Fitzgerald (2006). For an anthropology of mobility see Lelièvre and Marshall (2015). For a discussion of the anthropological literature on migration see Tilman Lanz (Last Modified: 24 July 2013 DOI: 10.1093/obo/9780199766567-0098).
13 Overt translation - Definition: translation, which is intended to be recognized as a translation, e.g. because it is clearly bound to the source culture; it may have a different function from that of the original (compare "covert translation" In contrast, covert translation – Definition: translation that aims to present itself as an original, concealing its nature as a translation (House, 1981).
14 http://integratiebeleid.vlaanderen.be/lokale-inburgerings-en-integratiemonitor-editie-2018 (consulted 1309/2022) see also a report for 2022 on people of foreign origin on the same page.
15 http://integratiebeleid.vlaanderen.be/beleid (consulted 13/09/2022).
16 See Vološinov on the primacy of genre in conceptualising and analysing any speech event.
17 The use of a non-standard variety of Dutch can be considered as part of back-office behaviour which most applicants will probably not be privy to, specifically for that reason.

References

Angelelli, C. V. (2010). A professional ideology in the making: Bilingual youngsters interpreting for their communities and the notion of (no) choice. *Translation and Interpreting Studies*, 5(1), 94–108.

Angelelli, C. V. (2016). Looking back: A study of (ad-hoc) family interpreters. *European Journal of Applied Linguistics; Berlin*, 4(1), 5–31.

Bistra, A. (1997). A typology of interpreter-mediated events. *The Translator*, 3(2), 153–174. doi:10.1080/13556509.1997.10798996

Bourdieu, P. (1980). *Le sens pratique*. Paris : Les éditions de minuit.

Burawoy, M., Blum, J. A., George, S., Gille, Z., Thayer, M., Gowan, T., Haney, L., Klawiter, M., Lopez, S., & O'Riain, S. (2000). *Global Ethnography. Forces, Connections, and Imaginations in a Postmodern World*. Berkeley: University of California Press.

Butz, D., & Besio, K. (2009). Autoethnography. *Geography Compass*, 3(5), 1660–1674 [Peer Reviewed Journal].

Ellis, C. E., Adams, T. E., & Bochner, A. P. (2019)) Autoethnography: An Overview at http://dx.doi.org/10.17169/fqs-12.1.1589 (consulted 15/02/2019).

French, R., McCrory, M., & McKay, K. (Eds.). (2019). *I Wouldn't Start from Here: The Second-Generation Irish in Britain.* London: The Wild Geese Press.

Hall, N. (2004). The child in the middle: Agency and diplomacy in language brokering events. In G. Hansen, K. Malmkjær, & D. Gile (Eds.), *Claims, Changes and Challenges in Translation Studies* (Benjamins Translation Library, 50, pp. 285–296). Amsterdam/Philadelphia, PA: Benjamins, 285–296.

Hall, N., & Sham, S. (2007). Language brokering as young people's work: Evidence from Chinese adolescents in England. *Language and Education,* 21(1), 16–30.

Heaney, S. (1998). Something to write home about. *The Princeton University Library Chronicle,* 59(3), 621–632. www.jstor.org/stable/26509355 (last accessed 24/05/2020).

Heller, M. (2006). *Linguistic Minorities and Modernity: A Sociolinguistic Ethnography.* London: Longman.

House, J. (1981). *A Model for Translation Quality Assessment.* Tübingen: Narr Google Scholar.

Hymes, D. H. (1972). On Communicative Competence. In J. B. Pride & J. Holmes (Eds.), *Sociolinguistics. Selected Readings* (pp. 269–293). Harmondsworth: Penguin.

Kiberd, D. (1996). *Inventing Ireland: The Literature of the Modern Nation.* London: Vintage.

Lafleur, J. M., & Marfouk, A. (2018). *Pourquoi l'immigration? 21 questions que se posent les Belges sur les migrations internationales au XXIe siècle* (Collection Carrefours, 9). Louvain-la-Neuve: Academia-L'Harmattan.

Lelièvre, M. A., & Marshall, M. E. (2015). 'Because Life It Selfe Is But Motion': Toward an Anthropology of Mobility. *Anthropological Theory* 15(4), 434–471.

Maryns, K. (2006). *The Asylum Speaker. Language in the Belgian Asylum Procedure* (Encounters v. 7). Manchester: St. Jerome Publisher.

Mufwene, S. S. (2001). *The Ecology of Language Evolution.* Cambridge: Cambridge University Press.

O'Toole, F. (1998). *The Ex-isle of Erin: Images of a Global Ireland.* Dublin: New Island Books.

Pennycook, A. (2007). *Global Englishes and Transcultural Flows.* London: Routledge.

Piller, I. (2016). Monolingual ways of seeing multilingualism. *Journal of Multicultural Discourses,* 11(1), 25–33. doi:10.1080/17447143.2015.1102921

Rampton, B. (1990). Displacing the "native speaker": Expertise, affiliation and inheritance. *ELT Journal,* 44, 97–101.

Silverstein, M. (2003). Indexical order and the dialectics of sociolinguistic life. *Language & Communication,* 23, 193–229. doi:10.1016/S0271-5309(03)00013-2

Slembrouck, S. (2011). Globalization theory and migration. In R. Ruth Wodak, B. Johnstone, & P. Paul Kerswill (Eds.), *The SAGE Handbook of Sociolinguistics* (pp. 153–164). London: Sage.

Some Tentative Conclusions

As was stated from the outset in the Introduction, it seems like there is nothing new to the relationship between translation, migration and the city. It is probably as old as cities themselves and most likely instrumental in their growth and power of attraction. The relationship may even give us a way of re-imagining the myth of Babel by framing it as a nostalgic yearning for an innocent pre-urban monolingual existence in which understanding was given and self-evident. Having said so, I must admit I know little or nothing about Babel save to note its inherent support for monolingualism. The sociolinguistic realities of urban life have long since made any form of monolingual dream impossible to realise, despite the many attempts by nation states to build their foundations on it. In fact, it may also be the monolingual bias underlying national and regional languages that has prevented us for so long from taking (urban) multilingualism seriously and examining its dynamics more pertinently, particularly from a translational perspective.

Assumptions and Underpinnings – Reprise

Multilingualism and its presence was one of the basic assumptions underlying this work from the beginning, but which forms it might take in the sites under scrutiny still remained to be seen. It was also assumed that the forms of multilingualism would play a role in the types of translation and interpreting discovered at the various sites. The studies of the various sites has thrown up various articulations of multilingual and related translation and interpreting practices: those on the tram or at the city office differ from those at the Irish pub or at the school, for example. The study as a whole has drawn attention to local factors that may have been either taken for granted or perhaps understood too simply as backdrop or surrounding context. As the delineations revealed in the various case studies show, a blanket notion of urban multilingual and related translation and interpreting practices is only useful as a point of departure. Forms of natural translation have been discovered in all the sites. Only in one instance did these forms overlap with professional translation and interpreting, i.e. at the school. At no time was it assumed that

DOI: 10.4324/9781003363811-11

(natural) translation could be reduced by the same essential socio-cognitive process. As Risku, Rogl and Milosevic point out,

> Now seen as an interaction process (Risku, 2014), the translation process then includes elements inside and outside the brain and the body, as well as objects within the environment.
> (Clark & Chalmers, 1998; Risku et al., 2019, p. 3)

In trying to discover instances of natural translation at the various sites, attention has been consistently paid to the "elements" and "objects" Risku, Rogl and Milosovic mention. Translation has been viewed and examined throughout from the point of view of its collective instantiation or as an "interaction process" (Risku, 2014). As Cronin remarks, "[t]herefore, any attempt to discuss translation and its role in human society and culture must take into account the essential relationship between *techne* and cultural development" (Cronin, 2002). Hence, care has been taken throughout this study to tie translation and interpreting practices to their immediate contexts and the activities they emerged from.

In this respect, genres, including their textual precipitates, have proved to be shaping factors in translation in each of the sites discussed above. Letters have served as translational/interpreting anchors in Chapters 4, 7 and 8, cookbooks, menus, beer mats and (televised) sports in Chapters 5 and 6. Various forms of personal documents including residence permits were vital elements in the translational interactions examined in Chapter 9, as were sport, music and cooking in Chapter 3. There is nothing unusual about this on the face of it, were it not for what emerged from the translational interaction with or within these genres.

Take the letters in Chapters 4, 7 and 8 for example. How were these letters dealt with and end up simply in terms of Vermeer's notion of *translatum* or "the result of translational action" (Vermeer, 2000, p. 221)? According to Vermeer, a translatum is oriented towards the target culture. In each of these cases, the source and target cultures occupy the same space, however, and the action required after translating each letter has to happen in the source culture, in a manner of speaking. Hence the goals of the letters and their translations are basically the same, but as Vermeer points out their formulation and the distribution of their content may differ greatly (Vermeer in Nord, 1997). The difference in distribution and content is clear in the three translations of the letters and each translation also brought with it a set of instructions on how to take further action. These instructions were not always specifically or implicitly present in the letters except perhaps to some extent in the letters in Chapter 9.

A link can be made in terms of interaction between Vermeer's functional approach to translation and Hank's take on genre as "orienting frameworks, interpretive procedures, and sets of expectations" (Hanks, 1987, p. 670). The letters opened and translated on the tram (Chapter 4) at the letterboxes (Chapter 7), or at the school gate (Chapter 9) were approached by the participants in each case with the discretion expected when viewing (someone else's) letter. The interpretive procedures (including translation) were carried out with a view to helping the recipient/owner of the letter take correct action, which is what he or she hoped for or somehow expected, as did they all. But these three letter translation / interpreting events all hinge on the primary everyday speech genre of requesting help (Bakhtin, 1986, p. 60): by the man at the letterboxes, the woman on the tram, the parents at the school gate. Those who provided help responded to these requests thereby completing the utterance, which also included translation. Furthermore, the responses at the letterboxes and school gate were anticipated and together with the requests have become structured parts of daily practices and exchanges. Those at the school gate can also be considered an expression of the school's ethos, those on the tram simply an interesting instance of everyday politeness, perhaps.

Globalisation has remained more or less the ghost in the machine in this study, something that somehow underpins much of what has been reported on in this work. At the same time no conscious effort has been made to connect it directly as a category to each of the cases in the research. It is visible in the globalisation of the Irish pub and hence the Irish pubs in Ghent. But I think it fair to argue that the global spread of Italian pizzerias is older than the more recent wave of globalisation. It is visible in the fast-food chains and coffee vendors on the high streets, which we did not visit. It is considered the driver of superdiversity (Vertovec, 2007) and is clearly audible and visible in the civil affairs office of the city and in the discourse for expats on the city website. If we take the link between globalisation and superdiversity to be given, superdiversity as such still remains hard to pin down because of the complexity of the phenomena the term encapsulates in relation to migration (Vertovec, 2007) and evidence of migration in various forms is visible in all the cases discussed above.

Our focus was on how superdiversity (as a manifestation of globalisation and migration) became visible in particular shapes of multilingualism and translation and interpreting practices. Various different shapes and practices have emerged from the case studies. This allows us to suggest that the civil affairs office is not superdiverse in the same way as the block of flats or the Irish pub or the inner-city school are. Superdiversity does not manifest itself in blanket terms in the same way everywhere in a city, which is in line with what Vertovec points out by way of recapitulation in a more recent article:

> Super-diversity is a summary term proposed also to point out that the new migration patterns not only entailed variable combinations of these traits,[1] but that their combinations produced new hierarchical social positions, statuses or stratifications.
>
> (Vertovec, 2019, p. 126)

We can turn to the description of the interpreting event in Chapter 9 to show how it illustrates "hierarchical social positions, statuses or stratifications" in the making, for example, i.e. the two migrant women trying to get their papers sorted and a not too bona fide employer who is trying to help them. We can mention the inner-city school in Chapter 8 in pointing to the precarious situations some migrant children find themselves in but on the positive side to the responses of the teachers working there and their attempts to alleviate the situation. These and other elements or articulations of superdiversity emerged in studying language and translation practices at the seven sites reported on here.

Cities and migration were mentioned with reference to the literature at the beginning of the book. What emerges from the various cases is a variegated picture of a city as a composite entity addressed through and emerging from local community practices. Its official face is visible in registration processes in the civil affairs office (Chapter 9), in the school (Chapter 8) and its connections with city educational policy, in the block of flats (Chapter 7) and the official letters the people have to respond to and the appointments they have to keep and in the sometimes troubled relations with the social worker in Chapter 3. Its dynamic multilingual face is visible at all the various sites reported on above along with the migrants and others who have helped create this dynamic.

Having returned to assumptions and underpinnings to see how they bore out across the various sites under scrutiny, it is now time to move on to the task of drawing a set of tentative conclusions based on what has emerged from this study. This will first involve an attempt at tracing similarities across the seven sites, second at outlining the distinctions they threw up and third, to the extent that the observations made, and materials gathered for this study allow, to draw lines of meta-connection between the tools and concepts used to examine them.

Tracing Similarities

Again to return to the beginning, the goal in this ethnography was to find and investigate natural translation and interpreting practices at a number of sites in the same city. How this study would fit into Marcus's recommendations for following things in doing a multi-sited ethnography was initially unclear. Among his other recommendations, might this study fall under the recommendation to "follow the people" or "follow the metaphor," for example (Marcus, 1998, pp. 90–98)? Marcus cites migrant and diaspora studies as examples of following people. Migrants are ever present in this work but it was more a matter of being at the places where they gather to observe and capture translation and interpreting events rather than following them in their own trajectories. Regarding metaphor, "[w]hen the thing traced is within the realm of discourse and modes of thought, then the circulation of signs, symbols and metaphors guides the design of the ethnography" (Marcus, 1998, p. 92). Following the metaphor would involve "trying to trace the social correlates and groundings of associations that are more clearly alive in language use and print and media" (Marcus, 1998, p. 92). But following the metaphor doesn't really fit either as it would entail tracing elements of discourse, signs or symbols in their journey across sites, the icons used in Irish pubs being a possible case in point. But this work involves chasing forms of discourse practices across different sites, i.e. translation and interpreting. The project grew out of an awareness of translation and interpreting practices in the local community, but there is a large difference between noticing and regularly being involved in something and studying it in any detail in situ. What certainly could be done in following Marcus's recommendation was to "trace the social correlates and groundings of associations" of which translation is a part. These correlates and groundings have been shown in each case in this work but what is it that ties them all together?

First, we have shown that translation is not an activity that takes place across national borders but across counters and tables in pubs and restaurants, across desks in city offices, on public transport and in classrooms, playgrounds and at school gates or next to the letterboxes or at kitchen tables in a multilingual block of flats. This finding is confirmed by other studies in natural translation (Harris, 2013) and in TS (Antonini et al., 2017).

But what mainly emerges from all of these sites is the binding role played by translation and also invoked by its use. Next to solving communication and other problems, intralingual translation (Standard Dutch to Ghent dialect) serves as a factor in strengthening social cohesion in the block of flats and also in the Irish pub (Standard English to Irish English). Translation in and out of Dutch from a variety of languages at the school brings school staff and parents together in their common concern for the well-being of the children. The shape of the translation project at the Italian restaurant is also a direct expression of their friendship with others and of their belonging to the local community. In a similar vein, the menus in the Irish pub were translated into Dutch by a local customer who is fond of Irish culture. The interpreting event at the civil affairs office also highlights interpreting as a binding factor that extends in at least two directions at the same time. The woman behind the desk reminds the young girl of her role as an interpreter (an interesting professional move) and even says she should be at school, judging by her age. This degree of familiarity shows a concern for the young girl's well-being that goes beyond professional decorum. At the same time the young girl binds the two migrant workers to her by translating for them into their shared language in a seriously face threatening official situation. The woman on the tram draws on a sense of belonging to the same community to ask for help. The act of translation then becomes a shared problem-solving project among seemingly total strangers. Even the seeming absence of translation in Chapter 3 stems from the idea of connectedness (as a project or goal), a connectedness that dispenses with the need for translation, which is a very interesting thought in a multilingual situation.

All of the translation and interpreting work discussed in this book was done by non-professionals, none of whom identified as translator/interpreter. As was mentioned earlier on, the term non-professional is problematic and needs to be revisited here at the end of the study. The term places those labelled by it beyond the pale of the professional, which is of course true but beside the point. The term natural translator is perhaps more apt but remains somehow inscrutable. Though it's highly laudable, we may rightly wonder what's natural about it. Natural invokes the relative ease with which someone acquires translation skills outside of professional training. We can hence trace it as part of someone's "indexical biography" (Blommaert & Backus, 2013) or as an acquired competence (Hymes, 1972) from a quite young age (Angelelli, 2016). In relation to this study, the term natural points in the direction of translation being something that happens by itself, as it were. It doesn't require a professional protocol to set it in motion. It is recognised as a (shared) resource that can be drawn on when needed, as a practice that is even structured or regular, as in the block of flats, the school, the civil affairs office, for example. It should also be noted it is also a designated resource. Not everybody translates in the school, block of flats, etc. It is tied to "the social correlates and groundings of associations" (Marcus, 1998, p. 92) and help them function as such, which explains its different articulations across the various sites. Though this is true of professional translation as well, taken together, the instances of translation examined here are tied to these social correlates and groundings in a different way, which cannot be simply passed off as the result of a lack of the financial resources associated with professional translation. It is perhaps their immediacy and degree of closeness to their social correlates and groundings as a problem-solving socially-cohesive resource that link the various articulations of translation discovered in this study. Even if their goals are similar, professional practices still stage and frame translation in a different way.

In terms of similarity, the translation practices studied in this volume also follow and mirror local and migrant population flows, as all the cases illustrate in some way. These practices have acquired a certain degree of permanence that belongs to and reflects the dynamics of family and community life (see especially Chapters 7 and 8).

In terms of a general rationale, we can point to a shared recognition of cultural and language differences as a positive force, at the same time an awareness of (sometimes harsh) economic realities and socio-political constraints, and an accompanying sense of the importance of the egalitarian and ethical in daily interactions.

Tracing Distinctions

Marcus's notion of "social correlates and groundings" (1998, p. 90) have been used in part to trace similarities across the various sites in this study. These social correlates and groundings are also markers of distinction between the sites. Natural translation and interpreting practices have indeed been found at all the sites but despite similarity of type the practices serve different purposes or functions. Intralingual translation at the block of flats is as immediate as intralingual translation at the Irish pub but it is a far more urgent affair in terms of human consequences in the former than in the latter. This hinges on longstanding issues of literacy. In contrast, the insistence of the use of non-standard and local varieties of language in translation at the Italian restaurant is not a literacy issue but a conscious choice taken by all in the interests of authenticity and inclusion. Not using professional translators and interpreters at the school, except in certain "official" situations, is also a conscious choice taken for the purpose of lowering the threshold of communication between the school, its pupils and their parents. The distinction made between discretionary (learning purposes, practice) and (usually designated) non-discretionary interpreting (necessary exchanges with local customers) at the Irish pub also illustrates different orders of communication and related constraints in terms of politeness and good relations with the local community. The intersemiotic translation in the pub and the translation/interpreting event on the tram both happened during encounters between strangers and hence can be considered as exercises in intercultural politeness; but again they did serve very different primary purposes, the former explaining (the rules of) a game, the latter solving a problem. The take on translation in social work can be understood as a weariness and wariness of the havoc language can wreak. The types of translation and interpreting that takes place at the civil affairs office ostensibly serve the purpose of sorting out an applicant's papers but they also index different degrees of belonging and senses of foreignness and other factors pointed out by Vertovec in defining superdiversity (Vertovec, 2007, 2019). There is no overarching answer to the why of all these forms of translation, however, but they do refract, in various ways, aspects of the superdiversity they are involved in and form responses to.

Lines of Meta-Connection

Transcribing and analysing the materials gathered during the course of this project has meant mustering and bringing into play a whole range of tools and concepts from TS, sociolinguistics, anthropology and other areas of study. The work of disassembling and reassembling the materials analytically mainly began by starting with familiar tools from TS and then moving outward (but also further inward). This involved drawing on concepts from other disciplines to explicate layers of context, among other things, and to help in trying to explain what had been observed and recorded. Using this set of tools on complex and at times ephemeral materials over a prolonged period not only allowed me to see connections in the data in and across the seven sites but also between the tools themselves or in terms of their rationale. During the analysis, links to larger social processes of translation and transfer also became apparent. These links require some attention even though they reach beyond the project as it was first conceived and hence lie outside the study proper. It must be pointed out that these links emerged from reflection on and only were made possible by what has been observed and what has been given by the participants during the project.

Zones, Places and Spaces

The closeness and immediacy of natural translation pointed to in Tracing Similarities allows us to take a closer look at various views on the notion of space: "translation space[2]" (Cronin, 2006), "translation zone" (Apter, 2006; Cronin & Simon, 2014), "the space of translation" (Hanks, 2014) and "mundane metrolingualism" (Pennycook & Otsuji, 2015, 2019) for their research at various places in cities. The purpose is to contrast these notions with de Certeau's notion of "space" (de Certeau, 1988, p. 117). Cronin's notion of "translation space" is highly flexible and can range from a "small theatre" to "voice recognition and speech synthesis technology" (Cronin, 2006, p. 68) and draws on Lefebvre's tripartite notion of space as perceived, conceived and lived (Lefebvre, 1991), which offers us a way into various forms of semiosis. In contrast, Cronin and Simon use the term translation zone "more specifically to refer to the cultural and geographical spaces that give rise to intense language traffic," and note that "[t]hese spaces are a product of the city's history" (Cronin & Simon, 2014, pp. 121–122). In relation to this work, there is indeed intense multilingual and translational traffic involved,[3] and there are definite links, especially with the history of working-class neighbourhoods. These are also places where migrants, as denizens "may move through and knowingly inhabit" (Cronin, 2008, p. 267). To be fair however, it is hard to use the term "translation zone" as it is used in Cronin and Simon (2014) to encompass the places discussed in this work as there are no zones beyond or encircling them that do not have some translational element as well. At the same time, each of the areas discussed in this work could be considered a translation zone but only to the extent that it fades into another. Perhaps the civil affairs office is the most dynamic of them all but then again only during office hours. Hanks in turn views the "space of translation" as being both inter- and intracultural and further states:

> Drawing on the semiotics of Roman Jakobson, C. S. Peirce, and Charles Morris, the paper argues that intracultural translation plays a constitutive role in the social life of any human group, and not only in mediating between different groups and languages.
>
> (Hanks, 2014, p. 18)

This view is in line with the findings of this study, the main difference being that intracultural and intercultural translation are happening in the same locality and both play "a constitutive role in the social life" of a human group, while also "mediating between different groups and languages" within it.

Pennycook and Otsuji address forms of multilingualism that coincide with this space of translation. To recap, in examining mundane (everyday) metrolingualism, which "describes the ways in which people of different and mixed backgrounds use, play with and negotiate identities through language" Pennycook and Otsuji wish to "show how it operates in markets, cafés, streets, shops and other social city spaces" (Pennycook & Otsuji, 2015, p. 3). In doing so, they factor in time to account for shifts in language use in the same marketplace during the same day, for example. This is a shorter time frame than the historical frame pointed to in Cronin and Simon (2014), however. The sites in this work share elements of both time frames, in different measure. This brings us to de Certeau's notion of space "as the effect produced by the operations that orient it, situate it, temporalize it" (de Certeau, 1988, p. 117). This is clearly a semiotic take on space as a meaningful entity, which includes a time factor as one of three ways of dealing with its operations, those related to translation in our case. We could then ask if and how the notion of space might apply to any neighbourhood or café or street within it as a meaning-making element of focus. By way of further explanation, de Certeau makes a distinction between space and place, place (lieu) being "the order of whatever kind in accord with which elements are distributed in relationships of co-existence" (de Certeau, 1984, p. 117). Taken together, these relationships define a place as a distinct location, like a market or a café, for example. Maintaining the distinction between place and space is important methodologically, as we can already suppose that a place will have an impact on the (potential) semiotic activity that goes on there (viz. a courtroom versus a café). In terms of the relationships that define it, a place[4] might also be or become a translation space – it all remains to be seen. For example, I never thought an Irish pub could be the translation space it turned out to be.

Images in Discourse

The next line of meta-connections I would like to address involves discursive image construction or invocation in some form, which allows me to bring together a small set of concepts that conceptualise such image construction or invocation. Discursive image construction was visible in the way the inner-city school presents itself to the public eye. This has been dealt with in terms of ethos in Chapter 8. Next to this, participants at the various sites drew on national, regional and cultural stereotypes as a means of characterising, explaining certain forms of behaviour, or typifying ways of speaking (viz. how people typify others from different counties in Ireland by their "accents" during banter in the Irish pub; how the people at the Italian restaurant explain regional differences in types of people in terms of the basic ingredients in their cuisine; how the girls on the tram index the woman as Bulgarian because of the way she spoke; how the people at the inner-city school create an image of themselves and their school in their discourse and actions; and how the people in the block of flats create an egalitarian self image in the way they talk about exchanges in the building.

Such image constructions have a metaphoric element to them in the basic sense of explaining one thing in terms of another, i.e. Irish therefore wild, for example. Image markers also function metonymically in that a single marker can index a whole set of characteristics, viz. associations connected with the word Sicilian, for example. Stereotyping is omnipresent in all types of writing about and representations of people around the world, and these writings and representations have been studied in great detail (Beller & Leerssen, 2007). Beller and Leerssen's analyses run in and across languages and cultures, which is important for this brief discussion here. Based on their analyses, they begin by positing two basic forms of stereotyping: one constructing an image of the self or *auto (or self) image* and one constructing an image of the other or *hetero image* (Leerssen in Beller & Leerssen 2007, p. 343) The banter in the Irish pub mainly involves the friendly mocking of hetero images within the same Irish language and cultural context. The Italians in the restaurant construct both regional auto and hetero images distributed throughout Italy that are also predicated on distinctions between standard and dialects. The distinguishing hetero image of 'Bulgarian' used on the tram draws on varieties of the same language (Turkish) across two cultures with historical connections to the Ottoman Empire. In contrast, the constructions that emerge from the discourse of the people in the block of flats and the inner-city school are mainly self images. The hetero images in their discourse are those of officialdom marked by its use of standard Dutch. It must be noted here that these images make no claim to truth but they are taken at their face value in the course of interaction, face being the operative word. In terms of languages and cultures auto and hetero images may also overlap in the school. Auto and hetero image are being used here in relation to everyday speech and not writing.

Image construction and stereotyping as part and parcel of everyday speech have been studied in detail by Agha (2007). Examining these processes in terms of enregisterment, Agha considers a register of discourse as a

> cultural model of action (a) which links speech repertoires to stereotypic indexical values … In the case of registers of discourse, the relevant performable signs are speech repertoires; their stereotypic indexical values emerge through a reanalysis of speech variation in particular sociohistorical locales.
>
> (Agha, 2007, p. 81)

So when involved in interaction, among other things, we tie ways of speaking to (groups of) people and to their "particular socio-historical locales," whereby locale is a rather flexible designation of space. In a similar vein, in his work on indexicality, Silverstein also points to how "semiotic agents access macro-sociological plane categories and concepts as values in the indexable realm of the micro-contextual" (Silverstein, 2003, p. 193). Not only intra-social stereotypes but also national or ethnic stereotypes can be considered as belonging to these "macro-sociological plane categories."

The speech repertoires referred to by Agha are in no sense monolingual: people know how to switch code or translanguage depending on the register of the situation and the stereotypic indexical values at play. In the cases discussed in this book, stereotypic indexical work is scaled and complex in that it is intra-national (Ireland in Chapter 5; Italy in Chapter 6; Flanders (Belgium) in Chapter 7) and at the same time also intra-social and intercultural/international across the board in the local community (esp. but, not only, Chapters 8 and 9). This study has also shown that translating and interpreting are part of what Agha calls "the relevant performable signs" or "speech repertoires" (Agha, 2007, p. 81), not just practices that are added on to or standing outside these repertoires, as if such a thing were possible even in trained professional settings. In this sense, more structured stereotypic indexical work helps trigger a translational response, work that recognises the locale as being multicultural and hence multilingual. This is apparent in the block of flats (intralingual translation) and in the inner-city school (interlingual translation). It is an element of the indexical biographies of the two girls on the tram. At the same time, auto and hetero images are also at play in the local community and emerge from and are confirmed through translation.

Neighbourhoods are also often invoked in terms of their image and in adjacent terms of authenticity, down-to-earthness or some other stereotypical quality. This is another aspect of "being" a neighbourhood, which also applies to the people who live there. Working-class neighbourhoods become migrant neighbourhoods become gentrified neighbourhoods and/or remain all three, during which their speech repertoires and stereotypic indexical values (Agha, 2007, p. 81) shift and become increasingly layered (viz. the inner-city school as a mirror of this layeredness and its related translation policy). Image construction in groups and neighbourhoods can also be related to "scale" and to how "Distinctions are applied recursively to a fraction of a unit, as meaningful distinctions are played out to constitute a smaller group or individual with presupposed ancestry in the larger-scale unit" (Slembrouck, 2011, pp. 7–8). Furthermore, as Agha suggests, "a register is a cultural model of action" (Agha, 2007, p. 81), which brings us to another line of meta-connection.

Forms of Life and Genres

The third and final line of meta-connection I would like to draw is between Wittgenstein's "forms of life" and related "language games" (Wittgenstein, 2009) and the notion of genre as discussed by Bakhtin. Though Bakhtin wrote profusely on the topic, I will limit myself here to Bakhtin (2007, p. 60) and Bakhtin and Medvedev (1991, p. 129–134) with a brief reference to Vološinov (1986, p. 90). The early work on genre by Bakhtin, Medvedev and Vološinov has borne considerable fruit in which scholars have provided the term with further conceptual and methodological leverage, as the short section in Chapter 1 illustrates only in part.

This line of meta-connection may have been drawn by others elsewhere, but the connection emerged during engagement with Brian's social work and his commitment to cooking, music and sports. In trying to understand how Brian went about his work, I realised that it required some basic form of agreement about the state of play in any of the three activities for all concerned. This led first to Wittgenstein. To recap, here are some relevant quotes on forms of life and language games:

> *19. "It is easy to imagine a language consisting only of orders and reports in battle ... – And to imagine a language is to imagine a form of life."
>
> (Wittgenstein, 2009, p. 11^e)

> *23. ...There are *countless* kinds; countless different kinds of use of all the things we call "signs," "words," "sentences." And this diversity is not something fixed, given once for all; but new types of language, new language games, as we may say, come into existence, others become obsolete and get forgotten... The word *"language-game"* is used here to emphasize the fact that the *speaking* of language is part of an activity, or of a form of life.
>
> (Wittgenstein 2009, pp. 14^e–15^e)

> *241. "So you are saying that human agreement decides what is true and what is false?" - What is true or false is what human beings *say*, and it is in their *language* that human beings agree. This is agreement not in opinions, but in forms of life.
>
> (Wittgenstein, 2009, p. 94^e)

It is clear from these quotes that speaking and the activity it is part of is a form of life and that it is in forms of life that people agree. As I understand it, speaking is not an activity in itself but is tied to some form of life or other. The idea of tying language use to activity led further to Bakhtin's writings. Wittgenstein's reasoning bears a close resemblance to Bakhtin's views on genre which initially date from in or around the time Wittgenstein was working on Philosophical Investigations. Bakhtin opens his chapter on the Problem of Speech Genres as follows:

> All the diverse areas of human activity involve the use of language. Quite understandably, the nature and form of this use are just as diverse as are the areas of human activity.
>
> (Bakhtin, 2007, p. 60)

Wittgenstein speaks in his Philosophical Investigations of "countless different kinds of use," but then tied to just as many activities. In an earlier work (Bakhtin & Medvedev, 1991), we can find the following remarks:

> Each genre is only able to control certain definite aspects of reality. Each genre possesses definite principles of selection, definite forms for seeing and conceptualizing reality and a definite scope and depth of penetration.
>
> (p. 131)

> We might say that human consciousness possesses a series of inner genres for seeing and conceptualizing reality. A given consciousness is richer or poorer in genres, depending on its ideological environment.
>
> (p. 134)

Bakhtin connects inner speech genres to outward spoken generic activity involving speech or as Vološinov remarks: "… the whole route between inner experience (the "expressible") and its outward objectification (the "utterance") lies entirely across social territory" (Vološinov, 1986, p. 90). Wittgenstein makes a similar remark: "When I think in words, I don't have 'meanings' in my mind in addition to verbal expressions; rather, language is the vehicle of thought" (Wittgenstein, 2009, p. 329, 113[e]). The reasoning in Bakhtin and Vološinov further chimes with Wittgenstein's view on the impossibility of private inner speech (see Wittgenstein, 2009, *257, p. 98[e] for example). In relation to the study and by way of example, Bakhtin and Medvedev's notion of the poverty of inner genres matches the notion of textual poverty the artist refers to in the block of flats.

This study has shown how genre has anchored much of the translational interaction across the various sites. Forms of life allowed us to understand Brian's social life and the importance of music, cooking and sports.

Forms of life and (speech) genres (to the extent that they overlap?) can be considered basic units of interaction and hence of analysis. Again as Hanks points out, genres provide us with "orienting frameworks, interpretive procedures, and sets of expectations" with which to work (Hanks, 1987, p. 670). Following Wittgenstein and Bakhtin, this is an open system that can accommodate new forms of life and genres, many of which are now in the making or have already been made "online," and elsewhere

Three main lines of meta-connection – there are others — have been drawn in this section based on the materials that the participants provided. Their work and talk sparked these lines of connection.

Other Forms of Translation/Transfer

To conclude, I would like to address what could be called other forms of translation/transfer that have their origin outside yet also encompass the translation and interpreting practices discovered at the various sites and discussed in the chapters of this book. This involves moving beyond the limits of this study proper, as it also means addressing manifestations of what Marcus would call "the world system" (Marcus, 1998, p.78–104). Without going into detailed discussions of what the world system might entail, I wish to point to observations made during the study of phenomena that have a broader canvas than the local community but are still visible and operating within it. These phenomena are related to globalisation, the causes of which largely remain invisible to us in everyday life but nonetheless continue to be felt. In discussing what he calls the changed mise-en-scene of multi-sited ethnography along with an understanding of complicity as "complex or involved," Marcus draws our attention to:

> an awareness of existential doubleness on the part of *both* the anthropologist and subject; this derives from having a sense of being *here* where major transformations are underway that are tied to things happening simultaneously *elsewhere*, but not having a certainty or authoritative representation of what those connections are.
>
> (Marcus, 1998, p. 118)

Given this awareness, Marcus suggests the following:

> What ethnographers [...] want from subjects is not so much local knowledge as an articulation of the forms of anxiety that are generated by the awareness of being affected by what is elsewhere without knowing what the particular connections to what that elsewhere might be.
>
> (Marcus, 1998, p. 119)

This anxiety is apparent in the relations the residents of the block of flats have with the outside world (Chapter 7) and in the increasing precarity among children the school principal draws our attention to in Chapter 8. The anxiety comes together with an awareness that the social worker, the artist in the block of flats and the school principal are doing what they can to offset the effects of what is happening in their immediate neighbourhood. They too are also aware that it is happening elsewhere. It is argued here that these forms of anxiety are the result of the translation or transfer of macro-economic ideologies into the everyday workings of places like schools, social services and social housing schemes. There is absolutely nothing new in this, except that it is cast in terms of translation. But perhaps translation can offer an insight.

Translation is usually explained in terms of a source text from a source culture and a resultant target text that serves a purpose in a target culture. It has been shown already above, however, that all these can be found in the same locality. What was being translated in one case was a form of rationalisation that has long since become one of the catch-all solutions of neoliberal economic policy. Its "source text" is replete with promises of increased efficiency and economy but what its actual source text is, is hard to say.[5] It would require some archaeological work (Foucault) to find this source text or it would involve what Marcus calls "following the metaphor." The plan in this case was to apply/transfer a version of such a neoliberal (textual/ socio-economic) template to the cleaning of the buildings on a site shared by the school and other institutes. This would mean having the cleaning work done by a single team rather than the existing separate teams. This new single team would be selected from the existing teams.

It is often assumed that the resulting target text – here a new team – is something new in the target culture. In fact, it would have been something new, compared to the practices it planned to replace. But this means that, in a manner of speaking, the target culture already had its own source texts, albeit texts of a different bent and hue, which is sometimes forgotten in the translational magic of the moment. The crux of the matter was that the translation plan was drawn up by well-meaning people on the site. There was no neo-colonial enterprise calling the shots. By dint of Foucauldian irony, it was going to happen by itself, a self translation, as it were, conceived of and carried out by those who had suggested it. Such is the magic of the rationalisation template, it seems.

Or is there more to it? Certainly. Is it because, as Weber would have suggested, we have long since embraced the credo of efficiency such that we fail to see its detriment not only to community ties but also to existing viable solutions? It is up to those who might chase this metaphor to say whether this is the case or not. The school vetoed the plan, precisely because it had its own alternative translations (of other source texts?) that have arisen over time from confronting globalisation and superdiversity in real terms in the school.

The plan for the site was shelved but this doesn't remove the source text of rationalisation, which continues to be translated into a myriad of situations here and elsewhere. This is just one (translated) form of anxiety and precarity. The school's approach (Chapter 8) also illustrates a point made by Burawoy et al. in their Global Ethnography. Their book lays bare three elements they identified in studying globalisation across numerous sites: "external forces, connections between sites and imaginations from daily life" (Burawoy et al., 2000, p.5). The focus of which of these elements to study depended on particular experiences of globalisation, i.e.

> on whether people experienced globalisation as an external force to be resisted or accommodated, whether people participated in the creation and reproduction of connections that stretched across the world or whether people mobilised and/or contested imaginations that were of global dimensions.
>
> (Burawoy et al., 2000, p. 5)

In our case, members of the school staff have created and maintained connections with colleagues in other countries. They have also both mobilised and contested imaginations of the global in their everyday work.

To end on another positive note, I would like to draw attention to the imaginary surrounding the signing of the Bologna Agreement (a gigantic act of translation), which has since allowed students to continue their studies in other countries through the Erasmus programme. One knock-on effect of the programme is that it has allowed Spanish students to learn an Irish variety of English while serving Spanish tourists (in Spanish) in an Irish pub in Ghent (Belgium). The Spanish tourists are there to visit the birthplace of their former emperor, Charles the Fifth, who played a significant role in an earlier wave of globalisation.

Notes

1 Differential legal statuses and their concomitant conditions, divergent labour market experiences, discrete configurations of gender and age, patterns of spatial distribution and mixed local area responses by service providers and residents. The dynamic interaction of these variables is what is meant by "superdiversity" (Vertovec, 2007, p. 1025).
2 For a discussion of translanguaging space, see Wei (2011).
3 Blommaert also comments in detail on such neighbourhoods in his *Sociolinguistics of Globalisation* (Blommaert, 2010).
4 For a detailed discussion of "place as practised space" (de Certeau, 1984, p. 117) in relation to language use, see Higgins (2017, pp. 102–116).
5 Though Weber coined the term, it was something he feared and warned us against.

References

Agha. (2007). *Language and Social Relations* (Studies in the Social and Cultural Foundations of Language; 24). Cambridge: Cambridge University Press.

Antonini, R., Cirillo, L., & Rossato, L. (2017). *Non-professional Interpreting and Translation: State of the Art and Future of an Emerging Field of Research* (Benjamins Translation Library 129). Amsterdam: John Benjamins.

Apter, E. (2006). *The Translation Zone.* Princeton, NJ: Princeton University Press.

Bakhtin, M. M. (1986). *Speech Genres and Other Late Essays* (C. Emerson & M. Holquist, Eds. and V. W. McGee, Trans.). Austin: University of Texas Press.

Bakhtin, M. M., & Medvedev, P. N. (1978 [1928]). *The Formal Method in Literary Scholarship: A Critical Introduction to Sociological Poetics.* Baltimore, MD/ London: The Johns Hopkins University Press.

Beller, M., & Leerssen, J. (2007). *Imagology: The Cultural Construction and Literary Representation of National Characters: A Critical Survey* (Studia imagologica 13). Amsterdam: Rodopi.

Blommaert, J., & Backus, A. (2013). Superdiverse repertoires and the individual. In I. de Saint-Georges & J. J. Weber (Eds.), *Multilingualism and Multimodality: Current Challenges for Educational Studies* (pp. 11–32). Rotterdam: Sense.

Burawoy, M., Blum, J. A., George, S., Gille, Z., Thayer, M., Gowan, T., Haney, L., Klawiter, M., Lopez, S., & O'Riain, S. (2000). *Global Ethnography. Forces, Connections, and Imaginations in a Postmodern World.* Berkeley: University of California Press.

de Certeau, M. (1984). *The Practice of Everyday Life.* Berkeley/London: University of California Press.

Cronin, M. (2002). Babel's standing stones: Language, translation and the exosomatic. *Crossings: eJournal of Art and Technology,* 2(1) ISSN 1649-0460.

Cronin, M. (2006). *Translation and Identity.* London/New York: Routledge.

Cronin, M., & Simon, S. (2014). Introduction: The city as translation zone. *Translation Studies,* 7(2), 119–132, doi:10.1080/14781700.2014.897641

Hanks, W. F. (1987). Discourse genres in a theory of practice. *American Ethnologist,* 14(4), 668–692. http://www.jstor.org/stable/645320

Hanks, W. (2014). The space of translation. *HAU Journal of Ethnographic Theory,* 4(2), 17–39. doi:10.14318/hau4.2.002

Harris, B. (2013). An Annotated Chronological Bibliography of Natural Translation Studies with Native Translation and Language Brokering 1913–2012. https://www.academia.edu/ 5855596/Bibliography_of_natural_translation (last accessed 25/10/2020)

Higgins, C. (2017). Space, place and language. In S. Canagarajah (Ed.), *The Routledge Handbook of Migration and Language* (pp. 102–116). London/ New York: Routledge.

Hymes, D. H. (1972). On communicative competence. In J. B. Pride & J. Holmes (Eds.), *Sociolinguistics. Selected Readings* (pp. 269–293). Harmondsworth: Penguin.

Leerssen, J. (2007). The poetics and anthropology of national character (1500–2000). In M. Beller & J. Leerssen (Eds.), *Imagology: The Cultural Construction and Literary Representation of National Characters. A Critical Survey* (pp. 63–75).Amsterdam & New York: BRILL.

Lefebvre, H. (1991). *The Production of Space.* Oxford: Blackwell.

Marcus, G. E. (1998). *Ethnography through Thick and Thin.* Princeton, NJ: Princeton University Press.

Pennycook, A., & Otsuji, E. (2015). *Metrolingualism: Language in the City.* London/New York: Routledge.

Pennycook, A., & Otsuji, E. (2019). Mundane metrolingualism. *International Journal of Multilingualism*, 16(2), 175–186. doi:10.1080/14790718.2019.15 75836

Risku, H. (2014). Translation process research as interaction research: From mental to socio-cognitive processes. Minding Translation, guest edited by R. Munoz, 331–353. Special Issue 1 of MonTI. doi:10.6035/MonTI.2014.ne1.11

Risku, H., Rogl, R., & Milosevic, J. (2019). Translation practice in the field: Current research on socio-cognitive processes. In *Translation Practice in the Field* (Vol. 105). John Benjamins Publishing Company. doi:10.1075/bct.105

Silverstein, M. (2003). Indexical order and the dialectics of sociolinguistic life. *Language & Communication*, 23, 193–229. doi:10.1016/S0271-5309(03)00013-2

Slembrouck, S. (2011). Globalization theory and migration. In R. Wodak, B. Johnstone, & P. Kerswill (Eds.), *The Sage Handbook of Sociolinguistics* (pp. 153–164). London: Sage.

Vermeer, H. J. (2000). Skopos and commission in translational action. In L. Venuti (Ed.), *The Translation Studies Reader* (pp. 221–232). London: Routledge.

Vertovec, S. (2007). Super-diversity and its implications. *Ethnic and Racial Studies*, 30(6), 1024–1054. doi:10.1080/01419870701599465

Vertovec, S. (2019). Talking around super-diversity. *Ethnic and Racial Studies*, 42(1), 125–139. doi:10.1080/01419870.2017.1406128

Vološinov, V. N. (1973). *Marxism and the Philosophy of Language* (Studies in Language, L. Matejka & I. R. Titunik, Trans. and M. Silverstein, Ed.), New York/London: Seminar Press.

Wei, L. (2011). Moment analysis and translanguaging space: Discursive construction of identities by multilingual Chinese youth in Britain. *Journal of Pragmatics*, 43(5), 1222–1235.

Wittgenstein, L. (2009). *Philosophical Investigations* (Revised 4th ed., G. Anscombe, Trans.). Chichester: Wiley-Blackwell.

Index